Understanding
Adventures of Huckleberry Finn

The Greenwood Press "Literature in Context" Series

Understanding *To Kill a Mockingbird:* A Student Casebook to Issues, Sources, and Historic Documents
Claudia Durst Johnson

Understanding *The Scarlet Letter:* A Student Casebook to Issues, Sources, and Historical Documents
Claudia Durst Johnson

UNDERSTANDING
Adventures of Huckleberry Finn

A STUDENT CASEBOOK TO ISSUES, SOURCES, AND HISTORICAL DOCUMENTS

Claudia Durst Johnson

The Greenwood Press
"Literature in Context" Series

GREENWOOD PRESS
Westport, Connecticut • London

Library of Congress Cataloging-in-Publication Data

Johnson, Claudia D.
   Understanding Adventures of Huckleberry Finn : a student casebook
to issues, sources, and historical documents / Claudia Durst
Johnson.
      p.   cm. — (The Greenwood Press "Literature in context"
series, ISSN 1074–598X)
   Includes bibliographical references and index.
   ISBN 0–313–29327–9 (alk. paper)
   1. Twain, Mark, 1835–1910.   Adventures of Huckleberry Finn.
2. Literature and society—United States—History—19th century.
3. Adventure stories, American—History and criticism.
4. Mississippi River—In literature.   5. Race relations in
literature.   6. Boys in literature.   I. Title.   II. Series.
PS1305.J64   1996
813'.4—dc20   95–40031

British Library Cataloguing in Publication Data is available.

Library of Congress Catalog Card Number: 95–40031
ISBN: 0–313–29327–9
ISSN: 1074–598X

First published in 1996

Greenwood Press, 88 Post Road West, Westport, CT 06881
An imprint of Greenwood Publishing Group, Inc.

Printed in the United States of America

∞™

The paper used in this book complies with the
Permanent Paper Standard issued by the National
Information Standards Organization (Z39.48–1984).

10 9 8 7 6 5 4 3 2 1

Copyright Acknowledgments

The author and publisher gratefully acknowledge permission for use of the following material:

John Wallace, "The Case Against *Huck Finn*," in *Satire or Evasion? The Case Against Huckleberry Finn*, James S. Leonard, Thomas A. Tenney, and Thadious M. Davis, eds. Durham, N.C. and London: Duke University Press, 1992. Reprinted with permission.

Julius Lester, "Morality and *Adventures of Huckleberry Finn*," in *Satire or Evasion? The Case Against Huckleberry Finn*, James S. Leonard, Thomas A. Tenney, and Thadious M. Davis, eds. Durham, N.C. and London: Duke University Press, 1992. Reprinted with permission.

David Smith, "Huck, Jim, and American Racial Discourse," in *Satire or Evasion? The Case Against Huckleberry Finn*, James S. Leonard, Thomas A. Tenney, and Thadious M. Davis, eds. Durham, N.C. and London: Duke University Press, 1992. Reprinted with permission.

Kenny J. Williams, "*Adventures of Huckleberry Finn*; or, Mark Twain's Racial Ambiguity," in *Satire or Evasion? The Case Against Huckleberry Finn*, James S. Leonard, Thomas A. Tenney, and Thadious M. Davis, eds. Durham, N.C. and London: Duke University Press, 1992. Reprinted with permission.

Excerpts from "One Hateful Word," by Kenneth B. Noble, March 19, 1995. Copyright © 1995 by The New York Times Company. Reprinted by permission.

Excerpts from "We Give This Slur Its Power," by William Raspberry, April 11, 1995. © 1995, Washington Post Writers Group. Reprinted with permission.

Excerpts from "Civil Disobedience, the Draft and the War," by William Sloane Coffin, Jr., in *Christianity and Crisis*, February 5, 1968. Reprinted with permission.

"The Code of the Streets: An Interview with a Former Gang Member," by Professor Larry Watts. Interviewee anonymous. Reprinted with permission.

Contents

Introduction

The Concord (Mass.) Public Library committee has decided to exclude Mark Twain's latest book from the library. One member of
the committee says that, while he does not wish to call it immoral,
he thinks it contains but little humor, and that of a very coarse type.
He regards it as the veriest trash. The librarian and the other members of the committee entertain similar views, characterizing it as
rough, coarse and inelegant, dealing with a series of experiences
not elevating, the whole book being more suited to the slums than
to intelligent, respectable people. (Boston *Transcript*, March 17,
1885)

The Concord Public Library was not the only group to condemn
Mark Twain's *Adventures of Huckleberry Finn*. This novel about
the adventures of a fourteen-year-old boy has generated controversy in every year since it was published in 1884. "What!" the
newcomer to the novel might exclaim—"this popular boy's book
about a happy and wholesome young life in rural America?" Yet,
ironically, it is true. Even by the standards of the late twentieth
century, *Adventures of Huckleberry Finn* is one of the most radical
and darkly bitter books in the American canon. What does it present as good and worthy? For one thing, it represents the breaking
of a federal law as moral. It recommends disobedience and defi-

ance on the part of young people. It portrays churchgoers as hypocritical and their religion as silly; it shows respected community leaders to be cruel and immoral. The most admirable characters in the book habitually lie and steal and loaf. One is illiterate, and the other is a barely literate truant from school.

Yet Mark Twain's *Adventures of Huckleberry Finn* is one of the most recognized classics of literature in the world. Ernest Hemingway, a renowned writer of twentieth-century America, wrote that all modern American literature proceeded from one book, *Huckleberry Finn.* One would be hard pressed to find many Americans who have never heard of *Adventures of Huckleberry Finn,* even though many may not have read it. At the same time, it is one of those classics whose popular image has little to do with its realities. Direct a question about *Huckleberry Finn* to the man or woman on the street, most of whom have encountered Huck's story in a movie or an adaptation of the story for young children, and you will likely be told that Twain's novel is a boy's book about the happy, innocent times long ago of a barefoot boy in a straw hat and coveralls on the Mississippi River. While there is a grain of truth in such a characterization, the complete story of Mark Twain's novel is a far cry from this popular idea of it. In the first place, to classify *Adventures of Huckleberry Finn* as a boy's book is misleading. Although it contains some of the high jinks that made a true boy's book, *Tom Sawyer,* popular, and although Mark Twain might have first conceived of *Huckleberry Finn* as a boy's book, it evolved into a treatment of adult themes and profound intellectual questions which have made it the subject of university classrooms and scholarly conferences. Furthermore, when *Huckleberry Finn* first appeared, it was seen as anything but a *proper* boy's book: reviewers almost universally condemned it as so immoral and graphic in ugly detail that it should be kept away from boys as if it were poison. After all, Huck's grammar is atrocious; he smokes; he lies repeatedly; he steals like a pro; he doesn't go to church and isn't inclined to make up for the religious education he has never had; he inadvertently makes prayer, heaven and hell, churchgoers, temperance, revivals, and Bible stories appear ridiculous; he skips school; he describes drunkenness; he lies around the raft naked; he describes a pornographic stage show he witnesses; and he starts off his story with an account of joining a gang to terrorize the town.

No, *Adventures of Huckleberry Finn* is not exactly the typical young boy's book. Nor can it accurately be characterized as a happy, innocent tale. While many scenes on the river *are* idyllic, Huck and Jim's world is actually a brutal one by any standards. For instance, the story includes the description of a drowned person mistakenly believed to be Huck's father; Huck's faking of his own murder and the dragging of the river for a dead body; the cruelty of vicious child beatings; the discovery of the body of a naked man, shot in the back, in a shack once used by thieves and prostitutes; thieves threatening one of their gang with a pistol on another river boat—the *Walter Scott*—which eventually sinks and drowns them all; the murder before Huck's eyes of his good friend and others in a senseless feud; animal torture; the shooting down of a harmless, unarmed drunk in broad daylight; the digging up of a corpse to look for money; and the tarring and feathering of two con men. If a Hollywood studio made a movie of *Adventures of Huckleberry Finn* that visualized the violence that Huck relates, no child would ever be allowed to see it.

Even though the traditions about Twain's novel as an innocent boy's book are inaccurate, one tradition about it seems valid: that it is the first truly American novel. This is a puzzling statement at first glance because, of course, appearing as it did in 1884, it was neither the first novel written by an American nor the first novel with an American setting. Other American writers—Washington Irving, James Fenimore Cooper, Nathaniel Hawthorne, Harriet Beecher Stowe, Herman Melville, Louisa May Alcott, and dozens of others—had been writing novels with nineteenth-century American settings since the first American fiction appeared. For what reason, we may ask, is *Adventures of Huckleberry Finn* regarded as the first truly American novel?

The critical issue, as Twain specialist Bernard De Voto observed, is the novel's language. De Voto argued that with the first sentence—"You don't know about me without you have read a book by the name of *The Adventures of Tom Sawyer,* but that ain't no matter"—great literature was written in the language of Americans (*Mark Twain at Work* [Cambridge, Mass., 1942]). First, Twain uses the vernacular rather than a "literary" language descending from the English masters. One need only compare it with a page from Nathaniel Hawthorne's *The Scarlet Letter,* Herman Melville's *Moby Dick,* or Edgar Allan Poe's "The Fall of the House of Usher." The language found in Twain's novel was spoken by many Americans in the nineteenth century and nowhere else in the world. Second, its language is representative of a great variety of dialects from different regions, races, and classes. He used not only an African-American dialect, as Harriet Beecher Stowe had done in *Uncle Tom's Cabin* in 1852. According to the explanatory note that prefaced the first edition of the novel, he used at least seven different middle-American dialects, which students of language have subsequently identified.

While the message of the novel is universal, the particular subjects of *Adventures of Huckleberry Finn* are as uniquely American as its language. Central to the novel, set sometime between 1835 and 1845, are life on the Mississippi River, frontier society, and slavery. It is also about such American subjects as feuding in Tennessee, western-style gamblers, outlaws, and confidence men, small-town frontier entertainments like the circus, and frontier justice, that is, lynching.

The novel takes place in a thoroughly American landscape in the heart of the nation rather than in an East Coast town that looks back to Europe. In the heartland of America, on the Mississippi River, the characters seem to owe very little to European and English tradition. The exception is Tom Sawyer's obsession with Old World romantic fiction, which in this setting is made to appear ridiculous. The Mississippi culture, with its own distinct currents, characters, and vegetation, seems, by and large, free of the Old World which pervaded Massachusetts, Virginia, and South Carolina.

The present study begins in Chapter 1 with a literary analysis of *Adventures of Huckleberry Finn*, focusing on its point of view, major themes, and images. Chapter 2 is an exploration of the controversy over the novel's censorship, based largely on the use of racial epithets and racial characterizations. Here the student is asked to explore a variety of questions related to the issue before moving to arguments by African-American educators and journalists on both sides of the question of censorship and racial characterizations in the novel. Chapter 3 begins to place the novel in historical context, that is, the Mississippi Valley from 1830 to 1865. The context is established by people who lived in the period and wrote about life then. Included are reports of travelers and the childhood memories of an upstanding citizen, a professional gambler, and two men considered to be outlaws. Chapter 4 continues to explore the historical context of the novel in terms of one of its basic themes, the history of slavery in nineteenth-century America. The documents on slavery are divided into three main categories: (1) arguments in support of the perpetuation of slavery, and narratives of slaves themselves; (2) the text of two important legal documents in the history of slavery; and (3) public sentiment on whether laws should be obeyed, even if they are perceived to be immoral. Chapter 5 examines the nineteenth-century code of honor that shaped southern society, an important theme in *Adventures of Huckleberry Finn.* The code of the streets observed by youthful gangs in the 1990s is related to attitudes in the nineteenth century. Elements of the novel's satire, with particular reference to productions of Shakespearean plays, home decoration, and sentimental verse, are the subject of the final chapter. Each chapter contains projects and suggestions for oral or written exploration and a list of materials for reading further on various subjects.

NOTE

Page numbers in parentheses refer to the Signet Classic Edition of Mark Twain's *Adventures of Huckleberry Finn,* originally published in 1959.

1

Literary Analysis: *Adventures of Huckleberry Finn* and Forms of Enslavement

THE FLUID STRUCTURE

Mark Twain's *Adventures of Huckleberry Finn* is, in the way it is put together and in the various stories it tells, a repudiation of traditional forms of plot structure, the rules and manners of genteel society, and the restraints civilization places upon the free spirit. In looking at the way the novel is constructed, one can see that Mark Twain has dispensed with a tightly constructed plot in favor of an episodic narrative that takes its form from nature, in this case, the mighty Mississippi River flowing through the heart of America. A single, thoroughly American geographic feature not only contributes to the novel's endorsement of freedom and nature, it is also a key to and a reflection of the book's structure. The action of the novel is comprised of numerous episodes which are held together, not by the usual kind of plot, but by the river itself. Episodes occur on the river or close by the river, and there is always a return to the river. Because of its episodic nature, the novel's form can best be described as *picaresque,* meaning "a novel of the road," in this case, a journey on the river. The unifying elements in *Adventures of Huckleberry Finn* are the character of Huck, who relates the story and is always in the middle of the action, and the Mississippi River, in whose waters and on whose banks the episodes occur. The novel begins in a Missouri town located on the river and moves on down the river with Huck through Missouri, to Cairo, Illinois, then to Tennessee, Arkansas, Mississippi, and Louisiana; along the way Huck encounters other people traveling on the river itself and stops at towns on the river's banks.

Huckleberry Finn lacks what are called the "unities" of setting, character, and plot of the conventional narrative: there are many settings with many subplots involving many different sets of characters, instead of one plot, one setting, and a single set of characters. Most novels have what is called a dramatic structure. That is, they consist of (1) an exposition in which the characters and the situation are introduced (as an illustration, imagine this is a weekend party attended by a detective); (2) an initiating circumstance or action which introduces a complication (perhaps a murder at the party); (3) a single rising action during which each complication leads to another (for example, a detective investigating the murder discovers one thing and then another); (4) a climax, which is the turning point (when it is inevitably known who the murderer is); and, finally, (5) the denouement (as when the detective, in a conversation with the other houseguests after the arrest has been made, explains how he arrived at the identity of the murderer). *Adventures of Huckleberry Finn* does not have this kind of narrative form. It is not built on rising action with a single cast of characters in a single setting. A given action does not arise out of the one that precedes it or lead to the one that follows. Instead, the action is randomly episodic. The separate episodes, held together by the narrator, Huckleberry Finn, and by the river itself, include the following:

• The Tom Sawyer gang and Miss Watson

• Pap's imprisonment of Huck

• Huck's escape to Jackson's Island

• The meeting of Huck and Jim

• The dead man in the floating house

• The Sarah Williams/George Peters incident

• The *Walter Scott*

• The conversation about the Bible and royalty

- Huck getting lost in the fog and his apology
- Huck changing his mind about turning Jim in
- The Shepherdsons and Grangerfords
- The arrival of the king and the duke
- The revival scam
- The Boggs-Sherburn incident
- The circus
- The Shakespearean burlesque and the Royal Nonesuch
- The Wilks episode
- Huck's decision to go to hell
- The Phelps farm

The absence of traditional plot can be seen in that the characters and occurrences in one episode usually don't have a direct bearing on the action in other episodes. Note that the characters in the Grangerford feud, for example, do not appear again after that specific episode, as might be expected in a conventional narrative. Similarly, the settings of the various episodes change, from Missouri to Arkansas to Louisiana, while a conventional dramatic narrative would be expected to remain largely in the location where the initial action took place.

Despite its episodic structure, students of the novel have found elements that unify it. There is, for example, a central plot that does emerge throughout the story—the developing theme of Huck's growing up, his initiation into and attempt to survive the harsh realities of society. This is supported by the interplay of contrasting images (freedom on the raft as opposed to bondage in Pap's shack and on the Phelps farm, for example) and the repetition of various themes such as role-playing, which, as we shall see, also contribute to the coherence of the novel.

One of the most striking innovations in the novel is also an important unifying element: the point of view from which the story is told. Told by a young, uneducated boy, using language as it is spoken rather than read, *Adventures of Huckleberry Finn* was unique for its time and pointed the way for similarly told American masterpieces like *To Kill a Mockingbird* and *Catcher in the Rye*. Huck doesn't have the book learning or sophistication of the reader, so he is what is called an unreliable narrator in that his modern readers, for example, see the irony in what he has to say. The reader knows or is more aware than Huck about the cruelty of regarding slaves as property, whereas Huck merely accepts what his society has told him. The reader sees Huck as admirable in failing to turn Jim in, but for the same reason Huck thinks himself to be immoral and mean. What the reader recognizes as Miss Watson saying a prayer before eating is seen by Huck as "grumbling" over the food.

Though he is an unreliable narrator for these reasons, Huck has amazingly innocent insight and never lies to the reader. The effectiveness of his point of view, especially as a critic of society, is actually enhanced by his ignorance of social conventions, his position as an outsider. Because Huck, unlike Tom, hasn't learned a great deal about what he should think about cultural matters from teachers and books, he provides the reader with a fresh, insightful examination of society.

GROWING UP AND BREAKING FREE OF SOCIETY'S FORMS

Because the novel rejects traditional narrative form, it is a fitting vehicle for a story that repudiates society's forms—its rituals, polite manners, senseless, hypocritical rules of conduct, codes of honor, and, particularly, the institution of slavery. In following Huck and Jim's struggle against the forms of the slaveholding society, we note three major points: (1) the mythic course of Huck's initiation and development in this hostile world; (2) a characterization of the society in which Huck lives (or the novel as social criticism); and (3) the pretenses inherent in and demanded by this society.

Huck's Initiation

Mark Twain's notes indicate that he meant for Huck to be about fourteen years old, very near, then, to the age at which boys enter manhood in most societies. *Adventures of Huckleberry Finn* is essentially a story of one boy's becoming a man, his growing independence as he is initiated into the harsh realities of adult life. Huck's initiation has two important elements: his emergence from a fairly tranquil village boyhood into the brutal world of adult reality and, through his relationship with the slave Jim, the gradual awakening of his mature identity and of his moral sense, independent of the society in which he lives.

Huck as Outcast

In keeping with the tradition of the picaresque novel, the main character, in this case, Huck, is a kindhearted person who is a misfit in polite society and who, in most of his episodic encounters with people, is in some kind of trouble, or out of sympathy with the people who seem to control events. Although St. Petersburg is the idyllic setting from which Huck is awakened in his initiation, his childhood has scarcely been an idyllic one, nor has he lived the life of a typical carefree boy. From the first, before his adventures get under way, his outcast state is seen in his having experienced more of the ugliness of life than other children, like Tom Sawyer, have known. He has no supportive family and none of the softening, nurturing influence expected from a mother. His father, who fortunately for Huck is more often absent than present, is a drunken, abusive thief and con man. Huck has, except for a few months in his life, lived in various lean-tos in the woods, and has never had any kind of formal education in either school or church. At fourteen Huck has never heard of heaven or hell and doesn't know what prayer is. But he is what one might describe today as street smart. He has folk wisdom and common sense rather than book learning.

All of Huck's experiences in his story show him to be an outcast and an outlaw. His primary action in the story, running away with the slave Jim, finds him in violation of a law which holds that Jim is property that rightfully belongs to his mistress, Miss Watson. Though he longs to do the right thing and to be like Tom Sawyer, for example, Huck nevertheless continues until the end of the tale to help Jim reach freedom, contrary to all civil and religious law and expectation. Throughout the story he lies repeatedly, and he steals ("borrowing," he calls it). Even from the first he is an "outlaw" in Tom Sawyer's gang. At the Grangerfords' he is incapable of understanding their social code and breaks it by helping the daughter of the household to run away with young Shepherdson, with whose family the Grangerfords are feuding. In Arkansas, where his outlaw companions stage the Royal Nonesuch and where he feels sorry for the old drunk killed by the patriarch who runs the town, he is just one step ahead of the law. He then co-operates with his outlaw friends to cheat the Wilks family in Mississippi and in turn breaks *their* code to see that the Wilks girls get their money. Finally, he commits what he thinks is an illegal act by helping free Jim from the Phelps plantation. So Huck is continually at war with society, and with society's values.

Beginnings: Life in the Village

At the beginning of the novel, Huck is living the fairly protected and idyllic life of a young boy in a small town, having been taken in by the Widow Douglas. For a brief time, while his father, Pap, is mistakenly thought to be dead, Huck goes to school, sleeps in his own room in a comfortable house, eats regularly, and receives religious instruction. He has a group of friends his age with whom he enjoys a world of make-believe. His welfare is seen to by the Widow Douglas, who shelters and feeds him, and by Judge Thatcher, who manages his money and protects it from Pap.

But Pap, by kidnapping Huck and imprisoning him in a shack in the woods, puts an end to his life in St. Petersburg. Having been forced out of this fairly peaceful life, as he moves down the river he experiences a brutal side of reality outside village law and order. And he also begins to realize the brutality and senselessness that lie beneath the surface of human society, even in seemingly civilized villages very much like St. Petersburg.

Four key episodes specifically give Huck firsthand experience with the dark, ugly, violent side of human behavior after he and Jim escape from Pap and Miss Watson: the floating house, the *Walter Scott,* the feud, and the murder of Boggs.

The Horror of the Floating House

The first scene occurs when they discover a frame house floating down the river. A figure in the corner turns out to be a dead man, whom Huck discovers to be Pap only at the end of his journey. Jim describes a gruesome sight to Huck: "It's a dead man. Yes, indeedy; naked, too. He's ben shot in de back. I reck'n he's ben dead two er three days. Come in, Huck, but doan' look at his face—it's too gashly" (57). The scene that Huck sees for himself is a sordid one, suggesting a house frequented by thieves and prostitutes:

> There was heaps of old greasy cards scattered around over the floor, and old whisky bottles, and a couple of masks made out of black cloth; and all over the walls was the ignorantest kind of words and pictures, made with charcoal. There was two old dirty calico dresses, and a sun-bonnet, and some women's under-clothes, hanging against the wall, and some men's clothing, too. (57)

The Horror of the *Walter Scott*

The second harsh and ugly scene occurs on the sinking ship, the *Walter Scott*, where Huck and Jim overhear a band of thieves threatening one of their own number with a gun and then privately plotting to tie him up and let him drown as the boat goes down. One of them says, "Hear him beg! and yit if we hadn't got the best of him and tied him, he'd a killed us both. And what *for?* Jist for noth'n." Another one says, "I'm for killin' him—and didn't he kill old Hatfield jist the same way—and don't he deserve it?" Finally they decide to steal all the loot they can find from the staterooms of the sinking ship and leave their companion tied up to drown: "Now I say it ain't agoin' to be more'n two hours befo' this wrack breaks up and washes off down the river. See? He'll be drownded, and won't have nobody to blame for it but his own self" (75).

The Violence of the Feud

The third violent scene, one in which Huck is bruised psychologically by the senseless cruelty of the adult world, occurs in the Shepherdson-Grangerford sequence. Huck had become a contented member of the Grangerford family. The father of the family, unlike his own father, is a man he admires as "sunshine most always—I mean he made it seem like good weather" (109). And the young boy about his age, Buck, is Huck's playmate and friend. Still, the inevitable violence breaks out between the two feuding families and Huck learns in the middle of the battlefield that old Mr. Grangerford has been killed. Then he watches in horror as his friend, Buck, is gunned down like an animal. The impact on Huck is horrific:

All of a sudden, bang! bang! bang! goes three or four guns—the men had slipped around through the woods and come in from behind without their horses! The boys jumped for the river—both of them hurt—and as they swum down the current the men run along the bank shooting at them and singing out, "Kill them, kill them!" It made me so sick I most fell out of the tree. I ain't a going to tell *all* that happened—it would make me sick again if I was to do that. I wished I hadn't ever come ashore that night, to see such things. I ain't ever going to get shut of them—lots of times I dream about them. . . .

When I got down out of the tree, I crept along down the river bank a piece, and found the two bodies laying in the edge of the water, and tugged at them till I got them ashore; then I covered up their faces, and got away as quick as I could. I cried a little when I was covering up Buck's face, for he was mighty good to me. (117)

The Cold-Blooded Killing of Boggs

Finally, Huck sees an obnoxious but harmless town drunk shot down in cold blood in broad daylight. Townspeople describe Boggs as "always carryin' on like that, when he's drunk. He's the best-naturedest old fool in Arkansaw—never hurt nobody, drunk nor sober" (142). But Colonel Sherburn, the town aristocrat, the top of the social heap in this small world, who surely knew Boggs' character and habits, takes offense at the old drunk's ravings, though Boggs has not hurt him or put him in any danger, and comes calmly out of the store to warn Boggs that he is tired of his insults and to deliver an ultimatum: if Boggs says one word against him after one o'clock, he will hunt him down and kill him. One o'clock comes. Others in town have tried to control Boggs, and even Boggs himself, finally sensing danger, begins to hurry away from Sherburn's store with the help of two friends. Sherburn, true to his word, calls out from the middle of the street. By this time Boggs has to turn around to see Sherburn, but Sherburn has already made up his mind and shoots Boggs twice. Like Huck's recent shattering experience in witnessing the bloody death of Buck, this is not a pretty sight:

Boggs throws up both his hands, and says, "O Lord, don't shoot!" Bang! goes the first shot, and he staggers back clawing at the air—

bang! goes the second one, and he tumbles backwards onto the ground, heavy and solid, with his arms spread out. . . .

. . . They laid him on the floor, and put one large Bible under his head, and opened another one and spread it on his breast—but they tore open his shirt first, and I seen where one of the bullets went in. He made about a dozen long gasps, his breast lifting the Bible up when he drawed in his breath, and letting it down again when he breathed it out—and after that he laid still; he was dead. (144)

These and other experiences shock Huck from carefree boyhood into the ugly and cruel world of the adult. This initiation prepares the reader for Huck's decision at the end of the novel to leave civilization for a life in nature in the less inhabited "territory," freer from the cruelty of more established societies.

The Death of the Boy

As Huck travels down the river, his initiation can be seen not only in his experiences with the evils of the adult world, but also in his development of a personal identity and a moral stance, especially with regard to Jim. This transitional period in Huck's life, between boyhood and adulthood, is symbolized by his move down the river, a situation that never allows him to stay and stabilize in one place for very long. Like the river, he is always in flux, constantly changing, at times peaceful, at times turbulent, sometimes clear and sometimes foggy.

References to death and dying also symbolize his initiation: the child is dying and the adult is being born. The first time Huck "dies" is when he fakes his own death in order to escape Pap and Miss Watson. Similar to rituals in ancient times, he "sacrifices" a substitute for himself—only in Huck's case, it is a scape pig! The blood of the sacrifice is liberally spread around, and Huck leaves behind him his childhood, his hometown, and his father, and settles momentarily on Jackson's Island to observe the aftermath, when he speaks of the events as if he himself, rather than the pig, had actually died. As he is speculating about how the townspeople will react to the bloody scene he has left behind him, for example, he tells the reader, "And they'll follow that meal track to the lake and go browsing down the creek that leads out of it to find the robbers that killed me and took the things" (42). Shortly after, when the townspeople learn of Huck's supposed death, he also speaks as if his body is actually in the river: "You see, they was firing cannon over the water, trying to make my carcass come to the top" (46). Both Jim and Huck adopt the same attitude when they discover each other on Jackson's Island. Jim says, "I come heah de night arter you's killed." And Huck, explaining to Jim how long he has been on Jackson's Island, says, "Since the night I got killed" (49). Later, when, as Sarah Williams, he chats with Mrs. Loftus, he explains, "At last she got down to where I was murdered" (63).

Perhaps because his innocent former life and the child in himself are dying, Huck is somewhat obsessed with death, as many adolescents are. His frequent references to death illustrate this. Even before his mock death, his loneliness in the house of the Widow Douglas causes him to say, "I most wished I was dead" (13). And as he continues down the river, oblique references to his own death or his desire for death remain a part of his language. After Huck and Jim's hair-raising encounter on the *Walter Scott,* Huck says they "slept like dead people" (81). Lost in the fog, he says he had "no more idea which way I was going than a dead man" (86). Afterward, when his conscience tells him that he should have turned Jim in, he says, "I got to feeling so mean and so miserable I most wished I was dead" (92). And he reports Jim's remarks after the shattering Grangerford experience: "I 'uz right down sho' you's dead agin" (118). After Huck finds that Jim has been taken as a runaway slave, he is so lonely that "it makes a body wish he was dead, too, and done with it all. . . . for certain I wished I was dead" (214).

Surprising in a carefree book for young people, death, or faked death, is one of the most persistent presences in the novel, reminding Huck of the cruel world he is entering and of his own mortality. In addition to Huck's faked death, these images include the drowned woman mistaken for Pap; the people Tom Sawyer's gang intend to murder; Pap's death; the deaths of the parents of the assumed Sarah Williams; the drowning of the men aboard the *Walter Scott;* the pretended drowning of a ferryman and servant in Huck's story to save those on the *Walter Scott;* the deaths of Tom and Mort, the imagined brothers of George Jackson, another of his assumed identities; the deaths of the various Grangerfords and Shepherdsons (including Emmeline, who had been fixated on death, the Grangerford father, two brothers, Buck, and his cousin Joe on the day Huck leaves); the whole family of the boy whose story Huck fabricates for the king and the duke; Boggs; Peter Wilks; and a servant in the story of the steamboat wreck Huck fabricates for Aunt Sally—over twenty deaths, real or imagined, in the life of Huck and Jim in their relatively brief journey down the river.

Trying on Identities

Another theme that serves to accentuate the transition between the death of the boy and the emerging adult is that of Huck's several assumed identities. It is as if, in growing up, he must try on various identities before he can settle on one of his own. First, he pretends to be dead when he kills the pig; next he dons the clothes of a girl and pretends to be Sarah Williams. When that identity slips, he calls himself Mary Williams. Then, when he is discovered to be a boy, he takes on the name George Peters. All this occurs in the course of one afternoon.

After he escapes from the *Walter Scott* and it begins to sink, he asks for help in rescuing the thieves trapped aboard it by assuming still another identity, that of a boy whose family is on the sinking ship. Shortly after, when he goes ashore again to find out his location, he takes on the identity of another boy with a family that has smallpox. In the Grangerford household he becomes George Jackson. To the king and the duke he becomes an orphan whose father and brother have drowned. To the Wilkses he becomes an English valet. Finally, when he reaches the Phelps household, he is still sliding into other identities and needs to "find out who I was" (219). When Aunt Sally Phelps assumes that he is Tom Sawyer, Huck says, "But if they was joyful, it warn't nothing to what I was; for it was like being born again, I was so glad to find out who I was" (219). At the end, we finally see a stabilized Huck, presumably leaving behind the pretenses of civilization as well as the pretenses of boyhood.

Huck's Moral Development

Huck's initiation into adulthood is shown in his developing relationship with Jim. To grasp this, however, it must be understood that Huck is a young boy who has never known anything but a slave society in which black people are considered to be inhuman pieces of property. From beginning to end, Huck is painfully aware of prevailing social attitudes and believes them to be right. He never considers that society may be wrong, and even at the last is dismayed that Tom Sawyer so readily joins him in his illegal plan to free Jim, who is Miss Watson's property. The social attitudes with which Huck has grown up are summarized in extreme form by Pap in a tirade against free blacks and against a government that forbids the selling of free blacks. The great irony of the novel is that Huck always believes that it is his *conscience* that tells him that protecting Jim from being returned to slavery is wrong, and that the "right" and "moral" thing to do would be to see that Jim is returned to his owner, Miss Watson. Subsequently, he labels himself as immoral and a hopeless sinner when he remembers that he has not done anything to return Miss Watson's property.

While he never comes to suspect that society might be wrong or that black people as a whole are anything but property, his view of Jim as an individual human being changes, and he resolves to defy society to protect him. It is a resolution to which he comes gradually and painstakingly. Before he leaves town with Pap, while he is living at the house of the Widow Douglas, his view of Jim, Miss Watson's slave, does not differ significantly from the views of those around him, and Jim is portrayed as a stereotypical comical slave in the early chapters of the novel. He is superstitious, gullible, and slow-witted. In these opening chapters, Huck reluctantly goes along with Tom Sawyer in regarding Jim as a butt of practical jokes. Yet even at this early stage, Huck's association with Jim goes beyond Tom's, for Huck reports soliciting Jim's folk wisdom in trying to decide what to do about Pap.

As Jim and Huck go down the river together, Huck remains burdened and troubled with society's and Tom's view of Jim—that he is the property of a white woman and that he exists for the white man's amusement. But as Huck and Jim's relationship grows, these views of Jim become complicated and modified in Huck's mind.

When Huck and Jim first discover each other on Jackson's Island, they immediately form an alliance. Jim, with a little hesitancy, tells Huck his dark secret—he has run away from his owner. Huck, with no hesitancy at the time, promises not to reveal Jim's situation as a fugitive and immediately protects Jim by making him "lay down and cover up with the quilt'' so that no one will become suspicious by seeing a black man (58).

But only a few days later, on Jackson's Island, Huck behaves like Tom Sawyer by playing a practical joke on Jim that almost costs Jim his life: Huck puts a dead rattlesnake on Jim's blanket. What Huck had not planned on was that the snake's mate would be attracted there and would bite Jim. Huck is so ashamed that he keeps what he has done a secret from Jim.

Huck's instinctive alliance with Jim is cemented when, rather than running away alone and leaving Jim on the island to fend for himself, he wakes Jim up to run away with him: "Git up and hump yourself, Jim! There ain't a minute to lose. They're after us!" (68). Obviously, "they"—Mrs. Loftus' husband and his friend—aren't really after Huck; they are only interested in the reward they will get by capturing Jim. But Huck links his own fate with Jim's when he says, "They're after us!" It is a crucial moment in Huck's embrace of Jim as a human being and a comrade.

While Huck tries to teach Jim a garbled version of history and literature, primarily from the books they have found, Jim begins to instruct Huck further in folk ways, common sense, and, most of all, human decency. As Huck is impressed with Jim's concern and genuine affection for him, he seems to look to Jim for the guidance that he would have had, ideally, from a father. Huck writes that Jim "was most always right" (81).

A turning point in Huck's growth occurs after he pulls a second Tom Sawyer–like practical joke on Jim, leading Jim to believe that their separation in a storm has only been Jim's dream and that Jim's agony over Huck's possible drowning has been a delusion. When Jim realizes what has happened, he delivers a stinging paternal scolding to Huck:

When I got all wore out wid work, en wid de callin' for you, en went to sleep, my heart wuz mos' broke bekase you wuz los', en I didn' k'yer no mo' what become er me en de raf'. En when I wake up en fine you back agin', all safe en soun', de tears come en I could a got down on my knees en kiss' yo' foot, I's so thankful. En all you wuz thinkin' 'bout wuz how you could make a fool uv ole Jim wid a lie. Dat truck dah is *trash;* en trash is what people is dat puts dirt on de head er dey fren's en makes 'em ashamed. (90)

Huck, in response, goes against everything society has taught him about the relationship of black and white men by apologizing to Jim. "I done it," he confesses, "and I warn't ever sorry for it afterward, neither. I didn't do him no more mean tricks, and I wouldn't done that one if I'd a knowed it would make him feel that way" (90).

Ironically, in the episode that follows this turning point in Huck and Jim's father-son relationship, Huck, who begins feeling pressured by the values of the slaveholding society of which he is a part, contemplates turning Jim in—an action he views as doing the morally right thing:

> Well, I can tell you it made me all over trembly and feverish, too, to hear him, because I begun to get it through my head that he was most free—and who was to blame for it? Why, *me*. I couldn't get that out of my conscience, no how nor no way. It got to troubling me so I couldn't rest; I couldn't stay still in one place. It hadn't ever come home to me before, what this thing was that I was doing. But now it did; and it stayed with me and scorched me more and more. I tried to make out to myself that *I* warn't to blame, because *I* didn't run Jim off from his rightful owner; but it warn't no use, conscience up and says, every time, "But you knowed he was running for his freedom, and you could a paddled ashore and told somebody." (92)

When the moment arrives, however, Huck can't bring himself to turn Jim in and tells the slave hunters that Jim, who is back on the raft, is white.

By the time Huck leaves the Grangerford household, after the massacre of his friends, he and Jim are a solid team, enjoying life together on the raft, taking care of one another, and trying to cope together with the king and the duke. Jim takes on a greater human dimension, in Huck's mind, as one who errs and suffers, by telling of his discovery of his daughter's deafness, which he mistook for disobedience.

A further development in Huck's growth occurs when he discovers that Jim has been taken off the raft by bounty hunters. As Jim had cried when he thought he'd lost Huck in the fog, now Huck cries when he realizes that "old Jim was gone" (207). But Huck is again tormented by his "conscience," believing that his failure to turn Jim in to Miss Watson is immoral. He believes that his actions on behalf of Jim are so wrong that he will burn in hell for not turning him in. "I most dropped in my tracks I was so scared." He actually writes a letter exposing the whereabouts of Jim the slave, but then can't help but think back on the love and kindnesses of Jim the friend:

> And got to thinking over our trip down the river; and I see Jim before me, all the time, in the day, and in the night-time, sometimes moonlight, sometimes storms, and we a-floating along, talking, and singing, and laughing. But somehow I couldn't seem to strike no places to harden me against him, but only the other kind. I'd see him standing my watch on top of his'n, stead of calling me, so I could go on sleeping; and see him how glad he was when I come back out of the fog; and when I come to him again in the swamp, up there where the feud was; and such-like times; and would always call me honey, and pet me, and do everything he could think of for me, and how good he always was, and at last I struck the time I saved him by telling the men we had small-pox aboard, and he was so grateful, and said I was the best friend old Jim ever had in the world, and the *only* one he's got now. (209)

So Huck, upon reflection, tears up the letter and makes the momentous decision to go to hell rather than turn Jim in, as his world had taught him he should do. "All right, then, I'll *go* to hell" (210).

Though Huck seemingly does not discard the basic philosophical and social ideas held by his society, he does change. In becoming an independent adult, he dramatically shifts his view of one black man, coming to embrace him as a friend and father figure for whom he is ready to go to hell.

Huck's Good-Hearted Nature

The reader is prepared for Huck's humane self-sacrifice by his essential good-heartedness, his sympathy and compassion, especially for the lowly, the weak, and the outcast members of society like Jim. It is a sensitivity that is manifest as he makes his way down the river, seemingly unconscious of his own fundamental goodness: "I wished the widow knowed about it [his attempted rescue]. I judged she would be proud of me for helping these rapscallions, because rapscallions and deadbeats is the kind the widow and good people takes the most interest in" (80). The reader first sees an expression of this extraordinary quality of Huck's after he and Jim escape from the sinking *Walter Scott* on the little getaway boat owned by the frightening thieves and murderers who are looting the steamboat. He reports, "Now was the first time that I begun to worry about the men—I reckon I hadn't had time to before. I begun to think how dreadful it was, even for murderers, to be in such a fix" (77).

He is also deeply affected by Colonel Sherburn's murder of the foolhardy old drunk, Boggs—so much so that even the charade of the circus he attends afterwards terrifies him instead of amusing him. When a spectator at the circus who seems to be an old drunk, probably reminiscent of Boggs, staggers into the ring and mounts a horse which gallops wildly around, Huck is "all of a tremble to see his danger" (149).

His tenderheartedness also moves him to reveal the king and the duke's scheme to Mary Jane Wilks, and his eyes begin to "water a little" in remembering her crying beside her father's coffin.

Finally, Huck feels immensely sorry for even the king and the duke, who have made his life miserable, turned Jim in, and cheated every vulnerable person they could find. When Huck hears that the townspeople plan to run the king and the duke out of town, he and Tom rush to warn these "Royal Nonesuch rapscallions" (225). But by the time they get there, the king and the duke have been tarred and feathered. Huck is filled with genuine compassion for them:

> Well, it made me sick to see it; and I was sorry for them poor pitiful rascals, it seemed like I couldn't ever feel any hardness against them any more in the world. It was a dreadful thing to see. Human beings *can* be awful cruel to one another. (225)

The Evils of Civilization

Huck and Jim, a boy and a man, are, as social outsiders, attuned to nature and become a team that transcends race and cultural difference. They are pitted against a society that is both heartless and ridiculous. While Huck and Jim value freedom, society values rules, regulations, institutions, and slavery. One of the pervasive ironies of *Adventures of Huckleberry Finn* is that the most so-called civilized elements in society are often the most insensitive, brutal, and senseless. They are in contrast to the compassion and common sense of the uncivilized Huck and Jim. At the heart of civilization is the system of slavery that it rests upon—a system that separates families like Jim's, forces a man who would be independent to be a fugitive, and legalizes a man's imprisonment in a shed for no reason except that he "belongs" to someone else more powerful of a different race.

Miss Watson

The prime representative of civilization in the novel is Miss Watson. She is highly refined in her insistence on proper posture, table manners, and book learning. Though she is concerned with religion, hers is a cold, intolerant faith, full of hell and damnation and sin. Miss Watson is the chief imprisoner of both Jim, as her slave, and Huck, as the object of her teaching. Huck, in his early innocence, decides that he'd rather go to hell than to heaven, where he would encounter the pious Miss Watson. The religion of Miss Watson appears all the more negative and lacking in charity when she is compared to the Widow Douglas, Huck's kindly benefactor:

> Sometimes the widow would take me one side and talk about Providence in a way to make a boy's mouth water; but maybe next day Miss Watson would take hold and knock it all down again. I judged I could see that there was two Providences, and a poor chap would stand considerable show with the widow's Providence, but if Miss Watson's got him there warn't no help for him any more. (20–21)

The *Walter Scott*

The ironic mixture of the highly civilized and the barbaric continues throughout the novel. Take, for example, the implications of the steamboat named the *Walter Scott*. Here is a boat named for a cultivated, genteel writer whose romantic flair and chivalric code of honor were said to have influenced the elegant style of southern plantation life in slavery times. In short, the *Walter Scott* represents the height of civilization. Yet it is inhabited only by a band of thieves and murderers; moreover, it is sinking. The episode seems to say that the society created by the values of Sir

Walter Scott's works is the last refuge of scoundrels and is doomed to wreck.

The Grangerfords

The Grangerford household is another peak of civilization on the frontier. Here, in the eyes of a nineteenth-century middle-class American, is all the material evidence of an advanced society. Their everyday lives are marked by genteel rituals. Note the morning ceremony, for instance:

> When him and the old lady come down in the morning, all the family got up out of their chairs and give them good-day, and didn't set down again till they had set down. Then Tom and Bob went to the sideboard where the decanter was, and mixed a glass of bitters and handed it to him, and he held it in his hand and waited till Tom's and Bob's was mixed, and then they bowed and said "Our duty to you, sir, and madam." (109)

The family has all the entertainments expected of the aristocracy: overnight guests, picnics, cruises on the water, and dances because, with means and land and slaves, they live in material comfort. The Grangerfords could also be labeled a highly civilized family in that they are devout church attenders.

The Grangerford episode is rich in descriptions of the material comforts of the Walter Scott society. Colonel Grangerford, for example, always wears an impeccable white suit. And the house is decorated lavishly with clocks, figurines, pictures, and the books expected in the home of a family who are comfortably "well off." Furthermore, their deceased daughter had occupied herself with the refinements of art and literature.

Yet this height of civilization has also produced the most murderous and absurd circumstance imaginable for the family, in that, as far back as anyone can remember, it has been involved in a deadly feud with its neighbors. No one remembers why the feud started, but it is the focus of their entire lives and has escalated over the years into constant violent slaughter. The irony and contradictions in this seemingly highly civilized family are shown graphically in Huck's description of the two feuding families on Sunday morning when they drink in a sermon on brotherly love at church but carry their guns in case some incident gives them an opportunity to shoot each other:

> Next Sunday we all went to church, about three mile, everybody a-horseback. The men took their guns along, so did Buck, and kept them between their knees or stood them handy against the wall. The Shepherdsons done the same. It was pretty ornery preaching—all about brotherly love, and such-like tiresomeness; but everybody said it was a good sermon, and they all talked it over going home, and had such a powerful lot to say about faith, and good works, and free grace, and preforeordestination, and I don't know what all, that it did seem to me to be one of the roughest Sundays I had run across yet. (112)

As in the case of Miss Watson, so with the Grangerfords: the most civilized people in the novel—insistent on polite forms, including religious ones—are the people most lacking in brotherly love.

Colonel Sherburn

Colonel Sherburn's murder of Boggs is also evidence of the barbaric nature of society. The killer is not one of the town's deadbeats but the most gentlemanly looking man in his community. Colonel Sherburn was "a heap the best dressed man" in town (114). He is also the one with the most authority, for when he steps out of his store, "the crowd drops back on each side." This southern "gentleman," in a town of loafers and deadbeats, is the one who shoots down an unarmed drunk being led away from him.

The Code of Honor

The Sir Walter Scott civilization of the Old South was founded on personal honor and rigid principle. In the old days, "honor" produced endless wars and dueling. In the Grangerford and Sherburn cases, it results in human slaughter, as if to say: "You have injured me, and I am bound to retaliate; I give you my word that I will not allow you to insult me." The rigid codes of personal honor that were so much a part of southern antebellum culture (and which Mark Twain once said caused the Civil War!) are ridiculed not only by the feud and Colonel Sherburn but also in Pap's swaggering, self-righteous speech when he vows that he will refuse to vote to support a government that won't allow a free black to be sold: "I says I'll never vote again. Them's the very words I said; they all heard me" (35).

Finally, it is Tom Sawyer's adherence to the traditions of civilization he has picked up from books—the codes of chivalry and honor upheld by nobility and gentlemen—that begins the novel with the account of Tom's gang and leads at last to Jim's protracted imprisonment on the Phelps farm. Like the other members of polite society, Tom values the forms rather than the spirit of civilization.

The polite manners, the careful speech, the nice clothes, the sentimental literature, the codes of honor, the romance, and the religious rituals finally only serve to mask the cruelty.

Ironically, within these various communities in the slaveholding South, Huck and Jim, the lowly outcasts of society, are always less barbaric than other men. In fact, they are, Twain intimates, the only humane ones.

Lies and Pretense

This, finally, is a society that encourages game-playing (like the feud and other romantic rituals) and pretense. Often lies or pretenses come in the form of game-playing or role-playing, or "conning" someone in a more exploitative way. (The feud is, for example, a deadly game the two families play.) Occasionally the lie or the pretense has a great deal of truth in it. Sometimes society requires pretense, and sometimes the game-playing or pretense is a way to cover up unpleasant realities. Sometimes the pretense or game is a way of hiding from society. Huck, who is so concerned with truth and lies that he brings up the subject in the first paragraph of his tale, often pretends in order to manipulate others, as a way to survive in a dangerous setting. Obviously, in the landscape through which Huck travels, the truth is difficult to discern.

Game-playing and pretense are first assumed when Tom Sawyer comes on the scene to form a gang. Tom pretends that pigs are gold, vegetables are jewels, and a Sunday School picnic is a band of Arabs. Tom alters reality in the name of style and romance, and like much of the pretense and game-playing in the novel, his imaginings have a strong element of violence. In the case of Tom Sawyer's gang, the boys take oaths to cut the throats of members who betray the gang and to kill their families as well. (Huck generously offers up Miss Watson for himself since he has no family!) In associating violence with pretense, the business of the gang is "robbery and murder" (18). Tom's game-playing, shaped by the romantic fiction of his society, is in part his way of transforming a dull, small-town existence into something more exciting. For him, the style to which he pretends is everything; substance and truth are secondary. In many ways, Tom's schemes are unintended rehearsals for adult living in a violent world, even though the ugliness that pervades his world is largely made romantic.

Huck, however, is an outsider in Tom's society, which is shaped by the romantic tradition of the Old World; he is able to discern what he calls Tom's lies: "So then I judged that all that stuff was only just one of Tom Sawyer's lies" (23). At the same time, Huck is impressed with the way Tom does things "right" and with "style" and "by the books," which usually means pretending and role-playing.

At about the same time Tom is pretending that he is heading up a band of robbers, Pap is conning the new judge and his wife into believing that he is a reformed alcoholic when he is actually still a hopeless drunk. Pap plays the part in order to get what he wants. The judge and his wife believe him because they want the world to be more hopeful and the people in it like Pap to be more pleasant than they really are, just as Tom wants the world to be more romantic than it is.

While Tom is the master of pretense in the name of style and romance, the king and duke are masters of the lie known as the con game. Huck never seems to know their true identity. Nevertheless, just as he recognizes Tom's games for the lies they are, yet goes along with him up to a point, so he recognizes the king and the duke as "liars" and "just low-down humbugs and frauds," yet goes along with them to protect Jim (127).

The duke calls himself a stage actor. Actually, both the king and the duke are actors, not only in the Shakespearean parody and Royal Nonesuch they perform, but in the various roles they assume to con the public—reformed pirate, medicine man, preacher, and so on. And in a very real sense, all the characters are actors. Tom, of course, is an actor in his romantic schemes with the gang and in trying to free Jim (whom he knows is free anyway).

The hapless drunk Boggs ridiculously assumes the stance of a dangerous killer, and Colonel Sherburn accuses the lynch mob of pretending to be brave men instead of the cowards that they really are. And this scene is paired with the circus, in which a trained and sober acrobatic clown pretends to be a drunk in danger of being killed on a horse.

Jim and Huck must also take on roles to survive in this slave-holding society. While Huck admires Tom for his exciting ways of arranging events, even if they aren't real, Huck ironically has real, truly dangerous adventures, as is seen in the case of his escape from Pap, which in itself involves pretense and deception. Huck's secret plan of digging out of the shed, laying in supplies, spreading blood around, and escaping to an island is real and dangerous and necessary for his survival and his freedom. Curiously, this, Huck's escape to freedom, contains many of the same elements that Tom insists they pretend to, unnecessarily, to add more "style" to the freeing of Jim from the Phelps farm.

Just as Huck begins his journey with a pretense of being dead and with a lie of omission in failing to tell Jim that he put the snake's skin on his bedding, Jim also starts off their journey with a lie of omission by failing to tell Huck that Pap is the dead man in the floating house. Society also requires pretense and role-playing of Jim. He must play the role that the white man expects of him by shuffling and groveling, as he does at the first and last of the novel when they are in civilization.

Huck plays roles throughout the novel in order to survive in freedom from social restrictions and to protect Jim. All the roles he assumes reflect the truth of his experiences and his longings. In each case, when he takes on a false identity, Huck, who has never had a family, conjures up a family for himself. And each case involves some element of violence or tragedy which is the reality of his young existence. As Sarah Williams, Huck pretends to have a sick, down-and-out mother, and then, as George Peters, a mother and father who have died and an abusive guardian from whom he is fleeing. He pretends to have a family that is sinking aboard the *Walter Scott*. In his third pretense, he has a father with smallpox, and the fourth part he plays—that of George Jackson—also in-cludes a family, all of whom have run away or died, while he has almost drowned falling off a steamboat. To the king and the duke he pretends to have a family who drowned when their raft collided with a steamboat.

The reader of Huck's tale can conclude that the whole slave-holding society is made up of actors and pretenders—pretending to believe in brotherhood, gentleness, and Christian charity while killing, cheating, and imprisoning each other.

Perhaps this explains why Huck finally renounces civilization and leaves it behind him. Free of the forms, social games, and role-playing that restrict his freedom and cover over the inhumanity of the culture he has struggled in, he can live a life without pretense in the natural, unsettled territory in the West, which opens its arms to the outcast.

TOPICS FOR WRITTEN OR ORAL EXPLORATION

1. To attune your ear to dialect, try rewriting the first paragraph of *Adventures of Huckleberry Finn* in the language and dialect of your friends, family, or neighbors.

2. In his novel, Mark Twain uses some nineteenth-century American slang terms—words no longer used as they are here. Make a list of these words and their meanings.

3. Make a list of slang words and definitions that might be used today by teenagers.

4. Twain says in a prefatory note that he uses a number of dialects in the book. Identify the different dialects you find in the novel. How can you distinguish them?

5. Twain has used the Mississippi River as a symbolic geographical focal point for his work. Some students of Twain have called the river a god. Write a paper endorsing or refuting this claim.

6. Write a paper contrasting Huck's experiences on the land with those he has on the river. From this can you draw conclusions about the meaning of the river? Explain.

7. Write an essay on a geographical feature of the landscape in which you live, for example, a particular hill, mountain, pasture, garden, park, field, lake, or shoreline. Describe it and consider in your essay what meaning it has for you or for others.

8. In order to get used to examining the structure of narratives, study the structure of some sitcoms, soaps, or TV dramas for a couple of weeks. Make a list of those that are set in one place (like a house or an office) and those that have multiple settings. What are the maximum number and the usual number of settings used? What are the maximum number and the usual number of different characters used? the maximum length of dramatic time and the usual length of time that it takes for the plot to unfold? Does the story take place over a period of a few hours or a few weeks? Do any seem to be episodic, or have more than one story unfolding in one hour or one-half hour?

9. Write a paper on the theme of freedom and bondage in the novel, considering not only the issue of legal slavery, but the extent to which other characters besides Jim are slaves to certain people, situations, or ideas.

10. Notice Twain's repeated use of crowds in the novel. Pinpoint and describe them in a paper. Do any or all of these crowds have characteristics in common?

11. Why doesn't Jim tell Huck that the dead man in the floating house is Pap? Why doesn't Twain make it clear?

12. Imagine that Colonel Sherburn is eventually brought to trial. (In fact, the scene was based on an actual incident, and the shooter was tried by Mark Twain's father.) Stage the trial, having two students as lawyers—one to defend and one to prosecute.

13. Write an essay on the novel's women characters. Do they have characteristics in common? Are they as multidimensional as the male characters?

14. Mark Twain went on the lecture circuit and read parts of *Adventures of Huckleberry Finn* to his audience, as did actor Hal Holbrook. If you were a performer interested in making your audience laugh, which segments of the novel would you choose to read aloud? Take the next logical step and arrange and present a reading performance from the novel. Be prepared to tell your audience why you chose the particular scenes you present.

15. The ending of the novel—that is, the part taking place on the Phelps farm—has always been very controversial, some critics arguing that it is too long, that it is out of keeping with the rest of the novel, and that it has Huck going backwards from his amazing moral development. Write an opinion piece in which you either justify or criticize this section of the book.

16. Did your view of Tom Sawyer change after reading the final episode on the Phelps farm? Why did you (or why might someone else be more prone to) laugh and forgive his capers in St. Petersburg but not on the Phelps farm?

17. Look up a full definition of the term "realism" and its opposite, "romance." Which term most nearly describes the various episodes in *Adventures of Huckleberry Finn?* Explain exactly why you think so.

18. Is the fact that Jim gains his freedom at the end of the novel believable?

19. Is it believable that Miss Watson would free Jim? Why or why not?

20. Which situations—which Huck inevitably escapes from each time— can be said to have ended happily? which unhappily?

21. Look at the point of view in the novel. How do you think the story would have been told if Tom instead of Huck narrated it?

22. Huck thinks of Tom as the ultimate adventurer and the Widow Douglas as the ultimate doer of good. What irony do you find in this? Define irony before you begin.

23. If you have a criticism of the ending, how would you change what happens? In other words, rewrite the ending.

24. Make a comprehensive list of the superstitions referred to in the novel. Do any of the predictions come true?

25. Write an essay on the references to clothing in the novel and what it reveals about characters. Include in your discussion costumes and cross-dressing as well as the absence of clothes altogether.

26. Would you classify the novel as a tragedy or a comedy? If class members have different views, hold a debate on this matter.

27. Write a paper on the limitations of Huck's insights. Which of his statements show that he knows less about a particular subject or situation than the readers do?

28. Compare and contrast Huck with a typical "outcast" about his age in your own society. What elements of becoming an adult remain the same—are universal? What is specific to his time and is no longer relevant?

SUGGESTED READINGS

Baldanza, Frank. *Mark Twain.* New York: Holt, Rinehart and Winston, 1961.

Blair, Walter. *Mark Twain and Huck Finn.* Berkeley: University of California Press, 1960.

Budd, Louis, and Cady, Edwin H., eds. *On Mark Twain.* Durham: Duke University Press, 1987.

Camfield, Gregg. *Sentimental Twain.* Philadelphia: University of Pennsylvania Press, 1994.

Davis, Sara deSaussure, and Philip D. Beidler, eds. *Mythologizing of Mark Twain.* Tuscaloosa: University of Alabama Press, 1984.

De Voto, Bernard. *Mark Twain at Work.* Cambridge, Mass.: Harvard University Press, 1942.

Florence, Don. *Persona and Humor in Mark Twain's Early Writing.* Columbia: University of Missouri Press, 1995.

Geismar, Maxwell. *Mark Twain: An American Prophet.* New York: McGraw-Hill, 1970.

Kaplan, Justin. *Mark Twain and His World.* New York: Simon and Schuster, 1974.

Leary, Lewis. *Mark Twain.* Minneapolis: University of Minnesota Press, 1960.

———, ed. *Mark Twain's Wound.* New York: Thomas Y. Crowell, 1962.

Mandia, Patricia M. *Comedic Pathos.* Jefferson, N.C.: McFarland Publishing, 1991.

Smith, Henry Nash. *Mark Twain: The Development of a Writer.* Cambridge, Mass: Harvard University Press, 1962.

2

Unfit for Children: Censorship and Race

Adventures of Huckleberry Finn has the longest, most persistent, and most varied history of censorship of any book in America. It would be difficult to find another work banned by numerous groups in the year of its publication and still being challenged consistently 110 years later! In a study of banned books, Nicholas J. Karolides and Lee Burress found that it ranks ninth among the thirty most frequently censored books in America (*Celebrating Censored Books* [Racine: Wisconsin Council of Teachers of English, 1985], p. 6). Herbert N. Foerstel's research showed that in the 1990s *Adventures of Huckleberry Finn* was the fourth most frequently banned book in the nation (*Banned in the U.S.A.* [Westport, Conn.: Greenwood Press, 1994], p. 152).

People have persistently objected to the novel over the years for two major reasons: first, because they feel that it is unfit for children, even though its narrator and main character is a young boy; and second, because they find its language to be unsuitable or offensive. While these two objections have a long history, many of the other reasons for condemning the novel have changed over the years.

Although some reviewers thought well of Twain's novel when it first appeared in 1884, more of them condemned it resoundingly as immoral and unfit for children. On January 20, 1885, *Century* labeled it as coarse and in bad taste (p. 2), and on February 26 of the same year it published a sarcastic review, warning away children and morally upright people from several scenes in the book (119). The action that caused the biggest row, however, was the banning of the book in March by the Concord, Massachusetts, Library Committee, which was quoted as saying that *Adventures of Huckleberry Finn* was "rough, coarse and inelegant." The committee went on to describe the novel as "trash and suitable only for the slums" (quoted in *Chicago Tribune*, March 23, 1885, p. 5). Several newspapers applauded the action of the Concord Library. One of these was the Springfield (Massachusetts) *Republican*, which referred to the low moral level of the book (quoted in *The Critic*, March 28, 1885, p. 155). The Boston newspapers were especially unhappy with the book and with Mark Twain's influence on American humorists. On April 2, 1885, the *Boston Daily Advertiser* wrote of Twain and his imitators: "Nothing has been sacred with them, and over subjects dignified by age, tragedy and romance they have cast the slimy trail of vulgar humorist" (4).

During Twain's lifetime the novel was banned from the public libraries of Brooklyn, Denver, and Omaha. In 1905 the Brooklyn Public Library took the book out of its children's library on the grounds that Huck was a liar, was dirty and scratched himself, used terrible grammar, and said "sweat" instead of "perspiration." By 1907, when E. L. Pearson of the Library of the Military Information Division in Washington, D.C., wrote an article in defense of *Adventures of Huckleberry Finn*, children's librarians throughout the country were keeping the book off the shelves because they considered the dirtiness, ungrammatical English, vulgarity, mischievousness, and irreverence of Twain's characters to be a terrible influence on little boys. In fact, Pearson claimed that colleges and library schools taught prospective elementary teachers and librarians to get the novel off their shelves ("The Children's Librarian versus Huckleberry Finn," *Library Journal* 32 [July 1907]: 312–314).

While these unofficial efforts to discourage children from reading *Adventures of Huckleberry Finn* seemed to have continued quietly over the years, in many public schools the novel became part of the standard curriculum. But in the 1950s the effort to banish *Adventures of Huckleberry Finn* from required classroom reading lists came publicly to the fore again, now chiefly on the grounds that its depiction of black characters and the use of the word "nigger" were demeaning to African-American students. These objections continued to be raised throughout the rest of the twentieth century.

Before examining the arguments presented by educators and scholars on the matter of whether or how *Adventures of Huckleberry Finn* should be taught in public schools, students should explore the questions that follow. Most of these questions were designed for classroom discussion, but students who would like to express themselves on these issues in a more private and, perhaps, thoughtful forum, should be encouraged to respond on paper if they wish.

QUESTIONS FOR WRITTEN OR ORAL EXPLORATION

1. Is Mark Twain's voice Huck's? That is, does Twain seem to be expressing his own views through Huck? Or do we have a narrator (Huck) who is limited in his outlook and cannot speak for the author? Cite specific instances to illustrate.

2. Try your hand at a brief ironic narrative. As an exercise, for example, write a "show and tell" account from the perspective (and in the voice, or words) of a kindergarten child who reports something that occurred at home which he or she doesn't fully understand, but which any older reader (or the child's teacher) *would* understand from the child's report.

3. Write an ironic narrative of a controversial event (say, the Oklahoma City bombing, the O. J. Simpson trial, or some controversy in your school) from the point of view and in the words of someone whose interpretation of the event is totally different from yours. Your aim will be to make the narrator damn himself (or herself) with his own words, to make him look foolish or ignorant.

4. Look specifically at Huck's controversial conversation with Aunt Sally about the riverboat wreck in Chapter 32. Does Huck actually believe that a slave is a nobody killed in the explosion, or, as some critics argue, is he playing to Aunt Sally's prejudices?

5. Does Huck come to condemn slavery as a whole or just to stand up for his friend? Note that Huck is a fourteen-year-old boy—a poor white one, at that—who has no education to speak of and who has been told all his life by all those older and (he thinks) smarter and more moral than he is that slavery is right, even sanctioned by the Bible, and that the white race is superior. Is it realistic that he should suddenly become an abolitionist? that in a few months he should come to alter his views of race and slavery?

6. Versions of *Huckleberry Finn* have been written leaving out the "N" word (as well as the word "hell"). Would you recommend such versions of the story? Explain.

7. What would your response be to someone who argued that such versions merely pretty up the historical situation and whitewash the racists and the racist society of slaveholders, and their speech? Would you agree or disagree with such an objection to a rewritten version of the novel? Explain.

8. In your opinion, is *Adventures of Huckleberry Finn* appropriate for ninth graders? Or is the ironic point of view, with the *author's* voice being different from the *narrator's* voice, too difficult for readers that

young to grasp? Are students that young unable to see the reasons for Twain's characterization of Jim and of the use of racial epithets?

9. Columnist Russell Baker, among others, has stated that while *Tom Sawyer* is a book for kids, *Huckleberry Finn* "most emphatically is not" (*New York Times,* April 14, 1982). Discuss this view.

10. Discuss the idea presented by some who think that the novel should not be required reading in public schools because Mark Twain's ridicule and criticism of white society does not make up for the humiliation felt by black students who are required to study it.

11. Some critics have argued that studying the book worsens race relations among students. Discuss this.

12. What is your reaction to the characterization of Jim? Do you find yourself liking him? Admiring him? Respecting him? Laughing at him?

13. Is Jim portrayed as smart or slow-witted? Look specifically at their going past Cairo.

14. Does Jim seem to you a fully developed human character? a minstrel figure? or a mixture of both? Support your answers with specific references to the text.

15. Does the "French" discussion make fun of Jim or, as some have argued, does it make fun of white society?

16. Discuss this point: One critic, Julius Lester, writes that comparing Huck's enslavement by Pap to Jim's enslavement by Miss Watson is to apply "a veneer to slavery which obscures the fact that, by definition, slavery was a horror" ("Morality and *Adventures of Huckleberry Finn,*" in *Adventures of Huckleberry Finn* [Boston: St. Martin's Press, 1995], p. 342).

17. Another critic, Nat Hentoff, writes that students need to look past the racially inflammatory *words* to see what Twain was actually *saying.* "What's going to happen to a kid when he gets into the world if he's going to let a word paralyze him so he can't think?" ("Huck Finn and the Shortchanging of Black Kids," *Village Voice,* May 18, 1982). Does Hentoff have a point?

18. Much of the stereotyping of black people in *Adventures of Huckleberry Finn* has been caused, some readers contend, by the illustrations used in the original edition. Find a copy of the novel with the original illustrations and write a paper on their effect on one's reading of the book.

19. Some critics have argued that, far from promoting a stereotype, *Adventures of Huckleberry Finn* exposes the falseness of stereotypes. What do you think? Explain.

20. Would you classify the book as moral or immoral? In talking about this question, you need to define the word "moral."

21. Explore the difference between "immoral" literature and pornography. Having made a distinction (if you argue that there *is* a distinction), is there some literature that you would describe as immoral (even though it is *not* pornographic), that you think children should not read? You might want to make a distinction between children of different ages.

RACE AND *ADVENTURES OF HUCKLEBERRY FINN*

In the 1950s, not long after widespread desegregation had begun in the nation's schools, African-American children began studying the same material required of white children and were exposed to *Adventures of Huckleberry Finn* for the first time. Along with de-segregation, then, came challenges from the black community to the novel's place on the required reading lists of schools and its place on the shelves of libraries. In 1957 in New York City, the first major challenge to the novel on racial grounds developed when it was dropped from the approved list of books for elementary and junior high schools. In the same year the Philadelphia Board of Education replaced the full novel with an adaptation which not only toned down the violence and dialects, but cut all passages demeaning to African Americans. More public objections, on racial grounds, to requiring school children to read the novel occurred throughout the country: in Washington State in 1967; Florida in 1969; Chicago in 1976; Iowa in 1981; Texas in 1982; Pennsylvania in 1983; Springfield and Waukegan, Illinois, in 1984; Rockford, Illinois, Michigan, and Louisiana in 1988; Tennessee in 1989; Pennsylvania in 1990; Michigan, Oregon, Arizona, and Texas in 1991; North Carolina and California in 1992; Washington, D.C., and Connecticut in 1994. The most highly publicized challenge was begun in Fairfax County, Virginia, in 1982, by an educator named John Wallace who led a community objection to the book, chiefly because of its racial epithets. After long, public negotiations, the board of education decided that the book would continue to be taught in the Fairfax County schools, but would be supplemented with materials on African-American history. Because Wallace continues to believe that the book humiliates black students, he has taken his campaign against it throughout the country and written his own adaptation of the book, deleting the words "nigger" and "hell."

Challengers of the book have asked for or negotiated a variety of ways of dealing with *Adventures of Huckleberry Finn*. It has been removed from school library shelves in elementary schools and from required reading lists. Students who object to reading it have been allowed to substitute another text. It has been moved to the eleventh or twelfth grade from the junior high level and has been supplemented by texts that explain the history of the times, including books by or about slaves. Some schools use rewritten versions of the novel, or teach it with greater sensitivity to the feelings of black students by making fuller use of historical materials.

Peaches Henry of the University of Notre Dame has done the most exhaustive study of the various arguments for and against the use of *Adventures of Huckleberry Finn* since 1957 ("The Struggle for Tolerance: Race and Censorship in *Huckleberry Finn*," in *Satire or Evasion? Black Perspectives on "Huckleberry Finn*," ed. James S. Leonard, Thomas A. Tenney, and Thadious M. Davis [Durham: Duke University Press, 1992], pp. 25–48). She finds that most of the challenges on racial grounds fall roughly into four categories: (1) the use of the term "nigger"; (2) the depiction of blacks in general, and Jim in particular; (3) the difficulty young readers have in grasping the irony and ambiguity necessary to justify Twain's racial treatment; (4) the novel's potential for worsening race relations.

By far the most frequent objection to the book is its liberal use of the racial epithet "nigger." Those who protest the teaching of the novel on this ground contend that no amount of literary merit can make up for the humiliation that required classroom study of the novel, especially the reading aloud of passages, causes African-American students. They feel that placing the book on the required reading list gives an official endorsement of the use of a term now used by bigots. Finally, they state that African Americans cannot react objectively and coolly to the term. In his book *The Big Sea*, the noted African-American writer Langston Hughes explains the feeling the racial epithet evokes:

> The word *nigger* to colored people of high and low degree is like a red rag to a bull. Used rightly or wrongly, ironically or seriously, of necessity for the sake of realism, or impishly for the sake of comedy, it doesn't matter. Negroes do not like it in any book or play whatsoever, be the book or play ever so sympathetic in its treatment of the basic problems of the race. Even though the book or play is written by a Negro, they still do not like it.
>
> The word *nigger*, you see, sums up for us who are colored all the bitter years of insult and struggle in America. (New York: Thunder's Mouth Press, 1940, 268–269)

Those who defend the novel as required reading answer the objections to its use of an offensive racial term in the following ways: first, that students need to see past mere words to the *meaning* of the novel, which is clearly anti-slavery; second, to present a story of slavery in the nineteenth century and *not* use the word is to make these racists and their times appear less obnoxious than they actually were—that is, to "pretty up" the language of racists; and third, that Twain uses the term to show the contrast between society's dehumanization of slaves and Jim's nobility of character, a contrast that actually emphasizes society's heartlessness and Jim's humanity.

The second major objection to the novel is based on the portrayal of black characters in general and Jim in particular. In Twain's novel, critics contend, black characters, including Jim, are reduced to minstrel or childlike roles which deny their humanity and maturity. Furthermore, since the self-esteem of African-American children is so low anyway, they need positive role models, not stereotypical negative ones. Finally, while it may be conceded that Jim is presented as a noble character as he and Huck make their way down the river, the novel's ending cancels his humanity and undoes the progress made toward his brotherhood with Huck.

Many critics disagree with most of these assumptions, arguing that Twain was showing society and social attitudes *as they actually existed* and that he is supremely critical of those attitudes. They also seek to show that Jim's humanity is far greater than his caricature as a minstrel figure, that his innocence is used to poke fun at whites and show the falsity of stereotypes. Finally, the ending merely shows the power of society and Tom Sawyer to dehumanize Jim, which actually motivates Huck to leave civilization altogether.

Objectors argue that the novel cannot be defended if the student cannot grasp the concept of the ironic narrator. It is difficult enough for experienced scholars to see that Huck's voice is not necessarily Mark Twain's and that the young Huck mouths the opinions that he has been taught by society's authorities. It is far more difficult, if not impossible, objectors argue, for students, especially those as young as fourteen, to see this. Even after intensive classroom study, most young students continue to regard it solely as an adventure tale. One of the chief defenders of the novel, Nat

Hentoff, disagrees, saying that "at ten, or twelve, or fourteen, even with only the beginning ring of meaning, any child who can read will not miss the doltishness and sheer meanness and great foolishness of most whites in the book, particularly in their attitudes toward blacks" ("Huck Finn and the Shortchanging of Black Kids," *Village Voice,* May 18, 1982).

Finally, those who object to the teaching of the novel in public schools argue that the novel will tend to worsen race relations in every way—that black students will lose self-esteem, that white students will have their prejudices reinforced, and that studying the novel could result in racial violence, especially if insensitive teachers insist on having students read aloud passages heavy with dialect or racial epithets. On the contrary, studies have shown that, in the hands of a good teacher, the novel can actually have a positive impact on racial attitudes and increase interracial understanding. For example, the novel provides the opportunity to identify and examine stereotypes of all kinds and to explore their impact; to become more aware of language and its power, including racial epithets; and to examine the conditions under which interracial friendship and cooperation can flourish.

Two groups of documents follow: Those in the first group explore whether *Adventures of Huckleberry Finn* is a racist novel and whether it should be kept out of the junior high classroom. All of these comments, both for and against the novel, were written by African-American educators.

The second group, relevant to the impulse to ban *Adventures of Huckleberry Finn* because of its use of the word "nigger," is made up of excerpts from essays by African Americans on the use of what has become more commonly referred to as the "N" word.

JOHN H. WALLACE

African-American educators have taken a variety of positions on the teaching of *Adventures of Huckleberry Finn*, especially to black students. John H. Wallace and Julius Lester, as excerpts from their essays show, are clearly opposed to the teaching of the novel. Wallace, now a consultant for the Chicago public schools, is a well-known opponent of the novel, mainly on the basis of its language; he led the Fairfax, Virginia, challenge over its use in public schools.

He has written his own version of *Adventures of Huckleberry Finn,*
leaving out the words "nigger" and "hell."

FROM JOHN H. WALLACE, "THE CASE AGAINST HUCK FINN," IN
*SATIRE OR EVASION? BLACK PERSPECTIVES ON "HUCKLEBERRY
FINN"*
(James S. Leonard, Thomas A. Tenney, and Thadious M. Davis, eds.
Durham: Duke University Press, 1992)

The Adventures of Huckleberry Finn, by Mark Twain, is the most gro-
tesque example of racist trash ever written. . . .

My own research indicates that the assignment and reading aloud of
Huckleberry Finn in our classrooms is humiliating and insulting to black
students. It contributes to their feelings of low self-esteem and to the
white student's disrespect for black people. . . .

My research suggests that the black child is offended by the use of the
word "nigger" anywhere, no matter what rationale the teacher may use
to justify it. . . . Pejorative terms should not be granted any legitimacy by
their use in the classroom under the guise of teaching books of great
literary merit, nor for any other reason. . . .

. . . Of the two main characters depicted, one is a thief, a liar, a sacri-
legious corn-cob-pipe-smoking truant; the other is a self-deprecating
slave. No one would want his children to emulate this pair. Yet some
"authorities" speak of Huck as a boyhood hero.

Huckleberry Finn is racist, whether its author intended it to be or not.
The book implies that black people are not honest. . . . *Huckleberry Finn*
also insinuates that black people are less intelligent than whites. (17–21)

JULIUS LESTER

Julius Lester, a professor of Afro-American Studies at the Uni-
versity of Massachusetts, also opposes the teaching of the novel.
Unlike Wallace, whose chief objection is to the single racial epithet,
Lester bases his objections mainly on the characterization of Jim.

FROM JULIUS LESTER, "MORALITY AND *ADVENTURES OF
HUCKLEBERRY FINN,"* IN *SATIRE OR EVASION?*

Twain makes an odious parallel between Huck's being "enslaved" by
a drunken father who keeps him locked in a cabin and Jim's legal enslavement. Regardless of how awful and wrong it is for a boy to be held

physically captive by his father, there is a profound difference between that and slavery. . . . Twain did not take slavery, and therefore black people, seriously.

Even allowing for the fact that the novel is written from the limited first-person point of view of a fourteen-year-old boy, . . . the author must be held responsible for choosing to write from that particular point of view. . . .

Jim does not exist with an integrity of his own. He is a childlike person who, in attitude and character, is more like one of the boys in Tom Sawyer's gang than a grown man with a wife and children, an important fact we do not learn until much later. . . .

The novel plays with black reality from the moment Jim runs away and does not immediately seek his freedom. It defies logic that Jim did not know Illinois was a free state. . . . A century of white readers have accepted this as credible, a grim reminder of the abysmal feelings of superiority with which whites are burdened. (201, 202)

DAVID L. SMITH

The following excerpts from African-American scholars take the position that while educators need to be sensitive to the effect of the frequently used racial epithet in the novel and the portrait of Jim, *Adventures of Huckleberry Finn* is one of the world's great novels which criticizes slavery and upholds an ideal biracial friendship. The novel, they conclude, should be taught. David L. Smith, a professor at Williams College, argues that Twain uses the racially offensive material to condemn white society.

FROM DAVID L. SMITH, "HUCK, JIM, AND RACIAL DISCOURSE," IN *SATIRE OR EVASION?*

Twain adopts a strategy of subversion in his attack on race. That is, he focuses on a number of commonplaces associated with "the Negro" and then systematically dramatizes their inadequacy. He uses the term "nigger," and he shows Jim engaging in superstitious behavior. Yet he portrays Jim as a compassionate, shrewd, thoughtful, self-sacrificing, and even wise man. . . . (105)

Ultimately, *Huckleberry Finn* renders a harsh judgment on American society. Freedom from slavery, the novel implies, is not freedom from gratuitous cruelty; and racism, like romanticism, is finally just an elaborate justification which the adult counterparts of Tom Sawyer use to facilitate their exploitation and abuse of other human beings. . . . And this is the point of Huck's final remark rejecting the prospect of civilization. To become civilized is not just to become like Aunt Sally. More immediately, it is to become like Tom Sawyer. (115)

KENNEY J. WILLIAMS

Smith's opinion is shared by Kenney J. Williams, a professor of Afro-American literature at Duke University. Kenney contends that the novel uncovers a basic historical reality and that much of the racism that Mark Twain denounces in his novel is very much with us today. For this reason alone, he believes, *Adventures of Huckleberry Finn* needs to be studied.

KENNEY J. WILLIAMS, "MARK TWAIN'S RACIAL AMBIGUITY," IN
SATIRE OR EVASION?

While he demonstrates throughout the novel that he has learned the important lesson of masking his feelings, of living behind the veil, Jim is also a manifestation of an acceptable character type for American readers. At the end of the novel, when he could have saved himself from discovery, he comes out of hiding with the full knowledge that he is jeopardizing his freedom. Perhaps nowhere in American literature has the sacrificial nature of loyalty been more simply presented. Jim, however, is more than a shallow stereotype. When he first appears on Jackson's Island, he has outsmarted his owner. . . . (233)

. . . Jim displays an affirmation of life that goes beyond the ignoble laws created to enslave. No matter how foolish Jim may appear, and despite the number of times he is called "nigger," in the final analysis he cannot be burlesqued. But the fact that he is not absolutely part of that happy lot of plantation slaves who people American literature is lost on those who reduce the novel to an exercise in name calling. . . . (234)

. . . Whether or not he intended to do so, Mark Twain satirized those who would romanticize race problems and, in the process, prolong them. . . . Racial epithets are still—unfortunately—too much a part of the spoken and unspoken language of the nation. Notwithstanding desires to the contrary, many Americans' notions of superiority do not vary greatly from Pap's. . . . To ban the novel is to condemn the messenger for the message. (237)

CONTROVERSY OVER THE "N" WORD

The continuing challenges to *Adventures of Huckleberry Finn* are inextricably tied to its frequent use of an obnoxious racial epithet. It is, therefore, instructive to examine some of the public conversations about the word, especially as it is viewed by African Americans. As Alison B. Hamilton points out in an article published in the popular magazine *Image,* the word "nigger" was commonly used throughout the nineteenth century in America, though even then it was considered by many to be a term of derision, and those who wanted to abolish slavery and raise the position of black people substituted the more respectful "Negro" and "colored."

In the twentieth century the word came to be an unmistakably derogatory term used either by the insensitive and ignorant or by racist whites. Discussions of the use of the "N" word became more frequent in the mid-1990s for several reasons: the more open and frequent use of the word by African Americans themselves (especially rap artists); the beginning of widespread use of the term by white people to refer to themselves; and the issues the term raised in the trial of O. J. Simpson, a famous African-American athlete accused of murdering his former wife.

The opinions presented here were prompted by the Simpson trial. Two of the central attorneys in the trial were black men: one, Chris Darden, prosecuting O. J. Simpson, and another, Johnnie Cochran, Jr., defending Simpson. Cochran, in defense of Simpson, wanted to establish racial bias on the part of a leading investigator in the case by questioning him about his use of alleged racial epithets. Darden, for the prosecution, calling the "N" word "the filthiest, dirtiest, nastiest word in the English language," argued that bringing it into the courtroom discussion would appeal too strongly to the emotions of the mostly black jury to enable them to deliberate objectively.

KENNETH B. NOBLE

African-American journalists also got into the discussion about the "N" word. Kenneth B. Noble, prompted by reports of the O. J. Simpson trial, tries to explain why the word has such power, tracing it to the African American's experience with slavery and the discomfort most black people feel in discussing slavery.

FROM KENNETH B. NOBLE, "ONE HATEFUL WORD"
(*New York Times*, March 19, 1995)

It is as if all the country's tangled legacy of racial animosity, brutality and fear has been bottled up in two ugly syllables. The despair and anger simmer without them, but when those two syllables find their way into the open air, the explosive power of old emotions is unleashed, and that power can sweep rationality, wisdom and even common humanity out of its path. . . . The word "nigger" occupies a place in the soul where logic and reason never go. . . .

. . . At the same time, some blacks have tried to strip the word of its racist meaning by reveling in it. Gangsta rappers use it as a term of endearment like "homeboy." . . . The catch is that whites who mimic blacks in this way do so at their own peril. . . .

What is it about this racial slur that changes the dynamics of nearly every situation it is used in? Part of the answer certainly has to do with slavery. While many white parents dread the moment when they must speak frankly to their children about sex, many blacks find the subject of slavery similarly discomfiting. (Sec. 4, pp. 1, 4)

WILLIAM RASPBERRY

Another African-American journalist whose comments on the "N" word are included here is William Raspberry. Raspberry goes a step further than Noble, arguing that the word continues to be hurtful because African Americans give it too much power.

FROM WILLIAM RASPBERRY, "WE GIVE THIS SLUR ITS POWER"
(*Washington Post*, April 11, 1995)

Nigger. The word is almost magical in its negative power. Books—*good* books—have been banned because of its use. Race relations have been shattered, friendships broken and credibility destroyed by its mere utterance.

O.J. Simpson's defense lawyers have tried hard to prove that Los Angeles police detective Mark Fuhrman has said the word, knowing that if they succeed they effectively destroy him as a witness against a black defendant.

Its use by whites has been cited as justification for everything from tears to murder. It is that powerful.

Yet, the fascinating question for me is why have we given it such power?

Oh, yes, the power comes from us—black Americans. We can render it neutral (as when black friends use it in casual conversation); we can make it an obscenity as when one of us finds the word offensive even from the mouths of other blacks); and we can reduce it to banality (as a number of rap artists have succeeded in doing).

But the nuances apply only when the word is used by blacks. There's no benign or banal way for whites to use it. Mark Twain and "The Autobiography of Miss Jane Pittman" have been barred from some classrooms because reading them requires that the word be pronounced in racially mixed company. . . .

Some readers will object to my notion that the N-word's power is conferred by blacks. The power, they will argue, comes from the relative power of whites over blacks in a country that once legalized slavery and then sanctioned second-class status for the descendants of black slaves. "Nigger," they will insist, is a white-created word, expressly designed to show maximum contempt for black people.

No doubt. But isn't this interesting: No definition of the word—no synonym, no lexicographer's phrase—can come anywhere close to the insult of the word itself. . . .

That's what makes it "perhaps the most offensive and inflammatory racial slur in English." Our own dread—our own evocation of everything from being sold like cattle, treated like children, or lynched like something hideous and inhuman—has given the N-word such power that we are incapable even of fashioning an equivalent insult for the person who uses it.

Not that we haven't tried. It hasn't worked, I'm convinced, because it takes two to play the magic-name game. Not only must we intend the grossest insult we are capable of imagining; the person against whom we use it must share our sense of the insult. For the most part, the others have declined to play the game. What would happen if *we* stopped playing it—if we chose not to give the word such power?

I remember the day I accidentally cut off another vehicle—a battered pickup—at a Washington intersection. The driver, a young Hispanic man, rolled down his window and, in an accent suggestive of recent arrival, yelled at me: "NEEger!" He then sped away.

I spent five seconds in seething resentment—both at this young immigrant and at the country that had so quickly taught him contempt for people who look like me. And then I laughed, and whatever power the word possessed that day dissipated into the air at Georgia and Kalmia. Is that a start?

SUGGESTED READINGS

Brown, Sterling. *The Negro in American Fiction.* Washington, D.C.: Associates in Negro Folk Education, 1935.

Burress, Lee, and Edward Jenkinson. *The Student's Right to Know.* Urbana, Ill.: National Council of Teachers of English, 1982.

Ellison, Ralph. "Change the Joke and Slip the Yoke." In *Shadow and Act.* New York: Random House, 1964, 45–59.

English Journal. See the following issues: 50 (January 1961), 18 (November 1956), 57 (February 1968).

Foerstel, Herbert N. *Banned in the U.S.A.: Book Censorship in Schools and Public Libraries.* Westport, Conn.: Greenwood Press, 1994.

Hentoff, Nat. *The Day They Came to Arrest the Book.* New York: Delacorte Press, 1982.

Interracial Books for Children. See the following issues: 15, no. 4 (April 1984) 15, no. 5 (May 1984).

Jenkinson, Edward B. *Censors in the Classroom: The Mind Benders.* Carbondale: Southern Illinois University Press, 1979.

Leonard, James S., Thomas A. Tenney, and Thadious M. Davis, eds. *Satire or Evasion? Black Perspectives on "Huckleberry Finn."* Durham: Duke University Press, 1992.

MacCann, Donnarae, and Gloria Woodard, eds. *The Black American in Books for Children.* Metuchen, N.J.: Scarecrow Press, 1985.

Parker, Barbara, and Stefanie Weiss. *Protecting the Freedom to Learn.* Washington, D.C.: People for the American Way, 1983.

Sloane, David E. E. *"Adventures of Huckleberry Finn": American Comic Vision.* Boston: Twayne, 1988.

Twain, Mark. *"Adventures of Huckleberry Finn": A Case Study in Critical Controversy.* Edited by Gerald Graff and James Phelan. Boston: Bedford Books, 1995.

Wallace, John H. *The Adventures of Huckleberry Finn Adapted.* Falls Church, Va.: John H. Wallace and Sons, 1983.

For a complete annotated bibliography of articles on *Adventures of Huckleberry Finn,* racism, and censorship, see Thomas A. Tenney, "For Further Reading," in Leonard, Tenney, and Davis, *Satire or Evasion?*

Three national organizations collect materials on censorship for distribution: People for the American Way, Washington, D.C.; American Library Association, whose headquarters is in Chicago, Illinois; and the National Council of the Teachers of English, Urbana, Illinois.

3

Mark Twain's Mississippi Valley

CHRONOLOGY

1818	Missouri applies for admission to the Union.
1820	Missouri Compromise allows admission of Missouri as a slave state.
1829	Presidency of Andrew Jackson begins.
1829–43	Closing of reservations in eastern and southern areas and removal of Native Americans to lands west of Missouri.
1830	Book of Mormon published by Joseph Smith in Palmyra, New York.
1832	Reelection of Jackson.
1835	Birth of Sam Clemens, known as Mark Twain, in Florida, Missouri.
1836	Texas declares its independence from Mexico.
1837	Election of Martin Van Buren to presidency, sponsored by Jackson.
	Panic of 1837, financial depression resulting in bank failures, high costs of goods, riots, and widespread unemployment and poverty.

1841	Inauguration of President William Henry Harrison, who dies within a month and is succeeded by John Tyler.
1842	"Oregon fever" in Iowa, Missouri, Illinois, and Kentucky.
1843	First practical telegraph line built.
1844	William Miller predicts that the world will end on October 22; founds Seventh-Day Adventists.
	Polk elected President.
1845	Texas voted into the Union as a state.
	Illinois citizens murder Joseph Smith.
1846	Mormons abandon their home in Nauvoo, moving west to found Salt Lake City.
	Mexico's declaration of war over the annexation of Texas by the United States reaches Congress. President Polk seems to have baited Mexico into a war in order to acquire California.
1848	Peace concluded with Mexico.
	Seneca Falls (New York) Convention launches the women's rights movement.
	Gold discovered at Sutter's mill in California.
1849	Rush of prospectors to the gold mines of California.
	Zachary Taylor becomes President.
1850	Taylor dies and Millard Fillmore becomes President.
	Passage of the Fugitive Slave Act.
	Publication of Nathaniel Hawthorne's *The Scarlet Letter*.
1851	Publication of Herman Melville's *Moby Dick*.
1851–56	Formulation of the Republican Party.
1852	Publication of Harriet Beecher Stowe's *Uncle Tom's Cabin*.
	Franklin Pierce elected President.
1857–61	Mark Twain is a pilot on the Mississippi River.
1860	Lincoln elected President.
1861–65	Civil War.
1861	For a few weeks, Twain is a member of the Confederate Army, then goes to the far West.

1863	Emancipation Proclamation frees slaves in rebel states.
1864–67	Twain works as a newspaperman in California.
1865	First publication of Twain's "Celebrated Jumping Frog of Calaveras County."
1867	Twain moves to New York City.
1868–69	Publication of Louisa May Alcott's *Little Women.*
1869	Publication of *The Innocents Abroad.*
1870	Twain marries Olivia Langdon.
1872	Twain's son dies at age of two years.
	Publication of *Roughing It.*
1873	Publication of *The Gilded Age.*
1876	Publication of *Adventures of Tom Sawyer.*
1880	Publication of *A Tramp Abroad.*
1882	Publication of *The Prince and the Pauper.*
1883	Publication of *Life on the Mississippi.*
1884	Publication of *Adventures of Huckleberry Finn.*
1889	Publication of *A Connecticut Yankee in King Arthur's Court.*
1894	Twain's bankruptcy caused by failure of the firm that published U.S. Grant's memoirs, backed by Twain.
	Publication of *The Tragedy of Pudd'nhead Wilson.*
1896	Publication of *Personal Recollections of Joan of Arc.*
	Death of Twain's daughter Susy.
1904	Death of his wife, Olivia.
1909	Death of his daughter Jean Lampton Clemens.
1910	Death of Mark Twain.
1916	Posthumous publication of *The Mysterious Stranger.*

By the time of Sam Clemens'* birth in 1835, America had become a nation of movers; from New England, Virginia, and the Carolinas they traveled in search of a better life, the chance to have more land or to escape the confines of social class, the opportunity to have adventures or to look for wealth. A few moved to be out

---

*In this chapter, while discussing the biography of the author of *Adventures of Huckleberry Finn*, known under the pen name Mark Twain, I will refer to him by his birth name, Samuel Clemens.

of the reach of the law, to establish fresh, new identities. For them, the past was dead, or at least they had made an energetic attempt to leave the past behind. Many took on new names; some were known only by their given names or by nicknames.

All along the way, they established new communities for protection. With this in mind, *Adventures of Huckleberry Finn* can be seen as a story of an American experience in particular and in miniature. For, like the pioneering Americans, Huck and Jim are constantly on the move, escaping civilization, leaving their old lives behind, taking up new identities and even new names once in a while, running from the law as well as the oppressive past. To be successful in their adventure, they form new "communities" for their own protection.

Movie-makers have contributed to the impression that the western frontier has always lain in California and other states in the far West, defined by the dramatic terrain of the Rocky Mountains and the American deserts. But in 1835, the year of Samuel Clemens' birth, the western frontier actually began in Arkansas and Louisiana and the Missouri of his youth. In 1840 Missouri, Arkansas, and Louisiana were the westernmost areas under settlement and were designated "the near West." The areas immediately along the Mississippi River in Missouri had about 18 to 45 people per square mile at that time. The entire territory of Missouri, including inland areas, had no more than 18 people for every square mile. For hundreds of people this area provided a new life in every sense of the word, where cities, industry, and institutions were brand new. Samuel Clemens grew up in this exciting time in the nation's history and chose it as the setting of *Adventures of Huckleberry Finn.*

To get some sense of the world that Sam Clemens and Huckleberry Finn inhabited, the reader of the novel needs to have a sense of what was occurring in the nation as a whole between 1835 and 1860, and to look closely at the Mississippi Valley area. Some first-hand accounts of everyday life in the area written by Twain and his contemporaries help complete the picture. The chronology at the opening of this chapter provides an overview of some of the major national political and social events that occurred in Clemens' life, especially in his childhood years in Missouri, and will be useful in studying this and subsequent chapters.

The period before the Civil War, when Clemens was growing to manhood, was a time of immense industrial growth, a time when

America became not just a producer of raw materials like cotton, but a manufacturing power to be reckoned with. The manufacture of textiles, for example, was made possible by the constant improvement of transportation, the harnessing of natural resources for power, the invention of numerous machines, and the importation of a huge labor force from Great Britain and Europe. Accompanying the growth in industry was the move westward, made easier by improved transportation on canals, roads, and railroads, enabling pioneers from New York and New England, Pennsylvania and Kentucky, to move into Illinois and Indiana, where the rich land was suitable for raising grain and cattle.

Although different kinds of people moved west, many of them shared distinct characteristics that distinguished them from those they left behind in the East. They were a restless people, always on the move, impatient, and, ironically for citizens of the horse-and-buggy days, obsessed with speed, with getting things done in a hurry. They were typically optimistic, looking forward to improving their lives, even acquiring wealth by securing some portion of America's rich store of untapped land and resources. They were energized by the prospect of starting over, making new lives on the frontier. A person did not escape the law or a bad reputation by going "underground," as one might in the twentieth century; instead he or she went west. To survive in this brave new world at this time, Americans in the near West had to be materialistic and practical. It must also be conceded, however, that this practicality was often tempered with idealism, as can be seen in the growth of all sorts of religious and reform movements on the frontier, such as the temperance and abolition movements.

DEMOCRACY AND EQUALITY

> He said we ought to bow, when we spoke to him, and say "Your Grace," or "My Lord," or "Your Lordship"—and he wouldn't mind it if we called him plain "Bridgewater," which he said was a title, anyway, and not a name, and one of us ought to wait on him at dinner, and do any little thing for him he wanted done. (125)

Through the characters of the king and the duke, Mark Twain satirizes English and European aristocracy; by ridiculing the aristocratic tradition of bestowing titles and privilege on those with inherited position, he expresses the frontier ideals of equality and democracy. Twain's sharpest comment on an undemocratic, royal form of government comes when Huck says he knows that the king and the duke are just liars and frauds, but they couldn't be as bad as real kings and dukes.

The democratic idea grew as Americans of this period, especially western-bound travelers, encouraged greater class equality than their ancestors in the East had allowed. They were also more prone to tolerate lives and beliefs that might be very different from those of the majority. Of course, democracy was limited; all women, non-white citizens, and some recent immigrants (like the Irish) still did not enjoy equality before the law.

In many ways, the idea of the frontier, where Clemens lived, and the values it represented characterized the nation as a whole from 1835 to 1860. The figure who dominated the nation in Clemens' youth, President Andrew Jackson, was an embodiment of pioneer values. With the election of Jackson in 1828, six years before Sam Clemens was born, the presidency passed from the refined hands of New Englanders and Virginians, who always looked backward to England, to a man reared on the frontier in Tennessee. It was one of the most radical shifts of power in the nation's history, a time when many perceived that the country, long governed by a well-educated upper-class elite, was now shifting to the common people who comprised the vast majority of the country's population.

Andrew Jackson was identified with the frontier ideals of Mark Twain's youth. Jackson had his origins in the western frontier, having emerged from the newly settled areas of Tennessee rather than from the East Coast states formed by the high culture of England in the seventeenth century. Furthermore, Jackson was perceived as the first democratic representative of the common workingman, the ordinary laborer in rural and urban areas. Jackson was no stranger to physical labor himself and believed in equality (for white men at least), a broad franchise, and opportunities for advancement for the working classes, such as public education. The frontier lacked the great disparities in wealth and social conditions found in the East, and the legislatures of the various western territories placed fewer limitations on the voting rights of white males than did the other states. Reflecting frontier ideals, Jackson seemed uninterested in maintaining a rigid separation of social classes, as his predecessors from the South and the Northeast had done. This attitude was epitomized by his inaugural, when hundreds of ordinary people, not just Washington's elite, invaded the White House to celebrate.

As in Sam Clemens' boyhood world, however, Native Americans and African Americans were treated shoddily. Most notably, we see Jackson's brutal plan of uprooting Native Americans throughout the East and sending them on what were largely death marches to unfamiliar land west of the Mississippi in order to secure Indian land for white development. Many memoirs written by frontiersmen acknowledge the shabby treatment of the Native Americans and African Americans by the government, and portraits of Native Americans are curiously missing from memoirs of the near West at mid-century and from *Adventures of Huckleberry Finn*. It is as if they had already vanished from the earth.

CENTRALIZED GOVERNMENT VERSUS TERRITORIAL INDEPENDENCE

> Call this a govment! why, just look at it and see what it's like. Here's the law a-standing ready to take a man's son away from him . . . (35)

Pap's tirade against "the govment" is a parody of another frontier attitude carried to the extreme—the distrust of government interference with individual action. Jackson and Jacksonians were identified with a kind of rugged individualism and a lessening of central national control, a sentiment consistent with the frontier. Citizens wanted progress; they wanted canals and railroads, but they were suspicious of government interference in constructing them. Typical of the frontier tendency to decentralize and keep power with the individual and the states was Jackson's renowned political battle with the powerful centralized Bank of the United States, whose practices impeded independent western speculation. Jackson managed to block the renewal of the central bank's charter and deposited the funds of the federal government with smaller state banks. The issue of central versus state control was scarcely put to rest, even with the Civil War: it resurfaced in the period of civil rights agitation in the 1950s and again in the mid-1990s.

ACTION, NOT BOOKS

> And looky here—you drop this school, you hear? . . . Your
> mother couldn't read, and she couldn't write, nuther, before
> she died. None of the family couldn't before they died. I can't;
> and here you're a-swelling yourself up like this. (28)

Twain again uses Pap as the means of satire. In this case, he is
making fun of the anti-intellectualism of the woodsman by taking
it to an extreme. Young boys, in particular, were too eager to get
on with their lives, travel, seek action and adventure, and head for
the western territories, to spend time in a schoolroom. One
learned by living, they thought, not by reading books. And, of
course, life on the frontier was so hard that many, even if they
wanted some book learning, had to forego school to help support
the family.

Consistent with the tone of the frontier, Jackson preferred sim-
plicity and action to the bookish, literary, or philosophical frame
of mind of New England.

POLITICAL ISSUES

The presidents who followed Jackson were frontiersman of another kind. They believed in Manifest Destiny, which promoted
pushing the frontier westward to the Pacific and south to the Rio
Grande, by acquiring Texas, Oregon, and California. The war with
Mexico, which broke out on May 9, 1846, and for the most part
was waged to secure this territory, was very popular with residents
of the Mississippi Valley. Many near westerners volunteered for the
Mexican War, in contrast to those in older eastern states, where
opposition to the war was stronger.

Major political issues often split people along east-west or north-
south lines. Historians Charles, Mary, and William Beard identified
the following:

> The push for low tariffs by planters and farmers in contrast to the
> encouragement of high tariffs for the protection of American "infant
> industries."
>
> The support of state banks and state paper money as opposed to
> a centralized, national bank and national currency.

The endorsement of federal aid to make internal improvements—highways, canals, and railways as opposed to state aid, or no aid at all, to fund such enterprises.

The support for free land for western settlers as opposed to the sale of land for the nation's revenue.

The establishment of states without slavery as opposed to the establishment of states that allowed slavery. (*The Beards' New Basic History of the United States* [Garden City, N.Y.: Doubleday and Co., 1968], p. 241)

Slavery, the largest single national issue shaping the nation in Twain's teenage years and the issue at the heart of *Adventures of Huckleberry Finn,* will be treated in Chapter 4.

Other conflicts also gave the nineteenth century definition. These tensions ran along national, religious, and class lines. Besides the conflicts between North and South over slavery and tariffs, there were tensions between native-born white Americans and the many immigrants flooding into the country who would be competing with them for jobs. There were conflicts as well between Protestants, mostly white, native-born Americans, and Catholics, many of whom were immigrants. A new political party, the Anti-Masonic party, came into being specifically to oppose immigrants. A class conflict was also waged in the cities between upper-class Americans sympathetic to the English, and working-class Americans who despised everything English. This culture war reached a peak of violence when the public became caught up in the rivalry between Edwin Forrest, a popular American actor, and William Macready, a well-known British actor. A large group of working-class New Yorkers attacked a theater where the British actor was appearing.

A TIME WHEN NATURE REIGNED

Soon as it was night, out we shoved; when we got her out to about the middle, we let her alone, and let her float wherever the current wanted her to; then we lit the pipes, and dangled our legs in the water and talked about all kinds of things—we was always naked, day and night. . . . We had the sky, up there, all speckled with stars, and we used to lay on our backs and look up at them. (121)

Huck, a young boy far from civilization and even free of clothes, very simply communes with and celebrates unspoiled nature with the slave Jim, also a natural, as opposed to a civilized, man. And indeed, the most important American philosophers in the nineteenth century, the Transcendentalists, were unlike their Protestant forebears in finding nature and what was natural to be not brutal and cruel, an element to be overcome, but basically good. They believed that society destroyed innocence, corrupted human beings, and fostered delusions. But, they argued, people could find religious truth in nature without the help of civilization. God spoke to mankind, they thought, not so much through the church and scripture as through nature. Those who were closest to nature— children and peoples who were regarded as uncivilized—were most deserving of our admiration (at least in literature and other art forms). So, on the stage, the Native American or American Indian was frequently shown as more heroic than the European, and in such popular works as *Uncle Tom's Cabin*, the simple black man and the little child were revered. *Adventures of Huckleberry Finn*, with Huck and Jim as its heroes, is obviously in that philosophical tradition.

REFORMERS

> And after supper he talked to him about temperance and such things till the old man cried, and said he'd been a fool, and fooled away his life, but now he was agoing to turn over a new leaf and be a man nobody wouldn't be ashamed of. (30)

When Pap shows up in Chapter 5 to claim Huck and the money Huck has found and entrusted to Judge Thatcher, he has to go to court to get custody of Huck. The new judge in town and his wife are illustrative of another typical movement in nineteenth-century culture—social reform. In this instance, the judge and his wife are members of a temperance league and set out to convert Pap to a life of abstinence from alcohol. Pap signs a pledge that he won't drink again and, as a result, they tearfully give him great praise, new clothes, a fine meal, and a roof over his head. The good temperance couple is made to look foolish, however, when Pap sneaks out of their house, trades his new coat for whiskey, goes back to

wreck the room they have provided for him, and falls out of the
window—dead drunk—and breaks his arm.

The nineteenth century was peopled with reformers and religious visionaries of all kinds. The most prominent reformers, mentioned derisively by Huck Finn, were the abolitionists, who wanted
an immediate end to slavery (see Chapter 4). Another energetic
reform group, in keeping with the move toward democracy, was
the women's rights movement, which worked to secure for women
the right to vote and to own property. The women's movement
was also allied to the abolition of slavery and to the temperance
movement, which worked to outlaw the sale of alcohol.

RELIGIOUS ENTHUSIASM

> And people would shout out, "Glory—A-a-men!" And so he
> went on, and the people groaning and crying and saying
> amen. (132)

Mark Twain provides the reader with a picture of a religious
revival out in the woods—radically different from the formal ceremonies of the wealthy churches back East with their highly educated clergy. Religious reformers peppered the country from the
sedate eastern states to the wild frontier. Camp meetings and revivals, like the one the old king uses to bilk people out of their
money, flourished especially well on the frontier.

One of the most prominent religious groups in the frontier states
was the Mormons, led by Joseph Smith. The new group, unlike
many others, was perceived as a threat by the non-Mormon citizens
because of their suspicion about Mormon multiple marriages and
political power. As a consequence, Mormons were attacked
wherever they went in the Midwest and constantly moved from
place to place until they finally settled in Utah. When Mark Twain
was a boy of ten, he heard about Joseph Smith, who had been run
out of the state of Missouri and settled in northwestern Illinois,
where he was lynched in 1845. Clemens would also have heard of
the removal of the Mormons further west in 1846. In 1843 he
would have heard the stories of another religious leader, William
Miller, whose disciples dressed in white robes and gathered on
hillsides to await the end of the world, which Miller had led them
to believe would occur on or about that time. Twain was also fa-

miliar with the emotional religious revivals that occasionally sprang up in the Mississippi Valley. The frontier was usually hospitable to unorthodox religious sects, despite its hounding of the Mormons. Furthermore, the frontier was an area where pioneers could ignore religion altogether if they chose—unlike Puritan New England, where churches dominated daily life.

SETTLEMENT OF THE MISSISSIPPI VALLEY

The area along the Mississippi River, where Sam Clemens grew up and Huck and Jim had their adventures, had been Indian territory until 1682, when French explorers claimed the land for France. In 1803, after France sold the area to the United States in the Louisiana Purchase, part of it was designated the "Territory of Missouri." Following in the steps of the 1769 party of Daniel Boone, settlers poured into Kentucky and Tennessee, and later moved farther west into Missouri, Arkansas, and Mississippi. They came chiefly from the inland areas of the Carolinas and Virginia, and from Kentucky and Tennessee, bringing their slaves with them, as Sam Clemens' father did. The first settlements were right along the rivers, like the Ohio, Missouri, and Mississippi, where water and transportation were easily available and the land was good. The uplands, which were less fertile and more difficult to farm, were settled later. Many poorer people who did not own slaves also moved into the area to farm on a smaller scale. The new settlers began farming hemp, tobacco, and corn on the good soil they found. Not all settlers were farmers, however; many who had capital invested it in commerce—furs, timber, river transportation, and even in various stores and businesses to service the villages. The newly formed communities' leaders generally came from this group, and it was to this group that Sam Clemens' father, a lawyer and businessman, belonged.

In 1818 Missouri requested admission to the Union as a state. After a long and heated controversy between pro- and anti-slavery factions in Congress over whether Missouri's citizens should be allowed or forbidden to hold slaves, it was admitted as a slave state in 1820. The dispute over this issue was never really settled, however, and violence over slavery erupted continually.

The people who settled in the Mississippi Valley in the 1820s and 1830s were largely of Scotch or Northern Irish descent, and largely Protestant. They were different from the aristocratic planters they left behind in Virginia and the Carolinas, being more adventurous and perhaps more curious and ambitious for a better life. Few foreign-born immigrants found their way to the region around Hannibal, Missouri, where Samuel Clemens was reared. Even though most were modest farmers and merchants with relatively little wealth apart from their land, they had a high level of literacy. They were skilled at living under hard and often lonely conditions.

LIVING ACCOMMODATIONS IN THE NEAR WEST

> [I]t was woody and there warn't no houses but an old log hut in a place where the timber was so thick you couldn't find it if you didn't know where it was. (32)

Pap's hut on the edge of Hannibal is typical of the houses rapidly thrown up by the settlers when they first moved to the Missouri territory. In the early decades of the century, houses were usually primitive one-room log structures, and even in Clemens' childhood, when pioneers had learned to quickly construct frame houses with several bedrooms, many pioneers, like Huck Finn's father, lived in very primitive shacks.

The Widow Douglas' house, quite a step above the accommodations that Huck is used to, is more like the modest frame houses that went up in the decades following settlement. The widow's house has all the amenities, including fresh bed linen, a carpet, and a mirror, much of which had probably been brought from the East at the time of settlement. The Grangerford house, which Huck stumbles on in his journey, illustrates another step in the civilizing of the near West, for it is grandly furnished with the latest fashions, seemingly recently imported from the East.

AMUSEMENTS AND FRAUDS

> "What's your line—mainly?"
>
> "Jour printer, by trade; do a little in patent medicines; theatre-actor—tragedy, you know; take a turn at mesmerism and phrenology when there's a chance; teach singing-geography school for a change; sling a lecture, sometimes—oh, I do lots

of things—most anything that comes handy, so it ain't work. What's your lay?''

"I've done considerble in the doctoring way in my time. Layin' on o' hands is my best holt—for cancer, and paralysis, and sich things; and I k'n tell a fortune pretty good, when I've got somebody along to find out the facts for me. Preachin's my line, too; and workin' camp-meetin's; and missionaryin' around.'' (123)

In just a few lines of conversation between the king and the duke, Mark Twain summarizes most of the traveling entertainments of his day on the frontier, many of them subject to exploitation by frauds such as the king and the duke. Extended episodes dramatizing the traveling deceptions perpetrated on simple frontiersmen eager for cure-alls and stimulation include the king's "working" of a revival meeting, the duke's Shakespearean production, and the pornographic show they put on in Arkansas. One of the most notorious bandits of Sam Clemens' day, a man named John Murel, consistently used revival meetings to recruit a band of outlaws to steal, murder, and generally control the Mississippi Valley through terror. The much less dangerous king and duke also consider themselves good with cards. Like typical Mississippi River gamblers, the king and the duke always had to be on the move. When con men weren't fast enough in removing themselves from the people they had cheated, they were the objects of frontier violence.

Besides revivals and stage plays, there were many other group activities that brought the people in the community together. In the early days, they hadn't the advantages of the elaborate city theaters, symphonies, and universities, but they had other communal outings: storytelling, fiddle-making, quilting bees, cabin raisings, rail splitting, food preserving, spelling bees, camp meetings, pie auctions, court trials, public hangings, funerals, picnics, traveling circuses, Sunday Schools, group singing, patriotic orators, political speeches, and hunting and fishing expeditions. Many of these activities are alluded to in Mark Twain's work.

HANNIBAL/ST. PETERSBURG

In 1835, the year Sam Clemens was born, Hannibal was a well-established community on the Mississippi River at the edge of the wilderness. The town had well-stocked stores, an orderly local government (Sam's father was a judge), and a system of schooling. Still, disease and the dangers and loneliness of the wilderness were a constant force in the lives of Hannibal citizens. By far the greatest influence on life in the area was the river itself, which at that time was a mile wide at Hannibal. The river was a link with older, exotic places like St. Louis and especially New Orleans. Often it brought visitors from as far away as Europe. The river was also a means of escape from the small community and its law, and it was a playground of murderous but romantic outlaws who ruled it with absolute tyranny. The river brought to the town the colorful people who made their living on the water—people who manned the steamboats, the gamblers who worked them, and the wild eccentrics who made their living from rafts and small boats.

DEATH AND VIOLENCE

The death and violence that permeate *Adventures of Huckleberry Finn* are entirely in keeping with the character of the Mississippi Valley of the 1830s and 1840s. Very few settlers lived to old age there, and almost a fifth of the children died before the age of one year. Epidemics of cholera, yellow fever, and dysentery decimated frontier settlements. Hookworm and malaria were widespread and weakened the general condition of the population, making them more susceptible to other diseases, often fatal ones. Astute observations on the part of travelers in the area confirm this. Mark Twain singled out for special praise Mrs. Frances Trollope, an Englishwoman who published accounts of her travels in the near West in 1828. Some seven years before Clemens was born she found that disease and the poor living conditions in which disease thrived were everywhere to be seen along the lower Mississippi River:

> [W]e might have thought ourselves the first of the human race who had ever penetrated into this territory of bears and alligators. But still from time to time appeared the hut of the wood-cutter, who supplies the steam-boats with fuel, at the risk, or rather with the assurance of early death, in exchange for dollars and whiskey. These sad dwellings are nearly all of them inundated during the winter, and the best of them are constructed on piles, which permit the

water to reach its highest level without drowning the wretched inhabitants. These unhappy beings are invariably victims of ague,
which they meet recklessly, sustained by the incessant use of ardent
spirits. The squalid look of the miserable wives and children of these
men was dreadful, and often as the spectacle was renewed I could
never look at it with indifference. Their complexion is of a blueish
white, that suggests the idea of dropsy; this is invariable, and the
poor little ones wear exactly the same ghastly hue. A miserable cow
and a few pigs standing knee-deep in water, distinguish the more
prosperous of these dwellings, and on the whole I should say that
I never witnessed human nature reduced so low, as it appeared in
the wood-cutters' huts on the unwholesome banks of the Mississippi. (*Domestic Manners of the Americans* [New York: Alfred A.
Knopf, 1949], pp. 20, 21)

Even further up on the Ohio River, she found equally unhealthy
conditions:

Yet these fair shores are still unhealthy. More than once we landed,
and conversed with the families of the wood-cutters, and scarcely
was there one in which we did not hear of some member who had
"lately died of the fever."—They are all subject to ague. (p. 35)

Similar stories of death in the Mississippi Valley are related by
Alexander Majors, a pioneer businessman on the frontier. He re-
calls that deaths were a regular occurrence on the steamboats
themselves:

During the cholera days there was a heavy loss of life on the Western
steam boats. On the Missouri River some of the old boats had a
burial crew. At night-time, when the passengers were hardly aware
of what was going on, the boat would stop near a sand-bar. The
bodies of those who had died during the day were taken to the
sand-bar, where they were quickly buried. What would have been
the use of putting up even a pine board, for the rising waters would
soon have washed it away?

But this is not simply Western history. It is a part of the history
of the North and the South, for those who came never to return
were from those sections. In many an Eastern and Southern home
it is as unknown to them as to the people of the West where sleep
their dead on those old trails of the Western empire. (Alexander

Majors, *Seventy Years on the Frontier* [Chicago: Rand McNally, 1893], p. 263)

Lives were also taken by the ravages of nature, such as the flooding of the river, and, above all, by frontier violence. Historian Page Smith summarizes the presence of death on the frontier:

Americans, like other humans, were born, grew up in families, ventured into the world, succeeded or failed (and often did both successively throughout their lives), grew old and died—by disease, gunshot wounds, steam boiler explosions, and drowning. In their reckless disregard for life and limb, many Americans did not survive to old age. Infant and child mortality was distressingly high. It was not uncommon for only half the children in a family to reach maturity. (*The Nation Comes of Age* [New York: McGraw-Hill, 1981], p. 884)

STEAMBOAT ACCIDENTS

Two years ago last Christmas, your Uncle Silas was coming up from Newrleans on the old Lally Rook, and she blowed out a cylinder head and crippled a man. And I think he died afterwards. (216)

Adventures of Huckleberry Finn makes two references to steamboats, as a substantial part of the story's plot. The first is the *Walter Scott,* "a steamboat that had killed herself on a rock." The passengers and crew had all been evacuated, and even though Huck and Jim board it to look for plunder, they realize the danger of climbing on board this wreck, especially in a storm, which likely precipitated the wreck in the first place. They eventually see the ship sink so far into the water that the gangsters who boarded it, also for plunder, have obviously drowned.

The second reference to steamboat wrecks occurs when Huck arrives at the Phelps farm to rescue Jim. To explain why he's late, Huck concocts a story about a wreck caused by a blown-up cylinder head. In response, Aunt Sally recounts another similar story about a wreck her husband had been in. All three instances, real and imaginary, suggest a historical reality: that violence and death were closely associated with the river itself. Constant danger attended river travel, even for the well-heeled passengers on steamboats. Fires, snags in the water, and explosions of steamboat boilers were frequent, fatal occurrences. Records show that forty-nine boats were destroyed on the Mississippi River and its tributaries in 1841, sixty-eight in 1842, and thirty-six in 1846. The candles and lanterns used for illumination sometimes ignited the whole boat, which could become completely engulfed in flames in a few minutes, leaving few survivors. Hidden underwater snags frequently tore into the bottom of a boat, starting a fire.

The love of speed, culminating in races between steamboats as a regular part of many passenger trips, brought about one of the most common causes of fatalities in steamboat travel, the explosion of the boiler. To increase their speed, steamboat captains and their engineers deliberately kept the water level in the boilers low, and safety valves on the boilers were sometimes taped shut, a practice that measurably increased the risk of an explosion. And when explosions did occur, the whole boat would be blown to smithereens and few passengers survived (see Figure 3.1). The horror of such explosions came home to the Clemens family when Sam's brother was blown up in such an accident.

An English traveler named Thomas Cather reported his observations about steamboat travel in his *Journals of 1836,* the year after Mark Twain was born:

> Steamboat accidents are of very frequent occurrence in the Western waters; scarcely a month passes without a boat being blown up, burned down, or sunk. We passed four or five wrecks on our passage up the river. These boats are constructed very hastily, of bad materials badly put together. The Americans are always in such a breathless hurry that they will not take time to do things permanently. I was informed that many a steamboat had been launched whose timbers ninety days before were uncut in the forest, and whose ironwork was unfashioned in the dark mine. To use their own words, they do go ahead, though sometimes they get along too fast as their steamboat disasters testify. The engines are of the high pressure kind and as they extend under the cabin deck, if they should happen to burst, the passengers are sure to be blown sky high. Considering the flimsy state of the boilers, the carelessness of the engineers, and the spirit of emulation which prompts the captains to race against other boats, not to mention the danger of fires, and the snags and stumps which abound in the Mississippi, it is more likely that you should meet with an accident than that you

Figure 3.1. Sketch accompanying a news story about a horrible and frequent occurrence on the Mississippi River—an explosion and fire aboard a riverboat. The fate of those who escaped the burning boat was often death by drowning. Courtesy Roland Harper Photograph Collection, W. S. Hoole Special Collections Library, The University of Alabama.

should perform your voyage in safety. (*Voyage to America* [New York: Thomas Yoseloff, 1961], pp. 79, 80)

In *Paddle Wheels and Pistols,* a book about the Mississippi Valley in the nineteenth century, Irving Anthony describes the results of an explosion much like ones with which Clemens was all too familiar throughout his childhood:

> Many engineers not only made steam with the water as low as possible, but they tied the safety valve shut so that it could not blow off and relieve the pressure. Thus bottled, the boiler was compelled to stand stresses for which it was never designed. If luck were with the engineer his engines ran better than they knew how, but if luck were bad the rivets surrendered, the tubes gave way, and in the sudden expansion of the steam the unfortunate boat was rent from end to end. Men were blown through solid wooden bulkheads, were lifted from the pilot houses and thrown a hundred feet, and lived unhurt, like the survivors of a freak hurricane, but most of those on board a steam boat whose boiler burst died at once, or were horribly scalded or crushed. (New York: Grosset and Dunlap, 1929, pp. 223, 224)

Another student of the river, Marquis W. Childs, gives a similar version of a boiler explosion:

> When there was an explosion, or the awful cry of fire, inferno, nothing less, broke loose. There was utter panic, the most horrible pandemonium, with the weak and helpless clawing at the strong for a chance at being saved. The hope for any but the toughest and brawniest was very slight. Live steam from the bursted boilers was fatal to all those who breathed it. Within a few minutes the river would be swarming with clutching, screaming figures, many of them helpless against the surge of the current. (*Mighty Mississippi: Biography of a River* [New York: Ticknor and Fields, 1982], p. 60)

The English author Charles Dickens was not alone among foreign travelers who were so fearful of traveling by steamboat that they often delayed their journeys for several days while they tried to find out just which one was the safest.

RAFTING ACCIDENTS

> We could hear her pounding along, but we didn't see her
> good till she was close. She aimed right for us. Often they do
> that and try to see how close they can come without touching;
> sometimes the wheel bites off a sweep, and then the pilot
> sticks his head out and laughs. . . . There was a yell at us, and
> a jingling of bells to stop the engines, a pow-pow of cussing,
> and whistling of steam—and as Jim went overboard on one
> side and I on the other, she come smashing straight through
> the raft. (98)

Huck recounts this incident in which he and Jim are traveling at
night on the raft, on which they display a lighted lantern to call
attention to their presence whenever they see a steamboat. On this
occasion they realize that a boat is coming upstream, full speed
ahead, and instead of trying to avoid the lighted raft, it heads
straight for them. Huck believes that the steamboat intends merely
to shave or sideswipe them, but soon it becomes obvious that the
steamboat has misjudged the situation and will hit the raft
squarely. Turning off its engines at the last minute does not help;
it is too late. Huck and Jim dive off just as the steamboat hits and
splinters the raft. To save himself Huck has to dive for the bottom
of the river and try to stay down for a minute and a half so that
the steamboat will go clear over him. As he surfaces, he observes
that steamboat crews dislike raftsmen and that the steamboat has
started its engines back up immediately, speeding away without
stopping to see if it can help the two poor raftsmen, who are in
dire peril.

The river had heavy traffic in raftsmen, who were subject to similar violent and fatal accidents when their crafts were pulverized
by the much larger steamboats that roared over them, splintering
the rafts into a thousand pieces, killing those aboard, and going
on ahead as if nothing had happened.

ALCOHOL AND FRONTIER VIOLENCE

> After supper Pap took the jug, and said he had enough whisky
> there for two drunks and one delirium tremens. . . .
> By and by he rolled out and jumped up to his feet looking
> wild, and he see me and went for me. He chased round and

round the place, with a clasp knife, calling me the Angel of
Death, and saying he would kill me, and then I couldn't come
for him no more. (37)

Pap is an example of a man whose alcohol consumption feeds
his violence. In the reader's first look at him, Pap takes a dollar
from Huck to get whiskey. The following day he appears in town
drunk. At first his drink-caused violence takes the form of rowdi-
ness and verbal abuse: he "got drunk and went a-blowing around
and cussing and whooping and carrying on; and he kept it up all
over town, with a tin pan, till most midnight" (30). After this episode, Pap is jailed for a week. He boasts, however, that while other
people can force him to do certain things, *he* is boss of his son,
Huck, who can be forced to submit to a whipping whenever Pap
feels inclined.

Soon his rhetorical violence becomes physical as he catches
Huck whenever he can and thrashes him, eventually imprisoning
Huck in his shack. Pap trades everything he owns for whiskey, and
when he gets drunk, he beats Huck until Huck can no longer tolerate it. The end of Pap's life is a violent one in a house littered
with whiskey bottles.

Drunkenness on the frontier, which so often fed the violence of
the region, is also seen in the habits of the king and the duke and
in the confrontation of Boggs and Sherburn. Boggs, who is roaring
drunk and refuses to moderate his speech or to leave the area, is
shot dead by Sherburn.

In *Hardscrabble Frontier,* a statistics-based study of an Arkansas
county in the 1850s, Gene W. Boyett documents the very high
consumption of alcohol typical of the communities Jim and Huck
encounter on their river trip. Alcohol was extraordinarily cheap in
the area, so that even the poorest person (like Pap) could afford
it. Furthermore, the temperance movement, powerfully at work in
other parts of the country at the time to outlaw the sale of whiskey,
had little support in the South and areas like the near West, which
was settled by Southerners, for temperance leagues were strongly
linked to the movement for the abolition of slavery (Lanham, Md.:
University Press of America, 1990).

OUTLAW VIOLENCE IN THE NEAR WEST

> Now, we'll start this band of robbers and call it Tom Sawyer's
> Gang. Everybody that wants to join has got to take an oath,
> and write his name in blood. . . .
> . . . We ain't burglars. That ain't no sort of style. We are
> highwaymen. We stop stages and carriages on the road, with
> masks on, and kill the people and take their watches and
> money. (17)

Tom's gang was a comical parody of activity that was quite common and dangerous on the Mississippi River in the 1830s and 1840s, for travel on the river was violent not only because of collisions and fatal traffic accidents, but because of the dangerous characters who made their livelihood from the river. Raftsmen, for example, were rough people who came into towns to drink, carouse, and terrorize the populace. These boatmen often became outlaws or pirates. The river became a prime workplace for horse thieves, for example, and a site for selling all manner of other stolen goods. Gangs of outlaws, who were not of the harmless character of Tom Sawyer's crew, were known to kidnap for ransom, to steal slaves and sell them down south, and to print and distribute counterfeit money. They roamed the shores of the river, stealing and slaughtering on farms, where they weren't above the mean-spirited torturing of dumb animals as well. They also swooped down to rob and kill boat passengers, very much as outlaws robbed stagecoach passengers farther out west.

OTHER DANGEROUS CHARACTERS ALONG THE RIVER

> Jim throwed some old rags over him, but he needn't done it;
> I didn't want to see him. There was heaps of old greasy cards
> scattered around over the floor, and old whisky bottles, and a
> couple of masks made out of black cloth; and all over the walls
> was the ignorantest kind of words and pictures, made with
> charcoal. There was two old dirty calico dresses, and a sun-
> bonnet, and some women's under-clothes, hanging against the
> wall. (57)

While Huck and Jim are just starting out on their journey, they come across a house floating down the river in which Jim finds the body of a dead man. What they find in addition—women's clothing, whiskey bottles, and, seemingly, pornography on the walls—suggests that they have stumbled on another root of violence in the near West—a house of prostitution.

Violence also inevitably followed the many floating brothels that moored in the docks near cities or roamed up and down the river, out of reach of the law. Some of the most notoriously dangerous men along the river kept woodyards or stations stocked with wood for steamboat fuel. Typically, these men, who had escaped the law in the East, would rob or kill any steamboat passenger who was foolish enough to disembark while the engineers were taking on fuel at one of these stations.

The presence of gamblers in the river towns and on steamboats also contributed to violence in the area. These men made their living by cheating at cards, often playing with drunken and ill-tempered passengers who frequented the saloons on the frontier. As a result, for self-protection, gamblers had to be as skilled with pistols as they were with cards, and fights and killings inevitably followed in their wake.

THE LIFE OF SAMUEL CLEMENS

Into this Missouri scene—Florida, Missouri, to be exact—Samuel Clemens was born on November 30, 1835. In the works of few writers would the "place" of childhood be so thoroughly absorbed—the idyllic small rural town of childhood, the closeness of nature, the wildness of new settlements, and the excitement of the country's major waterway, the Mississippi River. Clemens' parents, typical of other settlers in Missouri, moved out to the frontier, stopping in one place and then another in search of adventure and a better way of life. Coming from the southern states of Virginia and Kentucky, they brought their slaves with them and continued to buy and sell slaves once they reached Missouri. They were in one of the earlier waves of settlers in Florida, Missouri, composed at this time of a few log structures in a community newly carved from the wilderness.

When Sam was four years old, the family moved from Florida to the older and larger community of Hannibal, Missouri, the town on which he based St. Petersburg in *Adventures of Huckleberry Finn.* Though this community had also been settled recently, it already had more farms and town businesses than wilderness, and more frame houses than log ones. The original Native American inhabitants of the region were no longer part of life in this area of Missouri, and even the pioneer trappers and hunters had been replaced by businessmen and farmers.

In Hannibal, Sam's father was a prominent citizen, even for a time a judge, but his numerous business ventures continually failed, and the family was always poor, often on the move within town, renting smaller, less convenient quarters.

While the rural nature of Hannibal in the 1840s and 1850s offered young Sam a certain amount of hometown nurture and protection, the town's placement on the river brought close all the excitement of a wider, exotic world on the move. At the same time, his frequent stays on his Uncle John Quarles' farm in Florida, Missouri, afforded him a true rural experience and a different view of slaves from the one he received in Hannibal. In Hannibal, slaves did the house chores of servants. In Florida, they worked the land, much as they did in the upper South. His uncle's farm served as a model for the Phelps farm in *Adventures of Huckleberry Finn.*

Sam was fairly small and sometimes sickly, but a bright, independent child with a mind of his own. Like Tom Sawyer, whom he seemed to model after himself, he was always curious, inventive, and mischievous. He had little use for school, chiefly because of an excessively strict, unsympathetic schoolmaster. When he was twelve years old, his father died, and his mother gave in to his pleas and allowed him to quit school. Like Tom, he put together a "gang" with his friends Tom and Ben Blankenship, the sons of the town drunk. Tom Blankenship was his model for Huck Finn. The river constantly drew Sam and his friends like a magnet. They swam, fished, explored islands and caves, and, with the rest of the town, excitedly came to meet the frequent steamboats that landed there, observing the colorful passengers from all parts of the country, most of whom embarked from the Europeanized cities of New Orleans and St. Louis. The boys were especially fascinated with the crews of the steamboats, who seemed to have a secret wisdom all their own. Every boy wanted above all else to be a steamboat captain.

Young Sam was a frequent witness to the horrible violence of his home area. One incident, on which he later based the Sherburn/Boggs episode, was the murder on Hannibal's Main Street of a man named Smarr. Sam saw him shot and then carried to a post office, where he died with a Bible on his chest. The young boy dreamed about Smarr's death agony for years. At another time, he watched a slave die after having been hit in the head with a piece of iron ore. Sam also observed a knife fight between two pioneers heading for California and saw one of the men die from a knife wound. In another scene reminiscent of the Boggs/Sherburn encounter, he saw a woman shoot to death a man who threatened to assault her daughter. He had yet another traumatic experience when he crawled through the window of his father's office one night to take a nap, only to discover that a corpse with glassy eyes and a gaping chest wound was keeping him company. Sam witnessed hangings and slave beatings as a regular part of life in Hannibal.

After Sam was allowed to quit school, he began to get the kind of education students receive from books—not at school, but from the reading he began to do as part of a job working for a printer. In these five years as a printer, he first began to try his hand at writing a few pieces for magazines.

In 1852, at the age of seventeen, he began his youthful travels, leaving Hannibal for work as a compositor on a newspaper in St. Louis. From there he traveled east for the first time, to work for a printing house in New York City, then in Philadelphia. Less than two years after he had left the Midwest, he returned to Missouri, then Illinois, and then Ohio. While working as a printer for his brother, Orion, in Keokuk, Illinois, he took his first step toward another career in which he would eventually be very successful— delivering humorous lectures on Mississippi life. Meanwhile, when he was at the end of his youthful career as a printer in the Midwest, he was introduced to literature and philosophy by an older friend who shared the same rooming house with him.

In April 1857, when he was twenty-one years old, he began a trip down the Ohio and Mississippi rivers toward New Orleans. It was on this trip that he was able to embark on the job he had wanted all his life, that of a riverboat pilot. After a lengthy apprenticeship to a famous and exacting captain named Horace Bixby, he was finally licensed as a pilot. In the three years that followed, he became a master of an ever-shifting, dangerous, mesmerizing river that presented him with perpetual challenge. The intimate knowledge he took on in those years is relived in Huck and Jim's trip from St. Petersburg to the deep South. In 1860 his career ended abruptly with the outbreak of the Civil War. It was expected that a Missourian with a southern background would join the Confederate Army, which Clemens did even though he did not believe in the Confederate cause. Within a very few months he decided that he was neither skilled nor dedicated to "the cause," and he and a number of his fellow soldiers left the Civil War far behind, for the far West. As he writes at the end of an account of his brief service in the army (in "The Private History of a Campaign that Failed"), "I knew more about retreating than the man that invented retreating" (*The Portable Mark Twain* [New York: Viking Press, 1946], p. 142).

He made his way to the Nevada territory, where promises of fortunes in the mining industry had begun to attract many squatters, including his brother Orion, who had been made territorial secretary of Nevada. Although the places and times he wrote about in *Adventures of Huckleberry Finn* were far behind him as he headed west, Sam was still in training to write the first really American novel: in the four years he lived in Nevada, he not only did mining and prospecting, he began working as a newspaperman for the *Territorial Enterprise* and the *Virginia City Enterprise*. Around this time, in 1863, he began to write under the name Mark Twain, a technical term used by steamboat crews on the Mississippi River.

In May 1864, he moved to San Francisco, California, where he became a writer for the *Morning Call* and the *Alta Californian*. He lived the wild life of a young writer in San Francisco, a stranger to neither the city's jails nor its saloons. One of his biggest stories as a reporter was on corruption in the city, especially in the police department. At the same time, he began selling fiction to national magazines and developed a name for himself as a lecturer. His first big literary success was a short story, "The Celebrated Jumping Frog of Calaveras County," which gained him a reputation even back east in New York City.

After five and a half years in California, he left the West to return to New York City. He was able from this time forward to devote his complete attention to his dual careers as writer and lecturer, and although he would always be associated with the near West of Missouri and the far West of California, for the rest of his life he lived in the East, with brief sojourns in England and on the European continent.

His first book, *The Innocents Abroad,* completed in 1868, was about a shipload of American tourists in Europe. Shortly after its publication Clemens married Olivia Langdon, a wealthy young woman with whom he remained very much in love for the rest of his life. Her father built a mansion in Buffalo, New York, for the two of them to move into after they married. After a brief residence there, they moved to Hartford, Connecticut, which would remain his home base for the rest of his life. Here in Hartford and in his association with novelist William Dean Howells and other intellectuals in the Northeast, he began to reevaluate the southern society of his youth and become cognizant of the continuing plight of African Americans after the Civil War. In 1871 he began work on his second book, *Roughing It,* which was drawn from his experiences in the far West. The publication brought him tremendous worldwide success. In 1873 he co-wrote, with Charles Dudley Warner, *The Gilded Age,* critical of the greed and opulence of his day. Shortly after this, he completed his first Tom Sawyer book, which was also a great success, and began working on *Adventures of Huckleberry Finn.* He was not able to continue working on it, however, and instead took his first extensive trip back to Missouri and the Mississippi River. Although he was shocked at the changes he found since he had worked there as a riverboat pilot, what he saw also reminded him of his days on the river and in Hannibal. The result was a nonfiction book entitled *Life on the Mississippi.* The experience also inspired him to take up Huck Finn again, but not until 1884 was *Adventures of Huckleberry Finn* published. In his life, he was lucky in a happy marriage and enjoyed tremendous worldwide recognition, wonderful friends, and considerable wealth. But he also lost several fortunes on various ventures and endured the excruciating pain of seeing the death of several children and his wife. As a result, at the end of his life, the darkly cynical side of Mark Twain (which is evident even in *Adventures of Huckleberry Finn*) completely crowded out the lighter, more humorous side. He died in 1910, a bitter man.

While Mark Twain was the author of many books, essays, and works of short fiction, and such novels as *A Connecticut Yankee in King Arthur's Court, Pudd'nhead Wilson, The Prince and the Pauper, Joan of Arc,* and *The Mysterious Stranger, Adventures of Huckleberry Finn,* his book drawing on his boyhood in Hannibal and the knowledge of the Mississippi River he gained in young manhood as a steamboat pilot, was to stand as his greatest masterpiece.

Included in this section on the history of the Mississippi Valley frontier are a number of firsthand accounts by people who lived in Missouri at the same time Sam Clemens did: David Dyer, who wrote the first account, became a lawyer and a legislator; Tom Horn became a scout (and sometime lawman and hired killer); Samuel Hildebrand became a Confederate soldier and a notorious raider; and George Devol, who left home at the age of ten to work on a riverboat, became a Mississippi riverboat gambler. Accounts of life on the Mississippi by observers from other countries were written by Harriet Martineau, an Englishwoman, and Frederick Gerstaecker, a German sportsman. Dyer, Hildebrand, and Horn provide accounts of childhood at the time, showing a variety of reactions to the hardships of frontier life in general—home, education, freedom, nature, and violence. Martineau provides another picture of concerns about the safety of steamboat travel and about disease and poverty along the river; Gerstaecker writes about crime and violent frontier justice in the area. In George Devol's work the reader finds firsthand testimony of every kind of cheating, deception, and violence connected with the life of the gambler on the Mississippi River.

MEMOIRS OF DAVID DYER

David P. Dyer, a prominent midwestern lawyer and judge, had many things in common with Samuel Clemens and his characters in *Adventures of Huckleberry Finn,* but he also provides the reader with a view of a different kind of childhood in Missouri in the 1830s and 1840s, the same years which Clemens and Huck were growing up in Hannibal/St. Petersburg. Dyer was born in 1838, three years after Sam Clemens. Dyer's parents like Sam's, traveled by wagon to the Mississippi Valley from the South, bringing with them modest belongings and slaves. From Dyer the reader gets firsthand details of the life of a pioneer family in Missouri—their efforts at turning virgin soil into farmland and constructing the first buildings on the soil—as well as the problems that beset them: flooding, disease, and early death.

Like the fathers of both Sam and Huck, Dyer's father died when he was still a boy. Like Sam, Dyer begins to deplore the slavery that his family has brought with them to Missouri. (See his comments in Chapter 4.)

In many ways, Dyer's childhood stands in contrast to Sam's and Huck's; unlike the Clemens family, who lived in a good-sized and fairly well established town right on the Mississippi River, the Dyers lived on an isolated farm some sixteen miles from the busy waterway. Dyer's childhood does not appear to have been as carefree as Sam's and Tom Sawyer's, and his difficulties were not the same as Huck's. Perhaps because of the isolation and poverty in a rural setting, Dyer had to work very hard on the family farm (unlike Tom and Huck on the Phelps farm). At fourteen, for example, Dyer became solely responsible for making the five-day, sixty-mile trek to St. Louis to sell the family's farm produce and to purchase staples that could not be produced on the farm. But along with the hard work, Dyer looks back on a farm community with simple, fairly innocent amusements.

Formal education was given a high priority back in the East, where the Puritans had lost no time in establishing Harvard College, but it was less emphasized on the frontier of Missouri where Huck Finn lived. Note that the qualifications of Dyer's teacher leave something to be desired. Dyer took to the schoolroom much more readily than either Sam Clemens or Huck Finn, but he describes a schoolmate who sounds very much like Huck.

FROM DAVID P. DYER, *AUTOBIOGRAPHY AND REMINISCENCES*
(St. Louis: William Harvey Miner Co., 1922)

I was the youngest of twelve children, and when I married, on the 15th of November, 1860, all twelve were living. Today I am the only survivor. There were five brothers and seven sisters, and of these, George, Joseph, Mary, Martha, and John were married before I, the twelfth, was born. I have nieces and nephews older than myself which does not occur very often in a family.

The five eldest children of David and Nancy Dyer left Virginia in 1840 and came to Missouri and settled in the counties of Warren and St. Charles. They were all farmers. In 1841 my father and mother, with the seven remaining children and a few slaves, left the old home in Henry County, Virginia, and after six weeks of hardship on the way, came to Missouri.

The means of transportation used by my father from Virginia to Missouri consisted of two large wagons (made by convicts in the Virginia Penitentiary in Richmond), each of which were drawn by four horses. In these two wagons were placed the household goods that had accumulated in the Virginia home. Everything being made ready, the "whip was cracked" and the start was made for Missouri, a thousand miles and more away. For six long weeks they journeyed before the goal was reached. Over hills and through valleys, over mountains and across rivers, they traveled from Virginia through Tennessee, Kentucky, Indiana and Illinois, until the great Mississippi River was reached and crossed.

The children (except the youngest) and the negroes "footed it" practically all of the way. At nightfall camps were made on the roadside, tents pitched, fires lighted, horses tethered, watered and fed, meals cooked on open fires, beds made in wagons and on the ground, prayers said, and beneath the twinkling stars sleep was eagerly sought by each and every one of the tired party composing that group of hopeful and joyous "movers." A place was temporarily rented in the southern part of Warren County. This had a brick dwelling on it, the only building of its kind in the county. It was known far and wide as the "Brick House Place."

The master, leader, who had turned his back on the thin land of Henry County, Virginia, was looking, as most Virginians did, for "bottom land and living water." In this search he passed over the rich and fertile uplands of St. Louis and St. Charles Creek in Lincoln County. Here he found the place he was seeking. He bought of a man named Chambers, two hundred and sixty acres of bottom and hill land. The bottom land was rich and productive, but the hill land, while splendid with timber, was thin and poor. There were a few acres of cleared land in the bottom that had been cultivated by Chambers and a cabin in which he had lived, that was situated near the clearing and close by a well of "living water."

Possession was taken and improvements began. In the bottom the growth was large sycamore trees—on the hill big oaks with some hickories. The sycamores were felled, cut in pieces, rolled together and burned and the land made ready for cultivation. On the high land oak trees were felled, cut to the proper length, hewn on two sides and built into houses for a residence and other purposes on a high hill that overlooked the bottoms. The residence was composed of four large rooms and was two stories in height. A stone chimney was built between four rooms (two below and two above) with a fireplace in each. The roof was made of boards cut and split by hand and the interstices or cracks between the logs were filled by a mortar composed of earth, straw and lime. In addition to this most pretentious dwelling, other buildings were erected in close proximity,—houses for the negroes to live in, smoke house, kitchen, etc., etc. Everything seemed to be moving along happily and well; clearings were made, stables and fences built and improvements of a substantial character were to be seen on all sides; prosperity apparent everywhere. But, alas, after three years of unremitting toil and the endurance of hardships only known to the pioneer, there came the great flood of 1844, a flood of a magnitude hitherto unknown and which has never been equalled since. The creek (Big Creek) was not only big in name but big in fact. Practically all of the improvements made on the bottom lands were swept away, together with the ungathered and ungarnered crops.

This unfortunate disaster left the owner, the courageous master, practically where he began three years before. In time this could have been righted by hard work, but there was a greater misfortune to follow—a misfortune that could not be remedied. The waters of the great flood receded, but over the land that had been deluged there lurked the insidious, treacherous and deadly malaria. This hideous monster got within its coils both the master and mistress—caught the devoted husband, the just and patient father, the considerate master, and the loving wife and mother. After weeks of pain and struggle, the master closed his eyes in death on the 8th of October, 1844. He was buried on the hill near the house he had built, and there for more than three quarters of a century his ashes have reposed. The wife and mother, after a long illness, finally recovered her health. The departure of the husband left the burden of family government, the new and strange home, the care of children, their support and education upon her who had been to him sweetheart and wife. This heavy burden she took and carried during a widowhood of forty-six years, with a courage and loving fidelity that justly entitled her to be crowned a "Spartan mother." . . .

I was but six years old at the time of my father's death, and consequently my recollections of him are very vague. My mother was very ill when he died, but recovered her health in a few weeks' time and assumed the duties and shouldered the burden that had fallen upon her. Remaining with her in this new but now desolate home, made so by the death of the master and the great disaster caused by the flood, were six children, James, Jane, Elizabeth, Louisa, Matilda, and myself. The six older children, namely, George, Joseph, Mary, Martha, John, and Sarah, were married and in homes of their own. James and Jane did not remain long after the death of my father, but married and moved away. This left the four younger children, three sisters and myself, at the home with our mother. The neighborhood was sparsely settled, as said elsewhere, there being not a mile of railroad in the State, and the closest point to a navigable river, the Mississippi, was sixteen miles.

There was one water-mill and one "horse-mill" in the neighborhood. The water-mill ran only two or three months in the year, and then only as the waters of Big Creek furnished the power. This mill would grind wheat and corn, but the flour made from the wheat was bolted by hand. The "horse-mill" was located some six miles from our home and the power used at that was two horses attached to a sweep. The burden of taking the grain to the mills and bringing back the meal and flour, most generally fell upon me after I reached the age of twelve years. . . .

On the farm were cultivated corn, wheat, and tobacco. Tobacco was the staple principally relied upon to furnish the means necessary to buy family supplies. However, in addition to the tobacco, some wheat, bacon, oats, poultry, butter and eggs were sent to market and sold. St. Louis, sixty miles away, was then, as it is now, the market for that section of the State. It took five days to make the trip, two in going, one day in St. Louis and two to return. After I reached fourteen years of age, the marketing for the succeeding four years fell upon me. Only two or three such trips were made in the year. In the winter I stood upon the streets in St. Louis and sold turkeys, geese, ducks, and chickens, and with the proceeds of such sales bought sugar, coffee, molasses, salt, etc. On one occasion I made the trip without spending a single cent. The Missouri River at St. Charles was frozen over and wagon and team crossed without difficulty. The feed for the horses was carried in the wagon, as were the meat, bread and coffee that I used. At night I slept in the wagon or on the ground, as the weather permitted. These details are given for the purpose of showing the opportunities of that day and this. Then five days, now less than five hours to make the trip; then over heavy and unimproved roads, now in comfortable coaches.

The most interesting and enjoyable meetings of neighbors were at "log rollings," "corn shuckings" and "hog killings." Here the neighbors joined together to help each other. While the men were engaged in this work, the women were spinning or quilting, and when the day ended, a hearty and joyous gathering was held around the dinner table and fire-place. It is a question as to whether the people were not happier then than now. In the old time, friendships were stronger and more sincere. There was less selfishness and more of the milk of human kindness in the make-up of people than now. . . .

The opportunities offered in the neighborhood for an education were very limited. About one mile south of my home was a school-house built of logs. It was about twenty feet square, with a door in one side and a chimney place opposite. This chimney was built of stone gathered from the hill-side, and the fireplace was of sufficient size to take large pieces of wood. On the third side of the room, a log in its entire length had been left out for the purpose of making a window. Beneath this window a writing desk was made of a long plank about eighteen inches wide. It was on this desk—this plank—that the children were taught to write. The seats were made of logs split in half and supported by legs driven into augured holes. The interstices or cracks between the logs in the house were filled by mortar made of earth, lime and straw. In winter, with blazing fire going, and the door shut, the room was fairly comfort-able. It was in this house, when I was about six years of age, I started to school. With me went my three sisters, Elizabeth, Louisa, and Matilda.

John M. Faulconer was the teacher. He was the father of a large family of children, all of whom were of school age. Among others that went to the school at the same time were the children of Messrs. Ross, Creech, Cahal, Blanton, Duncan Carter and others. Faulconer was an old resident of the neighborhood and while a most excellent man, had a very limited education. The books in use at the time were McGuffy's speller and read-ers, Pike's arithmetic, Smith's geography and grammar, and a copy plate that was followed in writing. The pens used were made by the teacher out of goose quills, as there was no such thing as a steel pen in those days. Usually the school year lasted for about four months, and the teacher was paid at the rate of $15.00 per month. He furnished his own board and lodging.

Those who attended this school were the children of poor people and knew what it was like to live on short rations. They were healthy and independent, and grew up to be strong men and women. Now and then there would be one who gave little promise of usefulness or who "would not take learning."

A boy by the name of Dick Blanton started to this school. His father was a farmer and conducted a diminutive distillery in connection therewith. Dick was twelve years old and did not know a letter in the book. He had, however, learned to swear, drink whiskey and chew tobacco. When he first came, he said to the teacher, "All I want is a good education and plenty of new white whiskey." After he had been coming for a week, I (much younger than he) ventured to ask him how he was getting along with his letters. He replied as follows: "I have learned them all except that d——d letter 'E', but I think I will harness that before long." Poor Dick! He drifted along in life until the Civil War and then very naturally joined the rebels (as we then called the Southerners) and was killed in battle. . . .

As I have said, Mr. Faulconer did not have much of an education. He could go so far but no further. For several years that I went to him I got only so far as the end of the "single rule of three" in Pike's arithmetic. At the end of that rule I was told to *review*. The intricacies of the *double* rule of three seemed to be unknown to the teacher and, of course, were unknown to me. His knowledge of the other studies he sought to teach was on a par with his scholarship in arithmetic.

MEMOIRS OF TOM HORN

> He had a gun which he had stole, I reckon, and we fished and
> hunted, and that was what we lived on. . . .
> It was kind of lazy and jolly, laying off comfortable all day,
> smoking and fishing, and no books nor study. . . . (32)
> . . . I reckoned I would walk off with the gun and some
> lines, and take to the woods when I run away. I guessed I
> wouldn't stay in one place, but just tramp right across the
> country, mostly night times, and hunt and fish to keep alive.
> (34)
>
> But, by-and-by pap got too handy with his hick'ry, and I
> couldn't stand it. I was all over welts. (32)

Huck's description of his life in the woods with his father resembles in many ways the kind of ideal existence out in nature for
which many boys on the frontier of Missouri longed. One example
of such a boy was Tom Horn, born in Scotland County, Missouri,
some twenty-five years after Mark Twain. Despite the difference in
ages, there are distinct similarities among the experiences of Huck,
Tom Sawyer, Sam Clemens, and Tom Horn. Most important was
their independence and intimate knowledge of the woods. Just as
Huck is able to exist on Jackson's Island without the help of the
civilized world by fishing and shooting game, so Horn is a master
hunter, going into the wood alone with only the company of his
dog, Shedrick. Like Sam Clemens and Huck, Horn's heart was
never in schooling; all he could think of was tracking game.

Tom Horn and Huck Finn were alike in another unfortunate way:
both had brutal fathers. That brutality, in both cases, is what eventually sends them away from home to the territories farther west.

FROM TOM HORN, *THE LIFE OF TOM HORN*
(Denver: Southern Book Co., 1904)

I was born near Memphis, Scotland County, Missouri, November 21,
1860—a troublesome time, to be sure; and anyone born in Missouri is
bound to see trouble—so says Bill Nye.

Up to the time I left home I suppose I had more trouble than any man
or boy in Missouri. We had Sunday schools and church, and as my mother

was a good, old-fashioned Campbellite, I was supposed to go to church and Sunday school, as did most of the boys and girls in the neighborhood. I had three brothers and four sisters, and there was not one of them that acted as if they really enjoyed going to those places. I had nothing particular going, if it hadn't been for the 'coons, turkeys, quail, rabbits, prairie chickens, 'possums, skunks and other game of that kind, with once in a season a fat, cornfed deer; and they were all neglected to such an extent by the rest of the family, that it kept me busy most every Sunday, and many nights through the week, to do what I considered right in trying to keep on proper terms with the game.

I would steal out the gun and take the dog and hunt all day Sunday and many a night through the week, knowing full well that whenever I did show up at home I would get a whipping or a scolding from my mother or a regular thumping from father.

My mother was a tall, powerful woman, and she would whip me and cry, and tell me how much good she was trying to do me by breaking me of my Indian ways, so she called them (though I had never seen an Indian, and did not know what their ways were). Then, if a skunk or a 'coon or fox came along and carried off one of her chickens during the night, at daylight she would wake me and give me the gun and tell me to take old "Shedrick," the dog, and go and follow up the varmint and kill it.

For a kid I must have been a very successful hunter. When our neighbors would complain of losing a chicken—and that was a serious loss to them—mother would tell them that whenever any varmint bothered her hen-roosts, she just sent out Tom and "Shedrick" and when they returned they always brought the pelt of the varmint with them.

To this day I believe mother thought the dog was of more importance against varmints than I was. But "Shedrick" and I both understood that I was the better for I could climb any tree in Missouri, and dig frozen ground with a pick, and follow cold tracks in the mud or snow, and knew more than the dog in a good many ways. Still I think, even yet, that there never was a better dog. I always thought "Shed" could whip any dog in Missouri (and at that time I did not know there was any other place than Missouri, except, perhaps, Iowa. I knew of Iowa because one of our neighbors came from there). But I had many a hard fight myself to keep up the reputation of old "Shed" for as he began to get old and wise, I do believe he thought I would always help him. Once in a while Dad would go to an election or a public sale or a horse race or something and "Shed" would go with him, and sometimes the dog would get whipped. When he did get whipped he always came home looking pretty badly used up, and after an occurrence of that kind, "Shed" would not leave me for days.

I recollect a family of boys named Griggs who had what they always claimed was the best 'coon dog and the best fighter in the world; (Missouri or our neighborhood was the world to them), and now I think he must have been a good dog and no mistake; but at that time I did certainly hate him. Whenever the Griggs boys and I ran together, we had a dog fight, and the termination of the meeting was always a fight between Sam Griggs and myself. I also distinctly recollect that on nearly every occasion "Shed" and I both went home pretty badly used up. Sam Griggs always said I helped "Shed" and he would try to keep me from doing so; then Sam and I would mix. I guess we fought a hundred times and he always quit when he "had his satisfy" for I never did nor could whip him.

The Griggs' dog was named "Sandy" (because he was yellow, I suppose), and my argument always was that my dog "Shed" knew more than "Sandy." To illustrate, once Sam Griggs was up in a tree to shake off a 'coon for "Sandy" to kill. A limb of the tree snapped and down came Sam, and "Sandy" jumped atop him, bit his ear and bit him in the arm and shoulder and used Sam up pretty badly before he could get "Sandy" to understand that he was not a 'coon or a wildcat. I always claimed that "Shed" would have had more sense than to jump on me if I had been fool enough to fall out of a tree.

My mother was anxious to have all the children go to school during the winter months, and I always had to go, or to start anyway; but all the natural influences of the country were against my acquiring much of an education. During the summer we had to work on the farm, and work hard and long hours putting in crops and tending to them. Thus I had little legitimate time to fish and hunt bee trees. So when winter came and the work was all done and the crops all in, I wanted to go and look after the game, but as I was ordered to go to school, I had to go.

The first natural influence of any importance was that the schoolhouse was a mile from the house we lived in, and there was always more or less snow on the ground in winter, and on the trail to school I would always be finding fresh rabbit or 'coon or cat tracks crossing the trail to school. I never could cross a fresh track for I would see one and the rest of the children would pay no attention to it, so I would follow it a little ways just to see which way it went, and then I would go on a little farther, and then I would say to myself, "I will be late for school and get licked." Then an overpowering desire to get that rabbit or 'coon or wildcat, as it happened to be, would overcome me, and I would go back in the orchard behind the house, call the dog and as he would come running to me, the stuff for school was all off, and "Shed" and I would go hunting. So you see, had the schoolhouse been nearer, I could have gotten there a great deal oftener than I did.

I could never keep my mind on my books when I was at school for if it happened to commence to snow I could not help thinking about how fine it would be to trail 'coon on the morrow, and I would speculate a good deal more about the skins of the varmints I could catch, and could see more advantage in having a good string of pelts than in learning to read, write and cipher.

Things were beginning to get rather binding on me about this time anyway, as a cousin named Ben Markley came to live with us. He was a son of my mother's sister and I guess he was the best boy in the world. Oh, how many hundreds of times I was whipped or scolded and asked by parent or schoolteacher, why I did not do as Bennie did.

Ben never forgot to wash or comb his hair. He never swore. He could walk to school and not get his boots muddy. One pair of boots would last him as long as four pairs would me. He never whispered in school; never used tobacco. He never went hunting nor fishing on Sunday, and never wanted to. He never had any fights and he would prattle all evening about what the lesson would be in Sunday school next Sunday. Those were some of his good points, but not all, for he was held up as a model of perfection by everybody. Of course, my opinion of him was different.

I knew he could not shoot. He could not climb a tree. He did not know a 'coon track from a cow track. He was afraid of bees when a bee tree was to be robbed. He said 'coon skins were nasty, and skunks he could not go at all. He did not know how to bait a hook to fish. He could not swim, was afraid of horses, and once he struck old "Shedrick" with a piece of hoop pole. I had known a long time before this that he was a failure, so far as I estimated boys, so when he struck the sharer of my joys and sorrows, I jumped onto him. I was about thirteen and he was about seventeen, but I had him whipped before my mother and the rest of the family could get me off him. Dad was there but he did not try to help the women pull me off, for I do think Ben was a little too good for him.

Well, after that, "Shed" and I left him alone and he put in a good deal of his spare time leaving us alone. That row with Bennie made me no favorite with the womenfolks; something that was of little importance to me.

The climax to my life at home came the next spring. Some emigrants were going along the road and behind the wagons were two boys on one horse, bareheaded, and one of them had an old, single-barreled shotgun. They met "Shed" and me on the road and stopped to talk to us. I remarked that a man who shot game with a shotgun was not good. The oldest one of the boys asked me if I called myself a man, and the answer I made him caused them both to get off their old mare, and tie her to the fence. The younger and smaller of the two held the gun while the big one and I started to scrap. Things were looking so unfavorable to the boy I was fighting with that the smaller boy laid his gun down on the ground and was going to help his brother. He gave me a kick in the jaw as a preliminary; but he never smiled again. Old "Shed" threw him down and bit him in the arm and shoulder in doing it. That stopped the fight between the bigger boy and me, as I had to let go to take care that "Shed" did not hurt the small one too much.

Well, I took the dog off and told them that they had better to get on their old mare and go and get the rest of the family if they wanted to win a fight, and then the big one picked up the gun and helped the small boy on the mare, and he raised the gun and shot poor, old "Shed." "Shed" whined and I could scarcely believe such a thing had been done. The big boy then got on the mare with the smaller one and they went galloping off. I carried "Shed" home, which was about a quarter of a mile away, and he died that night.

I believe that was the first and only real sorrow of my life.

Dad got on his horse and went and overtook the emigrant train that night, and I guess there was "something doin'," for he came home that night before "Shed" died and he was pretty badly done up himself. Dad was called the hardest man to whip in northwest Missouri, but when he came home that night he looked to me like a man who had had at least what I would have called enough.

I was about fourteen years old by this time and I wanted to go somewhere. I had heard of California and thought that would be a good place to go. Dad and I had a disagreement one day and he had the trace of a single buggy harness in his hand, and he struck at me with it. I grabbed it and then the fight was on.

Well, I tried to do something, but the old man was too much for me. When I saw I was in for a daisy, I told him to just help himself, as it was his last time, for I was going to leave home.

He helped himself, and when he got through, he said: "Now, if you are going to leave home, go! But always remember that the last time the old man whipped you, he gave you a good one."

"Go," he said, "but ask your mother for a lunch to take with you. You will be back by night if you start in the morning, and if you take a lunch with you, you won't miss your dinner."

This happened at the barn. I lay down on the hay and lay there all night. Next morning, mother and the girls carried me to the house and put me in bed where I lay for a week. Dad had done his work well.

As soon I could get around, I sold my rifle for $11.00, kissed my mother for the last time in my life, went out and took a look at old "Shedrick's" grave, got a lunch and started west. (17–24)

MEMOIRS OF SAMUEL S. HILDEBRAND

Your mother couldn't read, and she couldn't write, nuther, before she died. None of the family couldn't, before they died. I can't. (28)

And he said people allowed there'd be another trial to get me away from him and give me to the widow for my guardian, and they guessed it would win, this time. This shook me up considerable, because I didn't want to go back to the widow's any more and be so cramped up and sivilized, as they called it. (33)

Before Pap reappeared on the scene to take Huck away from the Widow Douglas, Huck had actually become reconciled to schooling and living a comfortable life in a nice house. So he feels great dread when Pap returns to berate him for learning to read. But once Pap spirits Huck away to a hidden shack in the woods and Huck becomes used to hunting and fishing again, he decides that he doesn't want to return to civilization ever again.

This, the lure of complete freedom away from civilization's restraints, is also seen in Sam Hildebrand's account of his childhood. Hildebrand, born in Missouri one year after Sam Clemens, was notorious as a Confederate soldier who resorted to brutal tactics during the Civil War and who continued cruel raids even after the war was over. Hildebrand went to prison for murder and thievery and often escaped from jail. Eventually he was able to flee out west and escape the law entirely.

The story he relates to Evans and Keith has much in common with those of Huck Finn and Sam Clemens. Like Huck and Sam, Hildebrand was a boy of nature. He despised school and any of civilization's other restrictions. Hildebrand could never be kept in school long enough even to learn to read or write. His innocent description of the two letters of the alphabet that he did learn to recognize is reminiscent of some of Huck's observations about book learning. Given the choice of back-breaking farm labor or schooling, Hildebrand chooses the farm.

FROM JAMES W. EVANS AND A. WENDELL KEITH,
*AUTOBIOGRAPHY OF SAMUEL S. HILDEBRAND, THE RENOWNED
MISSOURI "BUSHWHACKER" AND UNCONQUERABLE ROB ROY OF
AMERICA; BEING HIS COMPLETE CONFESSION*
(Jefferson City, Mo.: State Times Book and Job Printing House, 1870)

In regard to the early history of the Hildebrand family, I can only state what tradition has handed down from one generation to another. . . . They were a hardy race of people and always shunned a city life, or being cooped up in thickly settled districts; they kept on the outskirts of aggressive civilization as it pressed the redman still back into the wild solitudes of the West, thus occupying the middle ground or twilight of refinement. Hence they continually breathed the pure, fresh air of our country's morning, trod through the dewy vales of pioneer life and drank at Freedom's shady fountains among the unclaimed hills.

They were literally a race of backwoodsmen inured to hardship, and delighted in nothing so much as wild adventure and personal danger. They explored the hills rather than the dull pages of history, pursued the wild deer instead of tame literature, and enjoyed their own thoughts rather than the dreamy notions emanating from the feverish brain of philosophy.

In 1832 my father and mother, George and Rebecca Hildebrand, settled in St. Francois county, Missouri, on a stream called Big River, one of the tributaries of the Meramee which empties into the Mississippi about twenty miles below St. Louis.

The bottom lands on Big River are remarkably fertile, and my father was so fortunate as to secure one of the best bodies of land in that county. Timber grew in abundance, both on the hills and in the valleys, consequently it took a great deal of hard labor to open a farm; but after a few years of close attention, father, by the assistance of his boys who were growing up, succeeded in opening a very large one. He built a large stone dwelling house two stories high, and finished it off in beautiful style, besides other buildings—barns, cribs and stables necessary on every well regulated farm.

Father and mother raised a family of ten children, consisting of seven boys and three girls. I was the fifth one in the family, and was born at the old homestead on Big River, St. Francois county, Missouri, on the 6th day of January, 1836.

The facilities for acquiring an education in that neighborhood were very slim indeed, besides I never felt inclined to go to school even when I had a chance; I was too fond of hunting and fishing, or playing around the majestic bluffs that wall in one side or the other of Big River, the

whole length of that crooked and very romantic stream. One day's schooling was all that I ever got in my life; that day was sufficient for me, it
gave me a distaste to the very sight of a school house. I only learned the
names of two letters, one shaped like the gable end of a house roof, and
the other shaped like an ox yoke standing on end. At recess in the afternoon the boys got to picking at me while the teacher was gone to dinner,
and I had them every one to whip. When the old tyrant came back from
dinner and commenced talking saucy, I gave him a good cursing and
broke for home. My father very generously gave me my choice, either to
go to school or to work on the farm. I gladly accepted the latter, redou-
bled my energy and always afterwards took particular pains to please my
father in all things, because he was so kind as not to compel me to attend
school. A threat to send me to school was all the whipping that I ever
required to insure obedience. (29–32)

HARRIET MARTINEAU, FOREIGN TRAVELER

> I see they had the king and the duke astraddle of a rail—that
> is, I knowed it *was* the king and the duke, though they was
> all over tar and feathers, and didn't look like nothing in the
> world that was human—just looked like a couple of mon-
> strous big soldier-plumes. . . . Human beings *can* be awful
> cruel to one another. (225)

By the time Huck comes upon the king and the duke being run
out of town in tar and feathers, he has already witnessed many
dangerous situations in frontier life, including the gunning down
of a drunk in midday, the drowning of a group of men on a
wrecked steamboat, and the wholesale slaughter of two families
who are feuding with one another. The dangers and hardships of
frontier life, much like the incidents Clemens incorporates in *Adventures of Huckleberry Finn,* are described by two travelers from
foreign countries, both of whom are impressed by the hardships
of life on the frontier. The first is by an Englishwoman, Harriet
Martineau, who traveled throughout the navigable Midwest. The
voyage she writes about starts in New Orleans, Louisiana, in 1838
and proceeds up the Mississippi River by steamboat, ending in Cin-
cinnati, Ohio. The excerpts here describe the dangers of steamboat
travel and the primitive living conditions of many of the poorer
woodsmen who lived along the river.

FROM HARRIET MARTINEAU, *RETROSPECT OF WESTERN TRAVEL*
(London: Saunders and Otley, 1838)

MISSISSIPPI VOYAGE

About four o'clock in the afternoon of the 6th of May we were con-
voyed, by a large party of friends, to the "Henry Clay," on board of which
accommodations had been secured for us by great exertion on the part
of a fellow-voyager. The "Henry Clay" had the highest reputation of any
boat on the river, having made ninety-six trips without accident; a rare
feat on this dangerous river. As I was stepping on board, Judge P. said
he hoped we were each provided with a life-preserver. I concluded he
was in joke; but he declared himself perfectly serious, adding that we
should probably find ourselves the only cabin passengers unprovided
with this means of safety. We should have been informed of this before;
it was too late now. Mr. E., of our party on board, told me all that this

inquiry made me anxious to know. He had been accustomed to ascend and descend the river annually with his family, and he made his arrangements according to his knowledge of the danger of the navigation. It was his custom to sit up till near the time of other people's rising, and then sleep in the day. There are always companies of gamblers in these boats, who, being awake and dressed during the hours of darkness, are able to seize the boats on the first alarm of an accident in the night, and are apt to leave the rest of the passengers behind. Mr. E. was a friend of the captain; he was a man of gigantic bodily strength and cool temper, every way fitted to be of use in an emergency; and the captain gave him the charge of the boats in case of a night accident. Mr. E. told me that, as we were particularly under his charge, his first thought in a time of danger would be of us. He had a life-preserver, and was an excellent swimmer, so that he had little doubt of being able to save us in any case. He only asked us to come the instant we were called, to do as we were bid, and to be quiet. As we looked at the stately vessel, with her active captain, her two pilots, the crowds of gay passengers, and all the provisions for safety and comfort, it was scarcely possible to realize the idea of danger; but we knew that the perils of this extraordinary river, sudden and overwhelming, are not like those of the ocean, which can be, in a great measure, guarded against by skill and care. The utmost watchfulness cannot here provide against danger from squalls, from changes in the channel of the river, and from the *snags, planters,* and *sawyers* (trunks of trees brought down from above by the current, and fixed in the mud under water) which may at any moment pierce the hull of the vessel. . . .

On the evening of our first day on the Mississippi, Mr. E. told me of the imminent danger he and his lady had twice been in on board steamboats. His stories give an idea of the perils people should make up their minds to on such excursions as ours. On their wedding journey, the E.'s, accompanied by their relative, Judge H., went down the Alabama river. One night, when Mr. E. was just concluding the watch I have described him as keeping, the boat ran foul of another, and parted in two, beginning instantly to sink. Mr. E. roused his lady from her sleep, made her thrust her feet into his boots, threw his cloak over her, and carried her up to the deck, not doubting that, from her being the only lady on board, she would be the first to be accommodated in the boat. But the boat had been seized by some gamblers who were wide awake and ready dressed when the accident happened, and they had got clear of the steamer. Mr. E. shouted to them to take in the lady, only the lady; he promised that neither Judge H. nor himself should enter the boat. They might have come back for every one on board with perfect safety; but he could not move them. Judge H., meanwhile, had secured a plank, on which he hoped to seat Mrs. E., while Mr. E. and himself, both good swimmers, might push it before them to the shore if they could escape the eddy from the sinking vessel. Mr. E. heard next the voice of an old gentleman whom he knew, who was in the boat, and trying to persuade the fellows to turn back. Mr. E. shouted to him to shoot the wretches if they would not come. The old gentleman took the hint, and held a pistol (which, however, was not loaded) at the head of the man who was steering; upon which they turned back and took in, not only Mrs. E., her party, and their luggage, but everybody else, so that no lives were lost. Mrs. E. lost nothing but the clothes she had left by her bedside. She was perfectly quiet and obedient to directions the whole time. The vessel sank within a quarter of an hour. . . .

We passed Baton Rouge, on the east Louisiana bank, on the afternoon of this day. It stands on the first eminence we had seen on these shores, and the barracks have a handsome appearance from the water. A summerhouse, perched on a rising ground, was full of people, amusing themselves with smoking and looking abroad upon the river; and, truly, they had an enviable station. A few miles farther on we went ashore at the wooding-place, and I had my first walk in the untrodden forest. The height of the trees seemed incredible as we stood at their foot and looked up. It made us feel suddenly dwarfed. We stood in a crowd of locust and cottonwood trees, elm, maple, and live oak; and they were all bound together by an inextricable tangle of creepers, which seemed to forbid our penetrating many paces into the forest beyond where the woodcutters had intruded. I had a great horror of going too far, and was not sorry to find it impossible; it would be so easy for the boat to leave two or three passengers behind without finding it out, and no fate could be conceived more desolate. I looked into the wood-cutter's dwelling, and hardly knew what to think of the hardihood of any one who could embrace such a mode of life for a single week on any consideration. Amid the desolation and abominable dirt, I observed a moscheto bar—muslin curtain—suspended over the crib. Without this, the dweller in the wood would be stung almost to madness or death before morning. This curtain was nearly of a saffron color; the floor of the hut was of damp earth, and the place so small that the wonder was how two men could live in it. There was a rude enclosure round it to keep off intruders, but the space was grown over with the rankest grass and yellow weeds. The ground was swampy all about, up to the wall of untouched forest which rendered this spot inaccessible except from the river. The beautiful squills-flower grew plentifully, the only relief to the eye from the vastness and rankness. Piles of wood were built up on the brink of the river, and were now rapidly disappearing under the activity of our deck-passengers, who were passing in two lines to and from the vessel. The bell from the boat tinkled through the wilderness like a foreign sound. We hastened on board, and

I watched the woodcutters with deep pity as they gazed after us for a minute or two, and then turned into their forlorn abode. . . .

On the 11th we overtook another disabled steamboat, which had been lying forty-eight hours with both her cylinders burst; unable, of course, to move a yard. We towed her about two miles to a settlement, and the captain agreed to take on board two young ladies who were anxious to proceed, and a few deck-passengers. (36–39)

FREDERICK GERSTAECKER

A German traveler named Frederick Gerstaecker also reported on life in the Mississippi Valley, where he came solely to hunt and kill wild animals in the 1830s. In the instance excerpted here, Gerstaecker gives firsthand testimony of the hard drinking, brawls, thievery, and brutal justice that were part of the everyday life of the frontier.

FROM FREDERICK GERSTAECKER, *WILD SPORTS IN THE FAR WEST*
(Boston: Crosby, Nichols and Co., 1859)

The two hunters had finished their game, and were sitting with me over the whiskey, conversing about old times, when six more arrived, dressed like ourselves with leggings and moccasins, armed with rifles and knives; they brought several empty bottles, which they caused to be replenished, and they all seemed to be in a fair way of getting drunk. As they were rolling about, one of them tumbled over the feet of the sleeper, who just mumbled some indistinct words, and fell off again. This seemed to afford them much amusement, and they began to tickle him under the nose with blades of grass, laughing immoderately at the faces he made. The two other young Americans told them very civilly to leave off, alleging that the sleeper was their friend, that his sleepiness was a disease which he could not help, and begging them to leave him in peace. A scornful burst of loud laughter was the answer. They said they could and would do as they chose, and one of them had the goodness to say, that he could eat us up altogether. My blood was already on the boil. Still it was clearly no business of mine; a somewhat ruder practical joke at length awoke the sleeper, who was a strong-built man. He was still the butt of their wit, while yawning and stretching his limbs, till suddenly on looking around on the circle, he seemed to catch a glimmering of what had taken place. His yawning was checked, and looking round attentively, he listened to their remarks, when the greatest braggart amongst them stepped up to him, and laughing in his face, wished him a good morning; in another instant, he lay bleeding on the ground from a blow of the sleeper's fist. This was the signal for a general row, and nine blades glittered in the rays of the setting sun. My knife was out as quickly as any of the others, and we had a regular hand-to-hand combat; as long as I live I hope never to see such another. It all passed so quickly, that I can only recollect that I defended myself against two tall fellows, that my left hand pained me much, and that one of my opponents uttered a loud cry. At this instant a shot was heard and one of the strangers reeled and fell; it acted like an electric stroke on both parties; all the knives were lowered and every one appeared to be interested about the wounded man. . . . All were sobered in an instant, yet no one thought of giving chase; all were intent on endeavoring to save the wounded man. But in vain; as the sun sank behind a range of red clouds he breathed his last. . . . My left hand, which I had hastily bound up the night before, began to be very painful; I had received a thrust through the palm, and the sinews were exposed. Laying wood-ashes on the wound I bandaged it again. I had also received a slight cut on the left side. All the others were more or less hurt; indeed, I seemed to have come off the best. . . .

Just as we were about to start on the following morning, five horsemen drew up before the door. They dismounted, and Hogarth asked them to breakfast, though we had just finished. After breakfast, as they saw that we were ready to start, one of them asked us not to go shooting to-day, but to go with them, as they were on their way to execute an act of justice. The case was this: Some time since had settled on the banks of the river, a set of men who were found to be rather too fond of horseflesh, without inquiring particularly to whom the horses belonged. . . .

Two men now stripped Curly of his upper garments, tied him up to a tree, and began to belabor his back with hickory sticks. Curly had sense enough to see that if his head remained obstinate, his back would have to pay the score; so he offered to confess. . . .

Brogan, who had listened to it all with a contemptuous smile, was now questioned; all attempts to make him confess were in vain; he denied having had any share in the crime, and was tied up to a tree and dreadfully beaten. It was a horrible sight. At first he gave vent to volleys of oaths and abuse; then he was silent for a long time, and bore the severe blows with wonderful firmness; at length he gave a deep groan, and called out, "Oh, my poor wife and children."

Two negroes now made their appearance with spades and dug a grave; they were followed by a white man with a cord in his left hand, and a piece of tallow, with which he kept greasing the cord in his right, looking as unconcerned as possible all the time, though he knew it was intended to hang the poor wretch. This seemed rather too severe, and several of us now stepped forward, and persuaded those who seemed most open to pity, that if they had resolved to hang the man, they ought not first to have lacerated him so dreadfully: this seemed evident to the others, so it was put to the vote, and his life was spared on condition that he left the country within four weeks, and never returned to it again. He made no promise, and as he was cast off, he fell senseless on the grass. (350–352, 360, 362)

MEMOIRS OF GEORGE DEVOL, MISSISSIPPI GAMBLER

> They couldn't hit no project that suited, exactly; so at last the
> duke said he reckoned he'd lay off and work his brains an
> hour or two and see if he couldn't put up something on the
> Arkansas village; and the king he allowed he would drop over
> to t'other village, without any plan, but just trust in Providence
> to lead him the profitable way. (157)

The king and the duke, like the band of thieves who go down in
the *Walter Scott* and those who leave the floating house where Pap
is found dead, are among the many rapscallions who subsist by
looking for suckers to fleece on the Mississippi River. One of the
most revealing accounts of a true-to-life character who made his
living by cheating gullible passengers on Mississippi riverboats was
that of George Devol.

Devol was born on the edges of the frontier in Ohio in 1829,
six years before the birth of Sam Clemens. The title page of his
memoirs sums up his raucous life: at the age of ten he ran away
from home and began immediately to learn how to cheat at cards.
For the rest of his life he made his money in a frankly immoral
fashion. Like Huck and Jim and the king and the duke, Devol often
got what he wanted by pretending to be someone else. Although
he led the most violent kind of life on the river, and later on the
railroad, he lived to a ripe old age to record his memoirs.

FROM GEORGE H. DEVOL, *FORTY YEARS A GAMBLER ON THE
MISSISSIPPI*
(New York: George H. Devol, 1892)

*A Cabin Boy in 1839; could steal cards and cheat the boys at eleven;
stack a deck at fourteen; bested soldiers on the Rio Grande during the
Mexican War; won hundreds of thousands from paymasters, cotton buyers, defaulters and thieves; fought more rough-and-tumble fights than
any man in America, and was the most daring gambler in the world.*

My Dear Reader: I first saw the light of day in a little town called Mar-
ietta, at the mouth of the Muskingum River in the State of Ohio, on the
first day of August, 1829. I was the youngest of six children, and was the
pet of the family. My father was a ship carpenter, and worked at boat-

building in the beginning of the present century. I had good opportunities to secure an early education, as we had good schools in the West at that time. I had very little liking for books, and much less for school. When my parents thought me at school, I was playing "hockey" with other boys, running about the river, kicking foot-ball, playing "shinny on your own side," and having a fight nearly every day. I hardly ever went home that I did not have my face all scratched up from having been in a fight, which innocent amusement I loved much better than school. When I was hardly ten years of age, I would carry stones in my pocket and tackle the school teachers if they attempted to whip me. My father was away from home at his work most of the time, and my mother (God bless her dear old soul) could not manage me. She often called in some passer-by to help her punish me. I can now see I richly deserved all the punishment I ever received, and more too. When there was company at our house, and my mother would be busy preparing a meal, I would get my bow and arrows and shoot the cups off from the tables, and then run away. I guess I was about the worst boy of my age west of the Allegheny Mountains that was born of good Christian parents. I have often heard the good old church members say: "That boy will be hung if he lives to be twenty years old." But I have fooled them, and am still on the turf, although I have had some pretty close calls, as you will see by reading this book.

In the year 1839, while at the river one day, I saw a steamer lying at the wharf-boat by the name of *Wacousta*. The first steward said I could ship as a cabin boy at $4 per month. I thought this a great opportunity, so when the boat backed out I was on board without saying anything to my parents or anyone else. My first duty was to scour knives. I knew they would stand no foolishness, so at it I went, and worked like a little trooper, and by so doing I gained the good will of the steward. At night I was told to get a mattress and sleep on the floor of the cabin; this I was very glad to do, as I was tired.

About four o'clock in the morning the second steward came up to me and gave me a pretty hard kick in the side that hurt me, and called out: "Get up here, and put your mattress away." I did get up and put away my bed, and then I went to the steward who kicked me and said: "Look here! Don't kick me that way again, for you hurt me." He let go and hit me a slap in the face that made my ears ring; so into him I pitched. I was a big boy for only ten years old; but I struck the wrong man that time, for he hit me another lick in the nose that came very near sending me to grass, but I rallied and came again. This time I had a piece of stone coal that I grabbed out of a bucket; I let it fly, and it caught him on the side of the head and brought him to his knees. . . .

My cousin got me the position as barkeeper, so I quit our boat, and shipped on the Corvette. . . .

There was a man aboard, on our way down, who took a great liking to me. He was well posted on cards, and taught me to "stack a deck," so I could give a man a big hand. . . .

I soon got tired of the Rio Grande, and after cheating all the soldiers that I could at cards (as there was no one else to rob), I took a vessel, and came back to New Orleans. When I landed there, I was very comfortably fixed, as I had about $2,700, and was not quite seventeen years old. . . . I shipped as second steward, at twenty dollars per month.

The boat was full of people, and the card tables were going every night as soon as the supper tables were cleared. We had been out from New Orleans two days and nights before I picked up a game. . . .

. . . I used to make it a point to "cold deck" a sucker on his own deal, as they then had great confidence in their hands. My old paw is large enough to hold out a compressed bale of cotton or a whole deck of cards, and it comes in very handy to do the work. I could hold one deck in the palm of my hand and shuffle up another, and then come the change on his deal. It requires a great deal of cheek and gall, and I was always endowed with both—that is, they used to say so down South. . . .

I was on board of the steamer *Princess* on a down trip when she was carrying a large number of passengers, and there were fourteen preachers among them, on their way to New Orleans to attend a conference. The boat was making the fastest time she had ever made. I had a big game of "roulette" in the barber shop, which ran all Saturday night; and on Sunday morning, just after leaving Baton Rouge, I opened up again, and had thirty-five persons in the shop, all putting down their money as fast as they could get up to the table. I was doing a land-office business, when all of a sudden there was a terrific noise, followed by the hissing of escaping steam, mingled with the screams and groans of the wounded and dying. The boat had blown up, and was almost a total wreck. There was but very little left, and that consisted mostly of the barber shop, which was at the time full of gamblers, and not one of them was hurt. The steamers *Peerless* and *McRay* came to our aid; one boat looked after the dead and wounded, and the other took us lucky fellows out of the barber shop. One hundred souls were landed into eternity without a moment's warning, and among them were the fourteen preachers. It was a horrible sight; the bodies were so mangled and scalded that one could not have recognized his own brother or sister. . . .

Another time I was coming up on the steamer *Fairchild* with Captain Fawcett, of Louisville. When we landed at Napoleon there were about twenty-five of the "Arkansas Killers" came on board, and I just opened out and cleaned the party of money, watches, and all their valuables. Things went along smoothly for a while, until they commenced to drink pretty freely. Finally one of them said: "Jake, Sam, Ike, get Bill, and let us kill that d——d gambler who got our money." "All right," said the party, and they broke for their rooms to get their guns. I stepped out of the side door, and got under the pilot-house, as it was my favorite hiding place. I could hear every word down stairs, and could whisper to the pilot. Well, they hunted the boat from stem to stern—even took lights and went down into the hold—and finally gave up the chase, as one man said I had jumped overboard. I slipped the pilot $100 in gold, as I had both pockets filled with gold and watches, and told him at the first point that stood out a good ways to run her as close as he could and I would jump. He whispered, "Get ready," and I slipped out and walked back, and stood on the top of the wheelhouse until she came, as I thought, near enough to make the jump, and away I went; but it was farther than I expected, so I went down about thirty feet into the river, and struck into the soft mud clear up to my waist. Some parties who were standing on the stern of the boat saw me, and gave the alarm, when the "killers" all rushed back and commenced firing at me, and the bullets went splattering all around me. The pilot threw her into the bend as quick as he could and then let on she took a sheer on him, and nearly went to the other side. . . . I got up on the bank and waited for another boat [See Figure 3.2].

Figure 3.2. In this illustration from George Devol's account, men fire at him while he flees for his life after "cleaning them out" in a card game. From George Devol, *Forty Years a Gambler on the Mississippi*. New York, 1892.

QUESTIONS FOR FURTHER EXPLORATION

1. Write an essay, using *Adventures of Huckleberry Finn* and excerpts of memoirs of childhood included here, showing the conflict between civilization and nature in the early West.

2. Debate the question of whether nature, as it is depicted in *Adventures of Huckleberry Finn* and other memoirs, is peaceful and good or cruel.

3. Read *Narrative of the Life of Frederick Douglass,* written by an ex-slave who remembers his childhood at about the same time as that of Sam Clemens. Contrast Douglass' view of education with Huck's and Tom Horn's.

4. Huck Finn, Sam Clemens, Tom Horn, Sam Hildebrand, and George Devol all leave home at an early age. Compare and contrast their motives.

5. The theme of escape is fundamental to the move west in general and to Huck, Tom Horn, and George Devol. Enlarge on this in a paper.

6. Compare Huck's feeling about the river with George Devol's.

7. Violence was very close to home in the near West, especially as it was exhibited by the fathers of Tom Horn and Huckleberry Finn. Using these two accounts as reference points, debate the issue of corporal punishment.

8. From the fictional and nonfictional accounts of growing up in the near West, what assertions can you make about the longevity of childhood? Do these characters leave childhood behind much too young? Or are they escaping the adult responsibilities that hinder a prolonged childhood?

9. The frontiersmen of the Mississippi Valley are frequently described as being obsessed with speed at any cost, not only on the steamboats themselves, but in their lives and careers—getting ahead or getting what they want fast, for example, getting rich quick in the California gold fields. Discuss whether or not Huck and the authors of the memoirs are hungry for speed. Is Huck typically obsessed with speed, or is this an aspect of his culture that he is trying to escape?

10. The near westerner and the far westerner have been characterized as being rebellious against all authority. Examine elements of authority in Huck Finn and one other selection here. Write or discuss the reactions of the characters to one of the following: parents, educators, older people, church, home, or government.

11. The novel's reviewers in 1885 often declared it to be far too violent.

Using memoirs and excerpts from two travelers, discuss Twain's use of violence. By comparison, is *Adventures of Huckleberry Finn* excessively violent? Or is it realistic and accurate in its portrayal of violence? Or does Twain underplay the real violence on the frontier?

12. Discuss, by comparison, violence—its roots and its effects—in our own society.

13. Discuss the term "frontier justice," meaning justice rendered outside the law, especially as it unfolds in *Adventures of Huckleberry Finn,* Gerstaecker, and Devol.

14. Martineau presents a picture of gamblers on the river that is somewhat different from Devol's description of his own behavior after a horrible steamboat accident. Explore this difference and discuss the con men—that is, the king and the duke—against these two accounts. From what Huck says, how would the king and the duke probably have behaved in such a steamboat accident? Support your views.

15. Discuss the presence of class divisions in *Adventures of Huckleberry Finn* and other works in this chapter. Is there any evidence that upper and lower classes exist on the frontier?

16. Explore the way in which some characters in Twain's novel and in the excerpts in this chapter handle situations with the use of violence, while others use cunning.

17. Risk-taking in the Mississippi Valley was especially evident in the frequent horrible accidents encountered in traveling by steamboat. Explore these and other elements of risk-taking in excerpts in this chapter. How does the theme of taking risks, actually flirting with danger, pervade the novel?

18. Discuss the connection between violence (and bad behavior in general) and alcohol in the novel and excerpts from accounts of life in the Mississippi Valley.

19. Compare and contrast entertainments within your community today and those reported by Twain and Dyer.

20. Write a carefully crafted narrative of a day in your own childhood.

21. Compare your own childhood with Huck Finn's, especially the place of nature, the character of the community, the entertainments, and the violence. What different aspects of your lives do you think create different kinds of people? different attitudes?

SUGGESTED READINGS

Blair, Walter. *Mark Twain's Hannibal, Huck and Tom.* Mark Twain Papers. Berkeley: University of California Press, 1964.

Boyett, Gene W. *Hardscrabble Frontier.* Lanham, Md.: University Press of America, 1990.

De Voto, Bernard. *Mark Twain's America.* Boston: Little, Brown, 1932.

Ghent, William James. *The Early Far West: A Narrative Outline.* New York: Longmans, Green, 1931.

Hofstadter, Richard, William Miller, and Daniel Aaron. *The American Republic,* Vol. 1. Englewood Cliffs, N.J.: Prentice-Hall, 1959.

Marcy, Randolph Barnes. *Border Reminiscences.* New York: Harper and Brothers, 1872.

Marryat, Frederick. *A Diary in America.* New York: Alfred A. Knopf, 1962.

Paine, Albert Bigelow. *Mark Twain: A Biography.* New York: Harper and Brothers, 1912.

Perkins, Dexter. *The United States of America.* New York: Macmillan, 1968.

Pessen, Edward. *Jacksonian America: Society, Personality and Politics.* Urbana: University of Illinois Press, 1985.

Smith, Page. *The Shaping of America.* New York: McGraw-Hill, 1980.

Smith, Solomon. *Theatrical Management in the West and South for Thirty Years.* New York: B. Blom, 1968.

Twain, Mark. *Mark Twain's Autobiography.* Intro. by Albert Bigelow Paine. 2 vols. New York: Gabriel Wells. Vol. 1, 1925.

Wecter, Dixon. *Sam Clemens of Hannibal.* Boston: Houghton Mifflin, 1952.

4

Slavery, Its Legacy, and *Adventures of Huckleberry Finn*

CHRONOLOGY

1619	First recorded importation of slaves into Virginia from Africa.
1664	Adoption of Virginia's "Black Code," which legislated lifetime slavery for Africans.
1739	First recorded slave revolts.
1780	Outlawing of slavery in Massachusetts.
1808	Outlawing of importation of slaves into the United States.
1820	Missouri Compromise allows admission of Missouri as a slave state.
1831	First publication of William Lloyd Garrison's *Liberator*, starting the abolitionist movement.
	Nat Turner's slave rebellion.
	Beginning of the Underground Railroad.
1838	Frederick Douglass escapes from slavery.
1845	Publication of *Narrative of the Life of Frederick Douglass*.
1846	Dred Scott sues for his freedom.

1849	Publication of Henry David Thoreau's "Civil Disobedience."
1850	Passage of the Fugitive Slave Act.
1851	Harriet Tubman escapes and makes the first of many trips on the Underground Railroad to free slaves.
1852	Publication of Harriet Beecher Stowe's *Uncle Tom's Cabin.*
1854	Passage of Kansas-Nebraska bill rescinds the Missouri Compromise and leaves decision to allow slavery in the territory up to the voters.
	Fugitive slave George Burns arrested in Boston.
1856	Murders by John Brown's gang in Pottawatomie, Kansas.
1857	Dred Scott decision, in which the U.S. Supreme Court rules that no slave has a right to the courts.
1859	John Brown's raid on Harper's Ferry federal arsenal in Virginia.
1860	Lincoln elected President.
	South Carolina secedes from the Union.
1861–65	Civil War.
1863	Emancipation Proclamation frees slaves in rebel states; Passage of Thirteenth Amendment, incorporating it into the Constitution.
1865–77	Reconstruction period.
1868	Fourteenth Amendment makes ex-slaves citizens.
1870	Fifteenth Amendment gives male former slaves the vote.
1884–85	Twain tours with George Washington Cable from November 1884 until February 1885.
	Publication of *Adventures of Huckleberry Finn.*
1885	Publication of Cable's "The Freedman's Case" and *The Silent South,* both highly critical of southern leadership.
	Cable departs from his native South to take up residence in New England.

Without a doubt, the issue that most profoundly shook the nation in the nineteenth century was slavery. Its effects were felt from

Kansas to New York, from Massachusetts to Georgia. Its presence shaped the nation, and continues to shape the nation, as no other issue has ever done. So it is not surprising that what many people regard as the first truly American novel, set in the 1840s and written after a civil war had been fought over slavery, should have at its heart the issue that divided a nation. Jim's escape from slavery, while not the only narrative thread in the novel, is the most persistent one, against which the entire theme of freedom and bondage is written.

HUCK FINN AND SLAVERY

The reader of *Adventures of Huckleberry Finn* does not come upon the theme of slavery until Chapter 2, when the author reveals that Huck and Tom live in a slaveholding community. The opening chapters comprise what can be labeled as Tom Sawyer's world, in which the reader is led to see the situation as Tom Sawyer does and as the civilization that Tom represents sees it. As a result, the slave Jim is regarded primarily as an object to laugh at and play jokes on, and slavery is presented as a natural institution. From this point of view, Jim is gullible and superstitious—a comic strip character rather than a human being with feelings and ideas.

As Huck and Jim leave the civilized world of Tom Sawyer and spend more time alone together on the river, Jim begins to shed the cartoon identity that he was saddled with in St. Petersburg. It is as if the author begins presenting Jim through Huck's eyes rather than Tom's and St. Petersburg's eyes. As Huck increasingly regards Jim as a more and more complex, full human being, Jim is presented to the reader as less of a stick, comic figure. Jim's grand human dimension is shown particularly in his heart-rending remorse over striking his deaf daughter, his declaration that Huck is his only friend, his joy at finding Huck alive after the separation in the fog, and the sermon he gives Huck for playing the last practical joke on him. When Tom Sawyer again takes over the scene in the Phelps episodes, however, Jim again is portrayed as if filtered through the overpowering consciousness of Tom Sawyer; in the end he is again an object to laugh at, a piece of property.

The background of Jim in slavery continues to be set in Chapter 4, as Huck, almost as much of an outsider in this society as Jim, goes to Jim for advice about his future when he suspects that Pap may have returned. In contrast to the civilized notions that Tom Sawyer gets from books, Huck and Jim are alike in depending on folk wisdom, superstitions that are given little credence in this civilized world.

The final scene that sets the stage for an escape from slavery is Pap's tirade against the government and black people in Chapter 6. Pap, in all his ignorance and mean-spiritedness, rails against a free black man who dares to dress in a white shirt, can speak several languages, and is a professor in a college. This harangue, put in the mouth of Pap, who is filthy, sadistic, a drunk, proud of his illiteracy, and determined that his son will remain illiterate, is the reader's first clue that the author's sympathies are not with the slaveholding society. A comparison of Pap to the black man he derides makes a mockery of the slaveholder's argument that black people are inferior to whites and are meant to be enslaved.

Indications that the reader's sympathy is enlisted for Jim rather than for the society that enslaved him appear early in the novel in the kinship between Jim and Huck. One sees here a parallel thematic development in the fate of the white boy and the black man, both of whom are casting off shackles. As Jim, the black man defined as property by civilization, escapes slavery, so Huck, the white boy who has always been an outcast, escapes from his own enslavement in the shack. Furthermore, both Huck and Jim are running away from the same person, Miss Watson. And both make their escape at the same time. The bonding between the runaway boy and the runaway slave happens immediately as they join forces for common survival.

The scene when they discover each other on Jackson's Island sets up a tension that recurs within Huck throughout the novel, one he never resolves intellectually: between the inculcated values of civilization—the law, the legalized morality of the slaveholding society (the rightness of which he never questions)—and his natural instinct to treat Jim humanely as a friend. The voice that urges him to do what society says is right, more precisely, to turn Jim in, is the voice he calls his conscience. To the very last, he sees his desire to protect Jim as his own weakness—the thing that makes him decide, at last, that he can never be civilized.

This tension is illustrated when Jim and Huck first encounter each other on Jackson's Island. When Jim, probably for his own safety, somewhat hesitantly reveals that he has run away from Miss

Watson, Huck is indeed shocked that Jim has broken the law. But Huck, who is already used to skirting the law himself, has no immediate problem in defying the rules to keep his promise to Jim not to tell anyone, even, he says, if "people would call me a low down Abolitionist" (50). Every household with which Huck comes in contact seems to have slaves: not only Miss Watson, but the Grangerfords, the Wilkses, and the Phelpses.

> I hear ole missus tell de widder she gwyne to sell me down
> to New Orleans. (50)

Jim's explanation of why he ran away, as well as Huck's reference to the abolitionists, grounds *Adventures of Huckleberry Finn* in the history of its time: the view of the slave as property; the practice of casually separating slave families; the activity of slave traders; the slave owners' precarious financial situation, which often led them to dispense with their "property" inhumanely; the slave's fear of being taken further south—to New Orleans—to be sold to cruel a master working a large plantation; the activity of abolitionists who worked to see an end to slavery and were hated by citizens in general; the constant hope of the adult slave that he or she would one day be able to escape and make enough money to free his or her family; and the support given the institution of slavery by the church. All this becomes the driving force of the novel.

Consistent with the facts of life in slavery, Twain shows that Jim's motivation for running away is threefold: he is separated from his family; he overhears Miss Watson's plan to sell him down south; and he is determined to buy the other members of his family and free them from slavery. If his family's masters refuse to sell them, then, Jim says, he will enlist the help of abolitionists. That slaves were always at the mercy of the misfortunes of their owners is graphically illustrated in the Wilks household when, after the death of the master, the king and duke, posing as the rightful executors to the estate, sell all the servants, separating families in doing so. The constant fear that Jim will be captured and returned to slavery (for example, by the husband of Mrs. Loftus), is also historically valid. The brutal treatment of the slaves, especially in the deep South, is illustrated when the Phelpses' neighbors continue to keep Jim chained hand and foot, with only water and bread to eat, even when they hear of his unselfish heroism in placing himself in jeopardy in order to save Tom Sawyer.

> [H]e would steal his children—children that belonged to a man I didn't even know. (93)

> I see it warn't no use for me to try to learn to do right. (95)

Two aspects of slavery are especially applicable to *Adventures of Huckleberry Finn.* One is the legal concept of the slave as property. Another is the endorsement and support of slavery on religious and moral grounds by the established church. Repeatedly in the novel the reader is reminded of the cruel absurdity by which one human being pretends to own another, much as he would own a cow or a horse. And that this is done in the name of religion—a religion of love—adds to it a special kind of horror. The idea is introduced immediately after Jim runs away when he speaks of himself as property: "I's rich now, come to look at it. I owns my-self" (54). At the same time, what continually bothers Huck is that in helping Jim escape, he is stealing Miss Watson's property and conspiring to help Jim steal his own children "that belonged to a man I didn't even know" (93). The only way that Huck is able to hold off those who would capture Jim, including the king and the duke, is to claim Jim as *his* rightful property (211).

> I judged I could see that there was two Providences, and a poor chap would stand considerable show with the widow's Providence, but if Miss Watson's got him there warn't no help for him any more. (21)

The peculiar notion that one person can actually own another, body and soul, is supported not only by the law and the government, but by the church and religion as well. It is no coincidence that Jim belongs to and is being sold down the river by the person in the novel who makes the greatest show of her religion, Miss Watson. Reflecting the religious notions of the slaveholding society, which believes that the Bible approves slavery, Huck thinks he hears the voice of God—"the plain hand of Providence"—telling him he should return Miss Watson's property (208). He attributes his final decision to go ahead with plans to help Jim get free, not

to his own good-heartedness and compassion, but to his fundamental wickedness, bad up-bringing, and failure to go to Sunday
School. Nor does Huck feel he is able to pray as long as he can't
bring himself to notify Miss Watson of Jim's whereabouts. Furthermore, his society's religion has taught him that he will be damned
to hell for helping a slave escape, a fate to which he resigns himself: "All right, then, I'll go to hell" (210).

Having reconciled himself to what he sees as his own wickedness, he determines to go to hell rather than follow society's rules
(which he mistakes for his conscience and the voice of God), and
is shocked that a "well brought up" boy like Tom would join him
in helping Jim escape. Finally, after all this, he comes to the conclusion that he doesn't give "a dead rat" what the authorities think.

SAM CLEMENS AND SLAVERY

Mark Twain had direct experience with the slavery about which
he wrote in *Adventures of Huckleberry Finn*. Although Twain's
family had been slave owners, and he himself had been a soldier
briefly in the Confederate Army, his well-known anti-slavery sentiments were formed by his recollections from childhood, his marriage into a family prominent in fighting slavery before the Civil
War, his circle of friends in Boston and New Haven, and his close
association with writer George Washington Cable. His biographer,
Albert Bigelow Paine, reports some of the childhood events that
influenced Twain's view of slavery: "He saw a slave struck down
and killed with a piece of slag for a trifling offense. He saw an
abolitionist attacked by a mob, and they would have lynched him
had not a Methodist minister defended him on a plea that he must
be crazy" (*Mark Twain: A Biography* [New York: Harper and
Brothers, 1912], p. 48). Twain himself, in his *Autobiography*, re-
calls another impression of slavery days in his youth:

I have no recollection of ever seeing a slave auction in that town;
but I am suspicious that that is because the thing was a common
and commonplace spectacle, not an uncommon and impressive
one. I vividly remember seeing a dozen black men and women
chained to one another, once, and lying in a group on the pave-
ment, awaiting shipment to the Southern slave market. Those were
the saddest faces I have ever seen. Chained slaves could not have

been a common sight, or this picture would not have made so strong and lasting an impression upon me. (*Mark Twain's Autobiography* [New York: Gabriel Wells, 1924], p. 124)

As Twain's close friend W. D. Howells writes in *My Mark Twain,* "No man more perfectly sensed and more entirely abhorred slavery" (New York: Harper, 1910, p. 903).

SLAVERY IN THE UNITED STATES

The historical context of slavery, so important to an understanding of *Adventures of Huckleberry Finn,* begins in the colonies in 1619 with the importation into Virginia of slaves from Africa. Early in the nation's settlement, slaves imported from Africa were chiefly brought by Spanish and Dutch traders to Florida and New York. In the colonial period slaves were imported for the specific purpose of securing workers to farm tobacco, rice, and indigo. The death rate in the rice fields was so extraordinarily high that more and more slaves were imported. In 1664, to increase the pool of slave labor, Virginia passed what was called the "Black Code," which stipulated that any black person in the colony was a slave for life, differentiating them legally from indentured servants, who were usually white. In 1681, however, there were already some free black people in the country.

The slave trade was brisk in the colonial period, when it was carried on chiefly by merchants and shippers from New England and New York. A clear cycle of trade developed: sugar was imported into New England from the West Indies and turned into rum, which was then exchanged for African slaves living in the West Indies, who were brought to the American colonies. Records indicate that black people tried to revolt from their slavery in the colonies as early as 1739. The response to an insurrection in 1741 discouraged slaves from seeking their freedom, for on the charge of suspected insurrection, thirteen black people were burned alive. By 1770, one-sixth of the entire population of the colonies was comprised of black slaves. In the 1780s, black slaves brought to the New World were also used as fighting men in the French and Indian and Revolutionary wars.

Soon the slave population became concentrated in the South, where the climate was favorable to the growing of tobacco, rice, and, eventually, cotton on large plantations. Fewer and fewer slaves were maintained in the North, where they had begun to be regarded as unprofitable. But the economy of the North as well as the South was buttressed by the system of black enslavement, for the cotton grown in the South with slave labor, for example, was in demand in northern textile mills like those in Lowell, Massachusetts, whose owners, in effect, subsidized slavery.

From 1776 onward, however, northern states, one at a time, made slavery unlawful within their borders. Among the the first were Massachusetts and Pennsylvania, which outlawed slavery in 1780. In 1827 New York State outlawed it. In 1808 the U.S. Congress outlawed the importation of slaves, but historians estimate that around 270,000 slaves were smuggled into the country in defiance of the law between 1808 and 1860. Major slave revolts continued in the nineteenth century, culminating in the insurrection by Nat Turner in Virginia in 1831, when 57 whites and 100 blacks lost their lives.

Although there was much sentiment at the time of the American Revolution to abolish slavery, legislators in the southern colonies succeeded in keeping slavery legal. By the nineteenth century, slavery was thoroughly established in the South. At first most slaves were held on moderate-sized farms, where they worked side by side with their white owners in the fields, but as the century wore on more and more slaves were concentrated on large plantations where rules were rigid and treatment shabby. Their position as possessions was nowhere more glaring than at slave auctions in the deep South, events at which they were often stripped and their bodies examined by prospective buyers in the most invasive and humiliating way. (See Figures 4.1 and 4.2.)

Even though there were laws to protect slaves from ill-treatment, overseers on large plantations were free to, and did, beat slaves brutally, often for trivial reasons. Few abusers were ever brought to justice. The absolute power of the owner and the overseer made sexual abuse rampant. Living conditions were primitive, and many slaves were malnourished, especially in light of the heavy labor demanded of them. They were sometimes forced to augment their diets by fishing, trapping, and growing their own food. Psychological as well as physical suffering was inevitably great on both the farms and the plantations, for very few slaves could ever look forward to having control over their own

Figure 4.1 (left) and Figure 4.2 (above). Posters illustrated with the stock figure of the fleeing black man. All are issued by dealers in human beings.

lives. Unlike indentured servants, they and their children and their children's children were usually doomed to servitude for the rest of their lives.

Intellectually and morally, the slave was regarded as an animal. Slaves were accused of being stupid, animal-like, and immoral, but at the same time they were beaten for trying to learn to read and write; they were forbidden to marry; they were used as "breeders" of more slaves and to satisfy the sexual appetites of their owners. Moreover, all sense of family was routinely and deliberately erased, as children were often sold away from their parents as soon as they were weaned.

Anti-slavery sentiment began with strategies of gradualism and colonization. Most of the early strategists who objected to slavery recommended a measured approach whereby planters would gradually emancipate their slaves and the government would pay slave owners for each slave who was freed. This method, which was advocated to appease slaveholders and to avoid the turmoil that might come from a large populace of African Americans suddenly being thrust out on their own, received almost no support in the South.

Those who called themselves colonists, on the other hand, thought the solution would be to relocate former slaves in Africa. This plan also met with little success and was unpopular with African Americans. By 1860, only 15,000 black people had been resettled in Africa.

By the nineteenth century, lines had been drawn between North and South on many issues. While a class system existed in the North, it was not as rigid or as pervasive as that in the South. On a political level, other disagreements divided the nation, especially with regard to tariffs, which hurt large southern plantation owners but helped northern industrialists. But the chief division, which was inextricable from cultural and political issues, and which grew increasingly important, was the maintenance of slavery in the South. It was this that drove a wedge between the two sections of the country and that created two distinct ways of life. The slavery issue ultimately extended westward to the new states coming into the Union.

In the political/economic/social struggle between the two sections of the country, as tension became increasingly intense, numerous compromises were made to keep a balance between free and slaveholding territories introduced into the Union and to hold the Union together.

In the early part of the century, a compromise was struck by Congress excluding slavery from some of the "New West" territory of the old Louisiana Purchase, above 36°30' north latitude. Below this latitude, roughly south of the Ohio River, it was permitted. By means of this legislation, called the Missouri Compromise of 1820, some new states were allowed to enter the Union as slave states while others were established as free.

PRO- AND ANTI-SLAVERY ARGUMENTS

In the years between 1830 and the beginning of the Civil War in 1861, while Mark Twain was growing to manhood in the slaveholding state of Missouri, many arguments for and against slavery constantly appeared in the public presses. Several grounds were repeatedly given for the maintenance of slavery, the most frequently used arguments being religious, strangely enough. Scripture, it was argued, held that slavery was morally justified. Furthermore, supporters of slavery argued, natural law allowed one person to hold another person as property. They further claimed that slaves were treated well because their masters did not want to damage their property. Those who supported slavery also contended that it benefitted the whole nation economically. Less often, it was argued that the enslavement of black people helped what was regarded as the more civilized white population to advance culturally by freeing it from drudgery. To those who supported slavery, black people were so vastly inferior that they were regarded as scarcely human. Even ministers of the gospel owned slaves and openly justified beating them.

Those who wanted the end or abolition of slavery also based their opposition to slavery on the Bible, basing their arguments more on the *spirit* of Christianity than on the letter of scripture, as the pro-slavery people did. To those opposing slavery, natural law dictated that no person could rightfully own another person's body or labor, that so doing was thievery. And in the realm of economics, it was argued that the reliance on slave labor kept poor whites, especially in the South, in a position of unending poverty. Even the effect on the most privileged class, the owners of the large plantations, was not positive, they argued; it was brutalizing. They insisted that slave owning lowered the morality of whites rather than raising it. It is significant, too, that while most of the pro-slavery factions based their arguments on theory, abolitionists based theirs largely on the individual, looking at the suffering of human beings in bondage: the separation of slave families; the frequency with which slave owners forced sexual attentions on black slaves; and the laws that prohibited slaves from marrying, learning to read and write, or receiving religious instruction.

THE ABOLITIONISTS

People would call me a low-down Abolitionist. (50)

While the campaign to abolish slavery had been under way for some time in England under the leadership of such people as the author of "Amazing Grace," John Newton, an ex-captain of a slave ship who, while studying the Bible at sea, became convinced that slavery was not God's will, and William Wilberforce, an Anglican cleric who pushed an anti-slavery bill through Parliament. In the United States, the official beginning of the movement came in 1831, when journalist William Lloyd Garrison delivered a sermon from the pulpit of the Park Street Church in Boston calling for the immediate abolition of slavery; at about the same time, he began publishing a newspaper devoted to abolition, the *Liberator*. To the ranks of the abolitionists came both northerners and southerners, men and women, white and black people. Many worked on a political plane to attempt to abolish slavery as an institution—to abolish it everywhere, in all the states, thus hitting slaveholders, plantation systems, northern mill owners who worked with southern cotton, and all others with a vested interest in the "peculiar institution" that had come to form the economic basis of a way of life where it hurt most: in the pocketbook. At the same time, they did not wait for laws to be passed in Washington: they went to work immediately to liberate individual slaves from their masters and from plantations, slipping them to freedom outside the areas of legal slavery—a movement guaranteed to exacerbate already frayed nerves. While the movement became exceedingly popular, attracting to its ranks a great host of idealists, practical workers, and martyrs—and especially intellectual writers and philosophers in the Northeast—most northerners, especially in the 1830s and

1840s, silently supported slavery—because their businesses depended on it, because they were morally indifferent to it, or because, for practical purposes, they found the abolitionists too extreme.

The abolitionist movement naturally came to include among its leaders a number of free blacks. Chief among these was Frederick Douglass, who escaped from slavery in 1838. His written account of his experiences in slavery became one of the most widely read records of the institution from the point of view of a slave. *Narrative of the Life of Frederick Douglass, an American Slave, Written By Himself* was published in 1845 by the Boston Anti-Slavery Society. William Lloyd Garrison was Douglass' mentor from the first, but as time passed the two abolitionist leaders began to disagree over tactics.

> [A]nd if their master wouldn't sell them, they'd get an Ab'litionist to go and steal them. (93)

Black abolitionists were most active in helping to free individual slaves through what was called the Underground Railroad, actually a system whereby activists assisted slaves in escaping from their masters, hiding the runaways in the houses of other sympathetic people along the way to freedom, often in Canada. The first "run" on the Underground Railroad was made in 1831. The most famous worker on the Underground Railroad was Harriet Tubman, who reached freedom on the Underground Railroad herself and brought her own first group out of slavery in 1851. From then until the end of the Civil War, she put her life at risk by returning repeatedly to the slave states to help others escape. It is estimated that she helped some three hundred people to escape, provoking southern slave owners to put a price on her head.

DECISIVE EVENTS

> [T]hat don't make no difference. I ain't agoing to tell. (50)

After years of agitation, the great turning point in American slavery came in 1850, when Congress passed laws—compromise measures—to keep much of the new territory free of slavery. Included in this compromise, however, was the Fugitive Slave Law, which legalized the return to their owners of slaves who had fled to free territory and threatened with arrest anyone who assisted fugitives. The 1850 law also pointedly refused to take into account the testimony of blacks *suspected* of having once been slaves, and it applied retroactively to slaves who had fled long before and had lived as free men or women for years. Furthermore, it allowed federal officials to compel any citizen to help in the return of slaves. Opponents of this act felt that now it would be virtually impossible for any slave to escape to freedom.

Far from solving the problem, however, this law, more than any other single action, so inflamed the situation as to make a peaceful solution impossible. The result was that vast numbers of people who had earlier been indifferent to slavery now actively supported abolition.

On March 20, 1852, some twenty years after William Lloyd Garrison's call to action, a second critical event occurred to heat up the battle for the abolition of slavery: the publication of Harriet Beecher Stowe's novel *Uncle Tom's Cabin*. Stowe's book, a carefully researched story of slavery, helped to galvanize public opinion in the North against slavery. Three hundred thousand copies of the book were sold in the first year, and the positive and negative responses to it were heated. It was almost immediately translated to the stage, where it became one of the great successes of the century. Stowe's fictional account brought home to many people, on a personal level, the evils of the system as never before, thus inflaming the passion for reform. At the same time, many who supported slavery, especially in the South, attacked the book as inaccurate, sensationalized, and even malicious. The debates were many and harsh. There seems to be little question, however, that the book itself served to hasten the armed conflict over slavery. In the middle of the Civil War several years later, when Stowe was invited to the White House, Abraham Lincoln greeted her by asking, "Is this the little lady that caused the great war?" In the 1880s, when Mark Twain was writing his novel about a young boy who puts his eternal salvation on the line to help free a black man from slavery, his neighbor and friend was Harriet Beecher Stowe.

In 1854, the passage of the Kansas-Nebraska Act further fueled antagonism between pro- and anti-slavery factions. This act rescinded the earlier Missouri Compromise of 1820, which excluded slavery from all the Louisiana Purchase territory above 36°30' north latitude. Now, instead, the issue of whether the Kansas-Nebraska territory would be free would be left to the ballot. Hundreds of hotheads on both sides of the issue flooded into Kansas territory, determined to decide the issue by force of numbers, thus insuring bloody violence. Raids and counterraids were immediate and savage. In 1856 pro-slavery forces destroyed the free-state settlement in Lawrence, Kansas; in retaliation, anti-slavery leader John Brown, determined to start a slave uprising and a civil war, attacked a pro-slavery settlement near Pottawatomie Creek, murdering five men. Brown, who believed that he was under orders from God, continued his work to abolish slavery, gathering many sympathizers, but eventually disturbing even his would-be supporters with his increasing violence.

As a direct consequence of the Fugitive Slave Law, 1857 marked another turning point in the history of slavery: the Dred Scott decision. In 1846 a slave named Dred Scott sued for his freedom, having at one time been taken by his master from Missouri into Illinois, where slavery was forbidden by the Missouri Compromise. But Scott remained a slave and was returned to Missouri and sold. Abolitionists and friends advised him that his previous residence in the free state of Illinois might allow him to sue for his freedom in the courts. The case reached the Supreme Court of the United States, which decided that Scott, because he was a slave, had no right to sue in the federal courts and had to remain in slavery. Furthermore, the Court announced that the Missouri Compromise itself, which designated free and slave states, was null and void. The decision meant that from the time of the Dred Scott decision, the institution of slavery was legally protected anywhere in the territories. The Dred Scott decision, like the Kansas-Nebraska Act, brought the already violent disagreement between pro- and anti-slavery forces to a dangerous pass.

In 1859 John Brown, along with a few followers, conducted an armed raid on the federal arsenal at Harper's Ferry, Virginia, expecting to bring about his longed-for slave revolt. No one rose up at all, and he was captured by marines and hanged in December of the same year.

In 1860 the victory of Abraham Lincoln and the Republican Party, which had come into being to protest the opening of the Kansas-Nebraska territory to slavery, made Civil War inevitable. By this time the issue between North and South was clearly slavery. In

December 1860, South Carolina became the first southern state to withdraw from the Union. Several compromises were proposed at this time to bring the Union back together, but each proved unworkable; and each one, once more, concerned the issue of slavery alone. Finally, when on April 12, 1861, Lincoln attempted to send provisions to Fort Sumter, a federal installation in the harbor in Charleston, South Carolina, state cannons opened fire on the fort. The Civil War had begun.

In 1863, after two years of unparalleled bloodshed and destruction, Lincoln, for tactical as well as moral reasons, issued the Emancipation Proclamation, freeing slaves in the rebel states. The bloody war dragged on for two more years, ending at last in 1865 with the surrender of southern forces. In that same year, the Thirteenth Amendment to the Constitution ended slavery forever.

In 1868 the Fourteenth Amendment made African Americans citizens, and in 1870 the Fifteenth Amendment gave the vote to African-American males.

CIVIL DISOBEDIENCE

> I don't give a dead rat what the authorities think about it nuther. (240)

The conflict between morality and legality in just about all its manifestations, especially as it concerns slavery and ownership, runs throughout all of *Adventures of Huckleberry Finn.* It comes to a climax when Huck decides, definitively, that he will disobey the law in order to help Jim escape. Huck has learned from Pap that he can justify breaking the law by taking what belongs to other people and calling it "borrowing." Then he learns from Tom when they are trying to free Jim from the Phelps shack that the form of lawbreaking known as stealing is all right as long as it is being done to free a prisoner. The supreme irony, for the reader, comes in Huck's discomfort with stealing Miss Watson's property, that is, Jim, in light of the fact that slavery itself is the theft of a human being's body and labor. Moral and natural law might dictate, then, that Miss Watson, not Huck, is the real thief.

Huck's dilemma raises a question that became especially prominent for virtually all of America in the 1850s after the passage of the Fugitive Slave Law: Is breaking the law ever justified? To put it another way: Can a law ever be so immoral that the only right action is to disobey it? To the abolitionists, the answer was a distinctive yes. Under the circumstances, then, it is no surprise that the abolitionists began wholesale illegal activities after the passage of the Fugitive Slave Law. As we have seen, the Fugitive Slave Law had made it illegal to refuse to turn in runaway slaves like Jim even when they had escaped to states where slavery was outlawed. To make matters worse, such slaves had no recourse to the courts. All a white person needed was minimal documentation to support his claim that a black person in free territory was his property.

Many people opposed to slavery believed intensely that the country's laws, no matter how objectionable, had to be obeyed. Law, it was thought, was sacred. It was the only thing that lifted mankind and civilization itself above savagery. They felt that chaos would ensue if citizens began selectively choosing which laws to obey and which to disobey on moral grounds.

Are some laws immoral? Are we obligated to obey immoral laws? These were the questions behind the debate over slavery, behind the condemnation of those who justified their allegiance to Adolf Hitler. Some of the most well defined arguments, along the same lines, can be found in the protests of massive numbers of Americans during the Vietnam War, many of them ministers of the gospel, who argued that it would be immoral to allow oneself to be drafted to fight in an immoral war. Thus, they too encouraged potential draftees to refuse to serve, and even to escape to Canada, Sweden, or other places where such refugees were accepted.

Ironically, Huckleberry Finn is cast in the mold of the abolitionists he so fears and despises. He is willing to break the law in order to obey a higher, contradictory law, though he is not aware that it is a higher law. Unlike the abolitionists, however, he acts not by theoretically challenging the institution of slavery, as they did, but by responding to the immediate needs of his friend. Even when he believes that such action will bring him eternal damnation, he decides, at last, "All right, then, I'll go to hell."

FREED SLAVES IN THE 1880s

Then what on earth did you want to set him free for, seeing he was already free? (280)

As more than one critic has noted, *Adventures of Huckleberry Finn* has as much to do with the legacy of slavery in the years after the Civil War—the years in which the novel was written and published—as it does with its pre–Civil War setting.

This postwar legacy of slavery is very likely alluded to in the final sequences of *Adventures of Huckleberry Finn.* Scholars Rita and Richard Gollin have noted that the Phelps chapters are a comment on the plight of African Americans right after the war. In this interpretation, Jim is intended as a representative of all African Americans and Tom Sawyer as a representative of the white ruling class in the South. Note that Tom Sawyer continues to act as if Jim is a slave even though he knows Jim has been freed by Miss Watson. This, the Gollins argue, is the attitude of postwar society, which accepts the emancipation of black people on paper, but continues to regard them as inferiors before the law and in society, almost as though nothing had changed. The argument that Twain targets specifically is the theory of gradualism, which advocated continuing the servitude of ex-slaves in all but name only, postponing equal education, equal opportunity for jobs, and decent living conditions, as well as respectability. This can be seen most graphically in Tom Sawyer's desire to keep up forever the game of getting Jim out. Perhaps, he speculates, he and Huck could leave "Jim to our children to get out" (193; Gollin and Gollin, "Huckleberry Finn and the Time of the Evasion," *Modern Language Studies* [Spring 1979]: 5–15).

What, then, were the actual conditions of African Americans observed by Mark Twain in the 1880s, at the time he was writing *Adventures of Huckleberry Finn?* In the years following the Civil War, in the period called Reconstruction, the South was further crushed economically, politically, and socially. Corruption was rampant; the old way of life as well as the economy was destroyed. And despite programs like the Freedman's Bureau designed to assist the newly freed slaves, many were plunged into a situation in which they could survive only with difficulty.

Immediately after the war, some of the newly freed slaves were allowed to acquire land and to sit in state legislatures (where, it is now agreed, they did a respectable job), but the national campaign of 1876, when the Democrats in Congress made a deal with southerners, ended all the progressive measures that had been begun. For a large majority of newly freed slaves, the legacy of slavery continued. Most were without money or land, training or income, in an economy that was already bleak for all the poor.

By 1880 Northern troops had been removed from the South, but to a large extent the old problems persisted. As a result of complex changes, the living conditions of the large majority of African Americans changed very little after they were freed. To survive, many remained on the farms and plantations where they had been slaves, continuing in slave/master relationships with whites and accepting their place on the bottom rung of the economic ladder. Successful attempts were made in the 1880s to keep ex-slaves in what has been described as virtual slavery by means of three economic and legal practices: the special labor contract system, the sharecropping system, and the convict labor system.

The contract labor system, which was put in place during Reconstruction and continued throughout the nineteenth century, was intended to supply much-needed cheap labor on the often devastated farms and plantations in the South. The process worked like this: plantation owners contracted with the federal government, acting on behalf of newly emancipated slaves, for a year's worth of worker's labor. With the old abuses in mind, the plantation owners were forbidden by law to discipline workers, this function being turned over to the occupying army. After Reconstruction, however, the process did not really die out; it merely became transformed. Even though the contracts were now formed between the individual workers and the plantation owner, the ex-slaves often found themselves bound forever just as before, this time by endless labor contracts. This was due in part to the fact that their very presence on the plantations was often regarded as legal evidence that they had agreed to a continuation of yearly contracts. Studies have shown, in fact, that the work was generally much harder than it had been in slavery times. The master/slave mentality thus continued in these situations while living conditions remained poor; and as long as the worker remained legally "under contract," there was not a remote chance for independence or a better life. Any ex-slave not at work on someone else's farm or plantation was subject to arrest. He or she had to carry a copy of this signed contract at all times to avoid being arrested for vagrancy.

Wages under the system were almost nonexistent. In what seems to have been a typical situation in Louisiana, a planter paid his workers for a year's work at the end of the year as follows: six of them received between $7.01 and $52.97 for the year; and twenty-eight of them were told at the end of the year that they owed money to their employer, rather than vice versa, for various rent, food, and medical expenses. Some owed amounts as large as $88.10.

The second means by which the newly freed slaves were kept in perpetual servitude was the sharecropping system, which had for years also kept poor whites in virtual bondage. By the 1880s, many former slaves, eager to have a little independence at all costs, had managed to become sharecroppers rather than plantation and farm hands, even though the situation offered little or no improvement for them financially. Sharecroppers worked plots of land belonging to someone else and then divided the crops with the landowner, who in turn supervised every aspect of the planting. So while the sharecropper had the illusion of independence, he generally had to take on so much debt to farm his plot and provide for his family's survival that he was often poorer at the end of the year than at the beginning.

By the 1880s, convict laws were also passed largely in an effort to reassert white supremacy and provide free labor. In the system, two economic conditions worked against the ex-slave: first, there were rigidly enforced vagrancy laws directed at newly freed slaves, especially those who were trying to escape their labor contracts with planters. These workers ended up in prison, working without recompense. Second, white politicians reclassified criminal laws (for example, making it grand larceny to steal any item as low in value as ten dollars). Both of these developments provided the white businessman with a rich pool of convict labor composed of both whites and blacks, but chiefly African Americans who had been born in slavery. Conditions for convicts were so abominable that the death rate was outrageously high. William Cohen found, for example, that "between 1877 and 1880, 285 South Carolina prisoners were sent to build the Greenwood and Augusta railroad. Of these, 128, or 44.9 percent, died in the three-year period" (*At Freedom's Edge* [Baton Rouge: Louisiana State University Press, 1991], p. 226). Cohen quotes Sir George Campbell, an Englishman who studied the Georgia convict system in 1878, as observing, "This does seem simply a return to another form of slavery" (*White and Black* [London: 1879], p. 365, quoted in Cohen, p. 227).

Illegal and secret militant organizations like the Ku Klux Klan (KKK) and the Knights of the Camellia sprang up everywhere. Though after the turn of the twentieth century most respectable southerners would denounce such organizations, in the 1870s and 1880s the general white population allowed them free rein. While mob violence during Reconstruction made ample use of intimidation and terror, it rarely resulted in murder. But after 1877, mob violence resulted in torture, mutilation, burning, and murder. In the 1880s, the number of lynchings rose by 63.5 percent—faster than at any other time in the nation's history. Between 1880 and 1884 there were 233 lynchings in the United States, almost all of the victims being black men in the South. Between 1885 and 1889, the number rose to 381. Between 1890 and 1894, 611 lynchings were recorded, acts which were rarely punished. "In many districts, particularly in the deep South, the killing of a Negro by a white man ceased, in practice, even to call for legal inquiry. But wherever and whenever the forms were still observed, the coroner or the jury was all but sure to call it 'self defense' " (Cash, *The Mind of the South,* p. 120).

During the 1880s, while Mark Twain was writing *Adventures of Huckleberry Finn,* many influences prompted him to examine the history and contemporary conditions of African Americans. One of the strongest influences to shape his portrayal of Jim's situation in the novel, especially the final Phelps episode, was his association with another writer, George Washington Cable. Twain traveled as a lecturer with Cable, a native of New Orleans and the foremost southern champion of justice for the African American, from November 1884 to February 1885, a time when Cable was most actively critical of the South's treatment of freed slaves. In January 1885, in the middle of their lecture tour together, Cable published "The Freedman's Case," and included it later the same year in *The Silent South;* both works deplored the continuing injustices under which the legally freed black person labored. There seems to be little doubt that Twain fully shared Cable's view.

Everything about the African American's plight, as Cable viewed it, illustrated that, though black people had been freed by an amendment to the Constitution, practically speaking, they remained slaves. Jim's enslavement on the Phelps farm represents the real situation of emancipated slaves at the time the novel was being written: that is, Jim has been freed by Miss Watson, but he remains a slave.

The Phelps episode also describes the reformer of the 1880s, who believed that justice had to come gradually. In connecting the attitude of these reformers with the ending of *Adventures of Huckleberry Finn*, Rita and Richard Gollin note that "what should be— and is for Huck and Jim—a matter of direct action is for Tom a question of rules and principles" (12). They observe that "central to the tangled and often absurd efforts of Tom and Huck to liberate Jim is Twain's indictment of polite society's continuing evasion, its conversion of action to liberate the freed black man into a satisfying game" (14).

While Huck's feelings and actions are always dictated by personal feelings rather than social and political beliefs, the reader should keep in mind the historical context of the 1880s in which the novel was completed. While one should not ignore the complexities of suddenly and fully bringing thousands of people enslaved for centuries into mainstream American society, as Cable insisted, simple justice was something that should not have been postponed.

The following groups of documents explore slavery and the civil disobedience that arose in the wake of the Fugitive Slave Law, as well as the issues of the continuing enslavement of African Americans after emancipation. The first group of documents sets forth the pro-slavery argument, which derives from the notion that one human being can be the property of another and that slavery is endorsed by religion. The second group of documents includes accounts by ex-slaves themselves and by a white man who observed slavery in Missouri. The third group includes excerpts from the text of the Missouri Compromise of 1820 and the Fugitive Slave Law of 1850. The fourth group includes arguments about law keeping and lawbreaking in the historical context of slavery, two contending that it was the duty of every right-thinking person to disobey the Fugitive Slave Law, two insisting that the law must be obeyed, and one explaining the difference the new law made in a slave's life. The final excerpt in the section on civil disobedience is an essay published in 1968 by William Sloane Coffin, Jr., on civil disobedience during the Vietnam War. Finally, with regard to the continued enslavement of the freedman in the post–Civil War

South, excerpts are included from ''The Freedman's Case'' by
Twain's friend, George Washington Cable.

THE PRO-SLAVERY ARGUMENT

An understanding of the pro-slavery stance is essential to get some sense of the heart-wrenching trauma faced by a boy who has been brought up in a society where the slaveholders' values prevail. The three pro-slavery arguments included here show the mental contortions performed by society to justify slavery. Huck believes he is going to hell for helping Jim escape because he has been imbued with assumptions he has never questioned. The two assumptions most important to *Adventures of Huckleberry Finn* are, first, that human beings can rightfully be the property of other human beings and, second, that the black race is inferior to the white. It followed that those who supported slavery would argue that Africans were meant to be enslaved by whites; it was virtually impossible for any black person to "own" himself. So a slave who ran away from slavery, or anyone who helped him or her escape, was breaking one of the Ten Commandments, "Thou shalt not steal." And there was a keen sense that the slave owners' property rights were sacred, God-given rights. It is not surprising, then, that many in the South, and in the North as well, presented religious arguments in support of slavery.

THOMAS RODERICK DEW

Thomas Roderick Dew was a member of the southern aristocracy, a professor of law who eventually became president of the College of William and Mary. He was also a Virginia planter and the owner of many slaves. Dew's 1832 response to a legislative move for emancipation, from which the following excerpt is taken, was one of the first treatises in America expressly countering anti-slavery sentiment.

Unlike most pro-slavery arguments, Dew's assertions were based solely on economic grounds. He was outraged chiefly because planters like himself would suffer if they were forced to relinquish valuable property—their slaves. Considering neither moral issues nor the welfare of slaves, he weighs the finances of the rich planter and the state alone. For the state of Virginia, he declares, emancipation would mean a loss of $100 million. In pressing that point, he acknowledges that the whole economy of Virginia subsists on the institution of slavery and warns further that without slavery "Virginia will be a desert."

FROM THOMAS RODERICK DEW, "ABOLITION OF NEGRO
SLAVERY," IN *THE PRO-SLAVERY ARGUMENT*
(Philadelphia: Lippincott, Grambo, and Co., 1853)

Some have attempted to evade the difficulties by seizing on the increase of the negroes after a certain time. Thus Mr. Randolph's plan proposed that all born after the year 1840, should be raised by their masters to the age of eighteen for the female and twenty-one for the male, and then hired out, until the neat sum arising therefrom amounted to enough to send them away. Scarcely any one in the legislature—we believe not even the author himself—entirely approved of this plan. It is obnoxious to the objections we have just been stating against voluntary surrender. It proposes to saddle the slave-holder with the whole burthen; it infringes directly the rights of property; it converts the fee simple possession of this kind of property into an estate for years; and it only puts off the great sacrifice required of the state to 1840, when most of the evils will occur that have already been described. In the mean time it destroys the value of slaves, and with it all landed possessions—checks the production of the state, (when 1840 arrives), when most of the evils will occur that have already been described. It imposes upon the master the intolerable and grievous burthen of raising his young slaves to the ages of eighteen and twenty-one, and then liberating them to be hired out under the super-intendence of government (the most miserable of all managers,) until the proceeds arising therefrom shall be sufficient to send them away. If any man at all conversant with political economy should ever anticipate the day when this shall happen, we can only say that his faith is great indeed, enough to remove mountains, and that he has studied in a totally different school from ourselves. . . . (38)

There is $100,000,000 of slave property in the state of Virginia, and it matters but little how you destroy it, whether by the slow process of the cautious *practitioner,* or with the frightful despatch of the self confident *quack;* when it is gone, no matter how, the deed will be done, and Virginia will be a desert. (39)

LETTER OF JAMES HENRY HAMMOND

The second pro-slavery argument included here was made by James Henry Hammond of South Carolina in 1845. Hammond was twice a United States congressman and a one-term governor of

South Carolina. He was considered one of the most articulate and creditable spokesmen for the cause of slavery. The excerpt below is from a letter Hammond wrote to a British opponent of slavery.

Using a reference in the Ten Commandments to "servant," which, he argues, means "slave," he asserts that it is both natural and biblical for a man to hold property in another man's person and labor.

FROM JAMES HENRY HAMMOND, "LETTER TO AN ENGLISH ABOLITIONIST," IN *THE PRO-SLAVERY ARGUMENT*

The wisdom of ages has concurred in the justice and expedience of establishing rights by prescriptive use, however tortuous in their origin they may have been. You would deem a man insane, whose keen sense of equity would lead him to denounce your right to the lands you hold, and which perhaps you inherited from a long line of ancestry, because your title was derived from a Saxon or Norman conqueror, and your lands were originally wrested by violence from the vanquished Britons. And so would the New-England abolitionist regard any one who would insist that he should restore his farm to the descendants of the slaughtered red men, to whom God had as clearly given it as he gave life and freedom to the kidnapped African. That time does not consecrate wrong, is a fallacy which all history exposes; and which the best and wisest men of all ages and professions of religious faith have practically denied. The means, therefore, whatever they may have been, by which the African race now in this country have been reduced to Slavery, cannot affect us, since they are our property, as your land is yours, by inheritance or purchase and prescriptive right. You will say that man cannot hold *property in man.* The answer is, that he can and *actually does* hold property in his fellow all the world over, in a variety of forms, and *has always done so.* I will show presently his authority for doing it. . . . (172)

. . . On Slavery in the abstract, then, it would not be amiss to have as little as possible to say. Let us contemplate it as it is. And thus contemplating it, the first question we have to ask ourselves is, whether it is contrary to the will of God, as revealed to us in his Holy Scriptures—the only certain means given us to ascertain his will. If it is, then Slavery is a sin. And I admit at once that every man is bound to set his face against it, and to emancipate his slaves, should he hold any.

Let us open these Holy Scriptures. In the twentieth chapter of Exodus, seventeenth verse, I find the following words: "Thou shalt not covet thy neighbor's house, thou shalt not covet thy neighbor's wife, nor his man-servant, nor his maid-servant, nor his ox, nor his ass, nor anything that is thy neighbor's"—which is the tenth of those commandments that declare the essential principles of the great moral law delivered to Moses by God himself. Now, discarding all technical and verbal quibbling as wholly unworthy to be used in interpreting the Word of God, what is the plain meaning, undoubted intent, and true spirit of this commandment? Does it not emphatically and explicitly forbid you to disturb your neighbor in the enjoyment of his property; and more especially of that which is here specifically mentioned as being lawfully, and by this commandment made sacredly his? Prominent in the catalogue stands his "man-servant and his maid-servant," who are thus distinctly *consecrated as his property,* and guaranteed to him for his exclusive benefit, in the most solemn manner. . . . (173)

I think, then, I may safely conclude, and I firmly believe, that American Slavery is not only not a sin, but especially commanded by God through Moses, and approved by Christ through his apostles. And here I might close its defence; for what God ordains, and Christ sanctifies, should surely command the respect and toleration of man. But I fear there has grown up in our time a transcendental religion, which is throwing even transcendental philosophy into the shade—a religion too pure and elevated for the Bible; which seeks to erect among men a higher standard of morals than the Almighty has revealed, or our Saviour preached; and which is probably destined to do more to impede the extension of God's kingdom on earth than all the infidels who have ever lived. Error is error. It is as dangerous to deviate to the right hand as to the left. And when men, professing to be holy men, and who are by numbers so regarded, declare those things to be sinful which our Creator has expressly authorized and instituted, they do more to destroy his authority among mankind than the most wicked can effect, by proclaiming that to be innocent which he has forbidden. (175)

ARGUMENT OF THE REVEREND BROWNLOW

For a full-blown justification of slavery on religious grounds we turn to the debate in 1858 between the Reverend W. G. Brownlow, a Virginia minister, and the Reverend A. Pryne, who opposed slavery. At this time the debate over slavery had reached a passionate level of intensity. Brownlow illustrates the commonly held view of southern, and even many northern, clergymen that slavery was approved by the Old and New Testaments. In the first paragraph cited here, Brownlow summarizes the main argument he will support in justification of slavery. He goes on to repudiate the Declaration of Independence, which claims that all men are created equal. He justifies slavery as natural and inevitable by contending that the institution always existed, that even the biblical patriarch Abraham owned slaves, and that the Christian slaves of the Romans had a duty to be humble and submit to their slavery without protest. Like Hammond and others before him, Brownlow uses the wording of the Ten Commandments to illustrate that God intended for slavery to be perpetuated. So, he charges, runaway slaves and those who assist them are not only stealing legal property, they are breaking one of the Ten Commandments.

He believes that slavery, "under the inspiration of God," is a system by which a superior race takes care of an inferior one. Brownlow goes even further in his concluding point to justify the beating of slaves.

Brownlow's argument is not published as part of a debate over specific points but as a single address, excerpts from which are quoted below.

FROM W. G. BROWNLOW, *OUGHT AMERICAN SLAVERY TO BE PERPETUATED? A DEBATE BETWEEN REV. W. G. BROWNLOW AND REV. A. PRYNE.*
(Held at Philadelphia, September, 1858. Philadelphia: J. B. Lippincott and Co., 1858)

Not only will I throughout this discussion openly and boldly take the ground that *Slavery as it exists in America ought to be perpetuated,* but that slavery is an established and inevitable condition to human society. I will maintain the ground that God always intended the relation of master and slave to exist; that Christ and the early teachers of Christianity, found slavery differing in no material respect from American slavery, *incorporated into every department of society;* that in the adoption of rules for the government of society, and of the church, they provided for the rights of *owners,* and the wants of *slaves;* that slavery having existed ever since the first organization of society, it will exist to the end of time. . . . (18–19)

When an unprejudiced and candid mind examines into the history of our race, and learns the fact which history develops, as the honest inquirer will, that a majority of mankind were *slaves,* he will be driven to the conclusion I have long since reached: namely, that the world, when first peopled by God himself, was not a world of *freemen,* but of SLAVES—the Declaration of American Independence, as usually construed, to the contrary notwithstanding.

Slavery was really established and sanctioned by Divine authority, among even God's chosen people—the favored people of Israel. Abraham, the founder of this interesting nation, and the chosen servant of the Most High, was the lawful owner, at one time, of more slaves than any cotton-planter in South Carolina, Georgia, Alabama, or Mississippi; or any tobacco or sugar planter in Virginia or Louisiana. This may strike you as a bold assertion, at first glance; but my competitor, who is familiar with the Scriptures, will *regret,* that there is more truth than poetry in the declaration.

That magnificent shrine, the gorgeous temple of Solomon, commenced and completed under the pious promptings of religion and ancient free-masonry, was reared alone by the hands of slaves! Involuntary servitude, reduced to a science, existed in ancient Assyria and Babylon. Egypt's venerable and enduring pyramids were all reared by the hands of slaves, and black negroes at that! The ten tribes of Israel were carried off to Assyria by Shalmanezar, and the two strong tribes of Judah were subsequently carried in triumph by Nebuchadnezzar to end their days in Babylon as *slaves,* and to labor to adorn the city. Ancient Phoenicia and Carthage, were literally overrun with slavery; the slave population outnumbering the free and the owners of slaves, nearly three to one! The Greeks and Trojans, at the siege of Troy, were attended with equal numbers of their slaves, to themselves. Athens, and Sparta, and Thebes—indeed, the whole Grecian and Roman worlds—had more slaves than freemen. And in those ages which succeeded the extinction of the Roman empire in the West, slaves, abject and degraded slaves, were the most numerous class. Even in the days of civilization and Christian light, which revolutionized governments, laboring serfs and abject slaves were distributed throughout Eastern Europe, and Western Asia—showing that slavery existed throughout these boundless regions. In China, the worst forms of slavery have existed since the earliest history of the "Celestial Empire." And when we turn to Africa, we find slavery, in all its most revolting forms, existing throughout its whole extent, the slaves outnumbering the free-men three to one! Looking then, to the whole world, I may with confidence assert, as I do today in your midst, that slavery in its worst forms, subdues by far the largest portion of the human race.

Now, my respected auditors, the inquiry is, how has slavery thus risen and spread over our whole earth? I answer—by the *laws of war*—the *state of property*—the *feebleness of governments*—the thirst for *bargain and sale*—the *increase of crime*—and last, but not least, *by and with the consent, knowledge, and approbation of Almighty God! Slavery, then, is an established and inevitable condition to human society....* (19–21)

In "that sacred book from Heaven bestowed," usually called the Bible, this call is made upon *slaves, or* servants, as you may choose to regard them:

> Let as many servants as are under the yoke count their own masters worthy
> of all honor, that the name of God and his doctrine be not blasphemed.—
> I *Tim.* vi:1

The scriptures, for the most part, were written in the Hebrew and Greek languages, and I flatter myself that my worthy competitor is familiar with these languages. If so, he knows that the word here rendered *servants* means SLAVES converted to the Christian faith; and the word *yoke* signifies the *state of slavery,* in which Christ and the Apostles found the world involved, when the Christian Church was first organized.

By the word rendered *masters,* we are to understand the heathen masters of those christianized slaves. Even these, in such circumstances, and under such domination, are commanded to treat their masters with all honor and respect, that the name of God, by which they were called, and the doctrine of God, to wit: Christianity, which they had professed, might not be blasphemed—might not be evil spoken of in consequence of their improper conduct. . . . (22)

The essential principles of the great Moral Law delivered to Moses by God himself, are set forth in what is called the Tenth Commandment, and will be found in the 20th chapter of the book of Exodus:

> Thou shalt not covet thy neighbor's house, thou shalt not covet thy neigh-
> bor's wife, nor his *man-servant,* nor his *maid-servant,* nor his ox nor his
> ass, nor anything that is thy neighbor's.

The only true interpretation of this portion of the word of God is, that the species of property herein mentioned, are *lawful,* and that all men are forbid to disturb others in the lawful enjoyment of their property. "Manservants and maid-servants," are distinctly *consecrated as property,* and guaranteed to man for his exclusive benefit—proof that slavery was ordained by God himself. I have seen learned dissertations from the pens of Anti-slavery men—and I expect to *hear* one equally learned, before this discussion closes—setting forth that the term "servant" and not "slave" is used here. To this I reply, once and for all, that both the Hebrew and Greek words translated "*servant,*" meaning "*slave*" also, and are more frequently used in this sense than in the former. Besides, the Hebrew Scriptures teach us, that God especially authorized his peculiar people to *purchase* "BOND-MEN FOR EVER"; and if to be in *bondage for ever,* does not constitute *slavery as perpetual as American slavery,* I yield the point to the gentleman who proposes to abolish the latter!

The visionary notions of piety and philanthropy entertained by many men at the North, lead them to resist the *Fugitive Slave Law* of this government, and even to *violate the tenth commandment,* by stealing our "men-servants and maid-servants" and running them into what they call free territory, upon their "under-ground railroads!" . . . (28–29)

For the present, I have only to say, that the institution of slavery was established for the benefit of that class of the human family who had not the *capacity to provide for their wants*—and of this class are the entire African race—a class that existed in the days of Moses—has existed ever since—and will continue to exist as long as man is clothed with the infirmities of mortality. Yes—the decree has gone forth, that fully *two-thirds* of the civilized race of man shall work for the rest in the capacity of *bond or hired* servants. It is a decree that pervades the dominions of civilization, not as the edict of duty, but of fallen humanity; and to meliorate the sufferings of the *dependant,* by affording them a competency during sickness and aged infirmity, *bondage* was instituted by Moses, under the inspiration of God! This form of slavery, then, is in perfect accordance with the will of God. And I shall be able to show that "American slavery" does not differ in *form* or *principle,* from that of the chosen people of God.

I endorse, without reserve, that much-abused sentiment of an eminent Southern statesman, now no more, Gov. McDuffie, that "slavery is the corner-stone of our republican edifice;" while I repudiate, as ridiculously absurd, that much lauded, but nowhere accredited dogma of Thomas Jefferson's, that "all men are born equal." God never intended to make the negro the equal of the white man, either morally, mentally, or physically. He never intended to make the *butcher* a judge, nor the *baker* president, but to protect them according to their claims as butcher and baker. Pope has beautifully expressed this sentiment, in these lines:

Order is heaven's first law, and this confess'd,
Some are, and must be, greater than the rest. (42–43)

In reference to *bad* servants, we read in Prov. xxix: 19.

A servant will not be corrected by *words;* for though he understand, he will not answer.

Here we are taught that a servant will not be corrected by *words,* and the inference is, that *stripes* must be inflicted. The Scriptures look to the correction of servants, and really enjoin it, as they do in the case of children. I esteem it the duty of Christian masters to feed and clothe their negroes well—to work them well, that is, constantly, but in moderation—and in cases of disobedience, to *whip well.* . . . (80)

FIRSTHAND ACCOUNTS OF SLAVERY

Nothing so quickly gives the lie to pro-slavery arguments than narratives of people who suffered through it, or who observed it through sympathetic eyes. Just so, the slaveholding society's preconceptions are belied for the reader by Jim's story of a family separated, by his fear of being sold down South by Miss Watson, and by the human greatness Jim achieves through his words and actions. By the end of the journey, Jim can no longer be regarded as a piece of property in the reader's eyes, and the religious justifications of slavery ring hollow.

FREDERICK DOUGLASS, ONCE A SLAVE

One of the first enlightenments that the general public received about slavery from the slave's point of view came with the publication in 1845 of Frederick Douglass' *Narrative of the Life of Frederick Douglass*. Douglass, son of a slave woman and her owner, managed secretly to educate himself, even though teaching a slave to read was absolutely illegal; an educated slave was a dangerous slave. Living under somewhat more lenient circumstances in Maryland than he would have found in deep South states like Georgia and Louisiana, Douglass was able to escape to freedom. In the North, he became an articulate leader in the battles for the abolition of slavery and for women's rights.

Douglass begins his narrative with a common fact of life in slavery—family separation. His experiences with slavery are blood-curdling refutations of Brownlow's and Hammond's assertions that the lives of black people were better under slavery. Brownlow's assertion that scripture recommends that masters whip slaves and "whip well" appears to be not only self-deluded, but cruel and cold-blooded in light of Douglass' hair-raising tales of the beatings he witnessed.

Along with other cruelties, Douglass somewhat delicately broaches the subject of the sexual abuse suffered at the hands of owners and overseers, as his own parentage and the story of his aunt illustrate. Finally he writes of the desperation of the runaway slave—without money, credit, home, family, or friends, always looking over his shoulder for slave hunters (see Figure 4.3). And

Figure 4.3. Sketch showing a family of runaway slaves being pursued by bounty hunters using dogs.

this was even before the passage of the Fugitive Slave Law of 1850.

FROM FREDERICK DOUGLASS, *NARRATIVE OF THE LIFE OF FREDERICK DOUGLASS*
(Boston: Boston Anti-Slavery Society, 1845)

My father was a white man. He was admitted to be such by all I ever heard speak of my parentage. The opinion was also whispered that my master was my father; but of the correctness of this opinion, I know nothing; the means of knowing was withheld from me. My mother and I were separated when I was but an infant—before I knew her as my mother. It is a common custom, in the part of Maryland from which I ran away, to part children from their mothers at a very early age. Frequently, before the child has reached its twelfth month, its mother is taken from it, and hired out on some farm a considerable distance off, and the child is placed under the care of an old woman, too old for field labor. For what reason this separation is done, I do not know, unless it be to hinder the development of the child's affection toward its mother, and to blunt and destroy the natural affection of the mother for the child. This is the inevitable result. . . . (18–19)

I have had two masters. My first master's name was Anthony. I do not remember his first name. He was generally called Captain Anthony—a title which, I presume, he acquired by sailing a craft on the Chesapeake Bay. He was not considered a rich slaveholder. He owned two or three farms, and about thirty slaves. His farms and slaves were under the care of an overseer. The overseer's name was Plummer. Mr. Plummer was a miserable drunkard, a profane swearer, and a savage monster. He always went armed with a cowskin [whip] and a heavy cudgel. I have known him to cut and slash the women's heads so horribly, that even master would be enraged at his cruelty, and would threaten to whip him if he did not mind himself. Master, however, was not a humane slaveholder. It required extraordinary barbarity on the part of an overseer to affect him. He was a cruel man, hardened by a long life of slaveholding. He would at times seem to take great pleasure in whipping a slave. I have often been awakened at the dawn of day by the most heart-rending shrieks of an own aunt of mine, whom he used to tie up to a joist, and whip upon her back till she was literally covered with blood. No words, no tears, no prayers, from his gory victim, seemed to move his iron heart from its bloody purpose. The louder she screamed, the harder he whipped; and where the blood ran fastest, there he whipped longest. He would whip her to make her scream, and whip her to make her hush; and not until overcome by fatigue would he cease to swing the blood-clotted cowskin. I remember the first time I ever witnessed this horrible exhibition. I was quite a child, but I well remember it! I never shall forget it whilst I remember any thing. It was the first of a long series of outrages, of which I was doomed to be a witness and a participant. It struck me with awful force. It was the blood-stained gate, the entrance to the hell of slavery, through which I was about to pass. It was a most horrible spectacle. I wish I could commit to paper the feelings with which I beheld it.

The occurrence took place very soon after I went to live with my old master, and under the following circumstances. Aunt Hester went out one night,—where or for what I do not know,—and happened to be absent when my master desired her presence. He had ordered her not to go out evenings, and warned her that she must never let him catch her in the company of a young man, who was paying attention to her belonging to Colonel Lloyd. The young man's name was Ned Roberts, General Lloyd's Ned. Why master was so careful of her, may be safely left to conjecture. She was a woman of noble form, and of graceful proportions, having very few equals and fewer superiors, in personal appearance, among the colored or white women of our neighborhood.

Aunt Hester had not only disobeyed his orders in going out, but had been found in company with Lloyd's Ned; which circumstance, I found, from what he said while whipping her, was the chief offence. Had he been a man of pure morals himself, he might have been thought interested in protecting the innocence of my aunt; but those who knew him will not suspect him of any such virtue. Before he commenced whipping Aunt Hester, he took her into the kitchen, and stripped her from neck to waist, leaving her neck, shoulders, and back, entirely naked. He then told her to cross her hands, calling her at the same time a d——d b——h. After crossing her hands, he tied them with a strong rope, and led her to a stool under a large hook in the joist, put in for the purpose. He made her get upon the stool, and tied her hands to the hook. She now stood fair for his infernal purpose. Her arms were stretched up at their full length, so that she stood upon the ends of her toes. He then said to her, "Now, you d——d b——h, I'll learn you how to disobey my orders!" and after rolling up his sleeves, he commenced to lay on the heavy cowskin, and soon the warm, red blood (amid heart-rending shrieks from her, and horrid oaths from him) came dripping to the floor. I was so terrified and horror-stricken at the sight, that I hid myself in a closet, and dared not venture out till long after the bloody transaction was over. I expected it would be my turn next. It was all new to me. I had never seen any thing like it before. I had always lived with my grandmother on the outskirts of the plantation, where she was put to raise the children of the younger women. I had therefore been, until now, out of the way of the bloody scenes that often occurred on the plantation. . . . (21–23)

Mr. Severe was rightly named: he was a cruel man. I have seen him whip a woman, causing the blood to run half an hour at the time; and this, too, in the midst of her crying children, pleading for their mother's release. He seemed to take pleasure in manifesting his fiendish barbarity. Added to his cruelty, he was a profane swearer: it was enough to chill the blood and stiffen the hair of an ordinary man to hear him talk. Scarce a sentence escaped him but that was commenced or concluded by some horrid oath. The field was the place to witness his cruelty and profanity. His presence made it both the field of blood and of blasphemy. From the rising till the going down of the sun, he was cursing, raving, cutting, and slashing among the slaves of the field, in the most frightful manner. His career was short. He died very soon after I went to Colonel Lloyd's; and he died as he lived, uttering, with his dying groans, bitter curses and horrid oaths. His death was regarded by the slaves as the result of a merciful providence. . . . (26–27)

. . . I was again seized with a feeling of great insecurity and loneliness. I was yet liable to be taken back, and subjected to all the tortures of slavery. This in itself was enough to damp the ardor of my enthusiasm. But the loneliness overcame me. There I was in the midst of thousands, and yet a perfect stranger; without home and without friends, in the midst of thousands of my own brethren—children of a common Father, and yet I dared not to unfold to any one of them my sad condition. I was afraid to speak to any one for fear of speaking to the wrong one, and thereby falling into the hands of money-loving kidnappers, whose business it was to lie in wait for the panting fugitive, as the ferocious beasts of the forest lie in wait for their prey. The motto which I adopted when I started from slavery was this—"trust no man!" I saw in every white man an enemy, and in almost every colored man cause for distrust. It was a most painful situation; and, to understand it, one must needs experience it, or imagine himself in similar circumstances. Let him be a fugitive slave in a strange land—a land given up to be the hunting-ground for slaveholders—whose inhabitants are legalized kidnappers—where he is every moment subjected to the terrible liability of being seized upon by his fellowmen, as the hideous crocodile seizes upon his prey!—I say, let him place himself in my situation—without home or friends—without money or credit—wanting bread, and no money to buy it,—and at the same time let him feel that he is pursued by merciless men-hunters, and in total darkness as to what to do, where to go, or where to stay,— perfectly helpless both as to the means of defence and means of escape,—in the midst of plenty, yet suffering the terrible gnawings of hunger,—in the midst of houses, yet having no home,—among fellow-men, yet feeling as if in the midst of wild beasts, whose greediness to swallow up the trembling and half-famished fugitive is only equalled by that with which the monsters of the deep swallow up the helpless fish upon which they subsist,—I say, let him be placed in this most trying situation,—the situation in which I was placed,—then, and not till then, will he fully appreciate the hardships of, and know how to sympathize with, the toil-worn and whip-scarred fugitive slave. (111–112)

HARRIET JACOBS, ONCE A SLAVE

The horrors of slavery outlined on the eve of the Civil War by Harriet Jacobs, author of the second slave narrative included here, are also a powerful contradiction of the pro-slavery argument. She especially stresses the separation of families and treats with greater frankness the sexual exploitation of slave women by their masters. Harriet herself was the target of her master's unwanted attentions and was, ironically enough, protected for a long while by her jealous mistress, who despised her. On her orders, Harriet slept in her mistress' chamber, thereby escaping the advances of her master. Soon, fearing that Harriet's life was in danger, her grandmother hid her until someone could spirit her to relative safety in New York City.

FROM HARRIET A. JACOBS, *INCIDENTS IN THE LIFE OF A SLAVE GIRL*
(Boston: Published for the Author, 1861)

Mrs. Flint, like many southern women, was totally deficient in energy. She had not strength to superintend her household affairs; but her nerves were so strong, that she could sit in her easy chair and see a woman whipped, till the blood trickled from every stroke of the lash. She was a member of the church; but partaking of the Lord's supper did not seem to put her in a Christian frame of mind. If dinner was not served at the exact time on that particular Sunday, she would station herself in the kitchen, and wait till it was dished, and then spit in all the kettles and pans that had been used for cooking. She did this to prevent the cook and her children from eking out their meager fare with the remains of the gravy and other scrapings. The slaves could get nothing to eat except what she chose to give them. Provisions were weighed out by the pound and ounce, three times a day. I can assure you she gave them no chance to eat wheat bread from her flour barrel. She knew how many biscuits a quart of flour would make, and exactly what size they ought to be.

Dr. Flint was an epicure. The cook never sent a dinner to his table without fear and trembling; for if there happened to be a dish not to his liking, he would either order her to be whipped, or compel her to eat every mouthful of it in his presence. The poor, hungry creature might not have objected to eating it; but she did object to having her master cram it down her throat till she choked.

They had a pet dog, that was a nuisance in the house. The cook was ordered to make some Indian mush for him. He refused to eat, and when his head was held over it, the froth flowed from his mouth into the basin. He died a few minutes after. When Dr. Flint came in, he said the mush had not been well cooked, and that was the reason the animal would not eat it. He sent for the cook, and compelled her to eat it. He thought that the woman's stomach was stronger than the dog's; but her sufferings afterwards proved that he was mistaken. This poor woman endured many cruelties from her master and mistress; sometimes she was locked up, away from her nursing babe, for a whole day and night.

When I had been in the family a few weeks, one of the plantation slaves was brought to town, by order of his master. It was near night when he arrived, and Dr. Flint ordered him to be taken to the work house, and tied up to the joist, so that his feet would just escape the ground. In that situation he was to wait till the doctor had taken his tea. I shall never forget that night. Never before, in my life, had I heard hundreds of blows fall, in succession, on a human being. His piteous groans, and his "O, pray don't, massa," rang in my ear for months afterwards. There were many conjectures as to the cause of this terrible punishment. Some said master accused him of stealing corn; others said the slave had quarrelled with his wife, in the presence of the overseer, and had accused his master of being the father of her child. They were both black, and the child was very fair.

I went into the work house next morning, and saw the cowhide still wet with blood, and the boards all covered with gore. The poor man lived, and continued to quarrel with his wife. A few months afterwards Dr. Flint handed them both over to a slavetrader. The guilty man put their value into his pocket, and had the satisfaction of knowing that they were out of sight and hearing. When the mother was delivered into the trader's hands, she said, "You *promised* to treat me well." To which he replied, "You have let your tongue run too far, damn you!" She had forgotten that it was a crime for a slave to tell who was the father of her child.

From others than the master persecution also comes in such cases. I once saw a young slave girl dying soon after the birth of a child nearly white. In her agony she cried out, "O Lord, come and take me!" Her mistress stood by, and mocked at her like an incarnate fiend. "You suffer, do you?" she exclaimed. "I am glad of it. You deserve it all, and more too."

The girl's mother said, "The baby is dead, thank God; and I hope my poor child will soon be in heaven, too."

"Heaven!" retorted the mistress. "There is no such place for the like of her and her bastard."

The poor mother turned away, sobbing. Her dying daughter called her, feebly, and as she bent over her, I heard her say, "Don't grieve so, mother; God knows all about it; and He will have mercy upon me."

Her sufferings, afterwards, became so intense, that her mistress felt unable to stay; but when she left the room, the scornful smile was still on her lips. Seven children called her mother. The poor black woman had but the one child, whose eyes she saw closing in death, while she thanked God for taking her away from the greater bitterness of life. . . . (17–24)

. . . [T]o the slave mother New Year's day comes laden with peculiar sorrows. She sits on her cold cabin floor, watching the children who may all be torn from her the next morning; and often does she wish that she and they might die before the day dawns. She may be an ignorant creature, degraded by the system that has brutalized her from childhood; but she has a mother's instincts, and is capable of feeling a mother's agonies.

On one of these sale days, I saw a mother lead seven children to the auction-block. She knew that *some* of them would be taken from her; but they took *all*. The children were sold to a slave-trader, and their mother was bought by a man in her own town. Before night her children were all far away. She begged the trader to tell her where he intended to take them; this he refused to do. How *could* he, when he knew he would sell them, one by one, wherever he could command the highest price? I met that mother in the street, and her wild, haggard face lives to-day in my mind. She wrung her hands in anguish, and exclaimed, "Gone! All gone! Why don't God kill me?" I had no words wherewith to comfort her. Instances of this kind are [of] daily, yea, of hourly occurrence.

Slaveholders have a method, peculiar to their institution, of getting rid of *old* slaves, whose lives have been worn out in their service. I knew an old woman, who for seventy years faithfully served her master. She had become almost helpless, from hard labor and disease. Her owners moved to Alabama, and the old black woman was left to be sold to anybody who would give twenty dollars for her. (25–27)

ACCOUNT OF DAVID P. DYER

The final account of slavery days is not by a former slave but by a white man, David P. Dyer, who had many things in common with

Sam Clemens. Born in 1838, Dyer was only three years younger than Clemens. Like Clemens' mother and father, Dyer's parents had traveled to the Mississippi Valley, bringing their slaves with them, and like Clemens, Dyer grew up in Missouri, which was a slave state. Dyer, who became a leading jurist, was also like Clemens in forming a distaste for slavery early in his life and in ridiculing frontier religions that encouraged and justified slavery.

FROM DAVID P. DYER, *AUTOBIOGRAPHY AND REMINISCENCES*
(St. Louis: William Harvey Miner Co., 1922)

It was while attending the country school that an incident occurred in the neighborhood that had much to do with forming my future political opinions. Slavery was a recognized institution in the State, and men, women, and children were treated as chattels and bought and sold at public and private sale. My mother had fallen heir to several by the terms of my father's will. Neither she nor my father ever sold one. Brought up as I was with the institution, I never questioned the right or the wrong of slavery until the incident of which I am about to speak, occurred.

I saw a family sold in Troy when I was a boy, probably ten or twelve years of age. It consisted of husband, wife, and three children. The sale was conducted by a little sharp-nosed man by the name of Joe Shelton. The father of the family was first placed upon the block and sold to a trader from the South. The wife and mother was then sold to a different person, as were the two daughters, aged about sixteen and fourteen, and the baby boy about five years old. When the baby was put up for sale to the highest bidder and the father held him in his arms while Shelton asked for bids, the tears coursed their way down the black face of the good and unoffending father as the auctioneer proceeded. This child, this baby, was sold away from the father and mother. I can still hear that tiny thing calling out, "I want my mammy!" As I stood there and witnessed the wreck of this family, I for the first time understood and appreciated the iniquity of the institution. I went home that night and told my mother what I had seen. I said to her that a just God would not countenance such a wrong—that the preaching of Mr. Wright and others that slavery was right and that it was a divine institution, could not be true, and as for me, if the time ever came when by word or act I could aid in striking a blow that would end it, the blow would be struck. I thank God that I kept the promise.

This was but one of the harrowing incidents of this accursed institution.

The country in and about the place my father bought was sparsely settled. The pioneers came mostly from Virginia and Kentucky, with now and then a family from a State farther south. In politics they were mostly Democrats, and in religion Primitive Baptists. Thomas Jefferson Wright (himself a Kentuckian) was the elder in charge of a congregation that met for worship two or three times each month in a log house then known as Sandrun Church. My father and mother were both members of this church and so continued up to the time they died.

Elder Wright officiated at the funeral of my father in October, 1844. He was a Southerner by birth, and his convictions on any subject were strong and generally expressed with great vigor. He believed in the institution of slavery, not only from a legal but from a religious and moral standpoint. He would preach sermon after sermon upon the subject and seek to prove by the Bible the correctness of his position. The right to his own slaves and the doctrine of baptism by immersion were the two principal things that he sought to establish by the Bible. He (representing his church) was opposed to missions, temperance and secret societies of all kinds, and Sunday schools. . . . (35–37)

It is a just tribute to the negro to say that they were faithful, obedient and loving to the whites, and there was no lullaby ever sung to the white child that was sweeter than that which the "old mammy" would sing. Surely, the good Lord will not forget them in the great hereafter.

An incident showing devotion to the wife and child by an old negro was never better exemplified than in that which I am about to relate. Christopher Carter was a neighbor of our family and owned a negro man by the name of John. John had a common-law wife by the name of Paulina, who belonged to my mother. Marriage between negroes was prohibited by law, and it was only by voluntary cohabitation that semblance was given to legality. These two persons, John and Paulina, were the father and mother of several children, all of whom under the law belonged to my mother. When the California gold excitement of 1849 was at its height, Carter's three sons, George, Tom and Rolla, determined to cross the plains to California in search of gold, and with the permission of their father, took John (the slave) with them.

Thus it was that the husband, without his consent, was taken away from the wife and children and made to work in the gold fields for his young masters. Had John seen proper to avail himself of his rights to freedom under the laws then existing, he could have remained in California a free man. This he did not prefer to do, but trusted to his master to take him back to slavery and his wife and children in Missouri. After being in California a year, the youngest of the Carter boys, Rolla, was taken very sick. It was thought best to send him home by water in care of the faithful old John. The two went on board ship at San Francisco and started for New York via Panama. This sick man was carried on the shoulders of John across the isthmus and placed in a vessel on the Atlantic side. In the course of time the vessel reached New York and the two passengers made their way from New York to Missouri. I was twelve years old when they returned, and I can never forget the joy that was overflowing in the cabin when John embraced his wife and children. Here was a husband so devoted to wife and children that he preferred them with slavery to freedom without. Monuments have been erected to many who are not so deserving as old John.

Carter owned another negro man by the name of Fred. He also had a wife at my mother's home, and her name was Rachel. These two were also father and mother of several children. Carter became involved in debt and had to sell Fred to get money to pay off his indebtedness. Fred was sold to a "negro trader" from the South. Thus it was that another family was separated for all time. One of the children followed my fortunes in the Civil War and took care of my horses while I was Colonel of the 49th Missouri. All of that family of negroes are dead, and only two years ago I contributed to the funeral expenses of the last one of them.

I have probably devoted more space to what I consider great wrongs done to the negroes than I should, but I confess that my sympathy for them has much to do with it all. . . . (40–43)

Having spent Christmas with my mother on the farm in Lincoln County, I was at the county seat on the 1st of January, 1858. The first day of the year was the time fixed by general consent for the sale and hire of negro slaves. There was a large assemblage of individuals there, some of whom went for the purpose of settling up accounts at the stores (settlements were usually made on that day), some for selling or buying of slaves, others for hiring of slaves, and many others were idle spectators.

An incident occurred that day that would never be forgotten by those who witnessed it. On the evening before Christmas a man by the name of Thornhill was stabbed to death by a negro slave belonging to him. The facts were briefly these: The merchants (there were four or five of them) of Troy got their goods from St. Louis via the Mississippi River to Cap-Au-Gris and thence by wagon across the country to Troy. Thornhill was engaged by the merchants to haul their goods. This he did with a wagon and four horses driven by a negro man named Giles. Giles had been to Cap-Au-Gris for a load of goods on the day before Christmas, and returning by way of his master's house, reached there late in the evening to stay overnight. Thornhill at the time was under the influence of liquor and for some trivial cause began to abuse Giles, and finally without any justification whatever, assaulted and beat him severely with a pair of "bridle bits." The assault was vicious and unprovoked, and the negro in absolute self-defense, and to save his own life, stabbed Thornhill with a small pocket knife. Thornhill died the next day from the effects of the wound. The negro was arrested and lodged in the jail at Troy. There he remained until the first day of January.

A neighbor of Thornhill's, by the name of Calloway, was in Troy on that day. Mounted on a block in front of Parker's store, he began to harangue the crowd about the death of Thornhill. He appealed to the people to go to the jail and take the negro out and burn him. A few hot-headed, vicious and drunken men responded to this appeal, and armed with hammers and bars went to the jail and overpowered, or rather over-awed the sheriff, Peach Shelton, broke open the door and led Giles (who was already shackled) out into the yard.

The only effort to stop the mob was feebly made by Shelton, who said, "Gentlemen, for God's sake, let the law take its course!" A great crowd of men stood silent, without even a protest, and witnessed the mob (a half dozen men) prepare for the burning of this faithful old negro. There was an old fence around the jail, made of rails that were dry as tinder. A post made of one of these was driven into the ground and Giles fastened to it. The mob then took more rails from the fence and built a three-cornered pen around the poor defenseless negro and set it on fire. He was burned to death and his body entirely destroyed.

In a few days after this, Aylett H. Buckner, who was the Judge of the Circuit Court, called a special grand jury to inquiry into the death of Giles, and to indict those who had caused it. The grand jury met but failed to return an indictment, not because the murderers were un-known, but simply because they were pro-slavery men and believed that the negro had no right to strike in self-defense. I witnessed this outrage but was powerless to prevent it. The grand jury failed to indict, but justice did not sleep. Each and every one of the ring leaders, including Calloway, Segrass, and others, in a little while met violent deaths.

This great wrong and the failure of the people of the County of Lincoln to enforce the law against the murderers, cast a stain on the county from which, after more than sixty years, it has not fully recovered. This great outrage upon the life of a human being, and the utter failure of those charged with the enforcement of law to prosecute the willful and delib-erate murderers was the necessary result of the teachings of those who advocated the right of a white man to own a black one, and to deny to the latter the inalienable right to life, liberty, and the pursuit of happi-ness, as expressed in the Declaration of Independence.

In the splendid memorial address of George Bancroft, the historian, delivered before the two houses of Congress in 1865 upon the life and character of Abraham Lincoln, he said, among other things, "In support-ing incipient measures for emancipation, Jefferson encountered difficul-ties greater than he could overcome and, after vain wrestling, the words that broke from him, 'I tremble for my country when I reflect that God is just, that His justice can not sleep forever,' were words of despair. It was the desire of Washington's heart that Virginia should remove slavery by a public act, and as the prospects of a general emancipation grew more and more dim, he, in utter hopelessness of the action of the State, did all that he could by bequeathing freedom to his own slaves. (69–72)

SLAVERY LAWS

THE MISSOURI COMPROMISE OF 1820

Excerpts from the texts of two important documents in the history of American slavery are included below. The first is the Missouri Compromise of 1820. As tensions mounted between slaveholding and free states, the two sides began to quarrel about whether new western territories annexed to the United States should allow slavery or outlaw it. Upon the application for statehood by Sam Clemens' own state, an agreement known as the Missouri Compromise was reached in Congress between pro- and antislavery factions. As part of the statute authorizing the admission of Missouri as a state, a section was included to allow slavery below 36°30' north latitude and forbid it above that latitude. Neither side was completely happy, though both sides regarded the agreement as acceptable. The exceptions were the abolitionists, who found it abominable because it sanctioned the spread of slavery on the continent. Even in this "compromise," however, there was a provision allowing slave owners to invade new, "free" territory to reclaim fugitive slaves.

FROM THE MISSOURI COMPROMISE OF 1820

SIXTEENTH CONGRESS—Sess. 1, Chap. 22, 1820.
STATUTE 1, MARCH 6, 1820
CHAP. XXII.—AN ACT to authorize the people of the Missouri territory to form a Constitution and State Government, and for the admission of such State into the Union on an equal footing with the original states, and to prohibit slavery in certain territories.

(All the previous sections of this Act relate entirely to the formation of the Missouri Territory in the usual form of territorial bills—8th section only relating to the slavery question.)

Sec. VIII. And be it further enacted, That in all that territory ceded by France to the United States, under the name of Louisiana, which lies north of thirty-six degrees, and thirty minutes north latitude, not included within the limits of the state contemplated by their act, slavery and involuntary servitude, otherwise than in the punishment of crimes, whereof the parties shall have been duly convicted, shall be, and is hereby, forever prohibited. Provided always that any person escaping into the same, from whom labor or service is lawfully claimed, in any state or territory of the United States, such fugitive may be lawfully reclaimed and conveyed to the person claiming his or her labor or service as aforesaid.

Approved March 6, 1820.

THE FUGITIVE SLAVE LAW OF 1850

Some thirty years after the Missouri Compromise, the application for admission to statehood by the Kansas-Nebraska territory brought to a boil tensions that had been simmering for decades. The South, desperate to retain its political hold, which rested on the institution of slavery, fought hard to gain slaveholders as political allies in new territories. The document that admitted Kansas to statehood, with its status as free or slave to be decided by a popular vote, included in it a large concession to southern slaveholders. This was the Fugitive Slave Law, passed by Congress in 1850.

While very few states (Ohio, for instance) had laws providing for the return of runaway slaves to their owners in the South, and while the Missouri Compromise allowed slave owners to hunt down runaways in the western territories labeled "free," slaves had been able to escape to most northern states without unreasonable concern that they would be hunted down and returned. But the passage of the Fugitive Slave Law altered the situation by expanding the fugitive laws to all states and territories. Moreover, while the old laws were almost casual in their enforcement of the return of fugitives, the new law of 1850 was aggressive, requiring cooperation from law enforcement and court authorities in free states. It required only minimal proof of "ownership" from the slave owner, denied the accused fugitive all rights, and subjected to prison and fines anyone who knowingly attempted to help a slave or kept secret the identification of a fugitive.

By the terms of this new law, to capture a slave who had run away to a free state, the owner or his representative, such as a bounty hunter, had only to secure an authorized affidavit from an authority *in the state from which the slave had escaped.* That seal, the law said, "shall be sufficient to establish the competency of the proof." To ensure even greater advantage to the slave owner, the fugitive was not allowed to testify on his or her own behalf: "In no trial or hearing under this act shall the testimony of such alleged fugitive be admitted in evidence."

FROM THE FUGITIVE SLAVE LAW OF 1850

THIRTY-FIRST CONGRESS—Sess. 1, Chap. 60, 1850.
SEPT. 18, 1850.

[A]nd all good citizens are hereby commanded to aid and assist in the prompt and efficient execution of this law, whenever their services may be required, as aforesaid, for that purpose; and said warrants shall run, and be executed by said officers, anywhere in the State within which they are issued.

Sec. 6. And be it further enacted, That when a person held to service or labor in any State or Territory of the United States, has heretofore or shall hereafter escape into another State or Territory of the United States, the person or persons to whom such service or labor may be due, or his, her, or their agent or attorney, duly authorized by power of attorney, in writing acknowledged and certified under the seal of some legal officer or Court of the State or Territory in which the same may be executed, may pursue and reclaim such fugitive person, either by procuring a warrant from some one of the Courts, Judges, or Commissioners aforesaid, of the proper circuit, district, or county, for the apprehension of such fugitive from service or labor, or by seizing and arresting such fugitive where the same can be done without process, and by taking, or causing such person to be taken forthwith before such Court, Judge or Commissioner, whose duty it shall be, to hear and determine the case of such claimant in summary manner; and upon satisfactory proof being made, by deposition or affidavit, in writing, to be taken, and certified by such Court, Judge, or Commissioner, or by other satisfactory testimony, duly taken and certified by some Court, Magistrate, Justice of the Peace, or other legal officer authorized to administer an oath and take depositions under the laws of the State or Territory from which such person owing service or labor may have escaped, with a certificate of such magistracy, or other authority as aforesaid, with the seal of the proper Court or officer thereto attached, which seal shall be sufficient to establish the competency of the proof, and with proof, also by affidavit, of the identity of the person whose service or labor is claimed to be due as aforesaid, that the person so arrested does in fact owe service or labor to the person or persons claiming him or her, in the State or Territory from which such fugitive may have escaped as aforesaid, and that said person escaped, to make out and deliver to such claimant, his or her agent or attorney, a certificate setting forth the substantial facts as to the service or labor due from such fugitive to the claimant, and of his or her escape from the State or Territory in which such service or labor was due to the State or Territory in which he or she was arrested, with authority to such claimant, or his, or her agent, or attorney, to use such reasonable force and restraint as may be necessary, under the circumstances of the case, to take and remove such fugitive person back to the State or Territory whence he or she may have escaped as aforesaid. In no trial or hearing under this Act shall the testimony of such alleged fugitive be admitted in evidence; and the certificates in this and the first (fourth) section mentioned, shall be conclusive of the right of the person or persons in whose favor granted, to remove such fugitive to the State or Territory from which he escaped, and shall prevent all molestations of such person or persons by any process issued by any Court, Judge, Magistrate or other person whomsoever.

Sec. 7. And be it further enacted, That any person who shall knowingly and willingly obstruct, hinder, or prevent such claimant, his agent or attorney, or any person or persons lawfully assisting him, her or them, from arresting such a fugitive from service or labor, either with or without process as aforesaid, or shall rescue or attempt to rescue such fugitive from service or labor from the custody of such claimant, his, or her agent, or attorney, or other person or persons lawfully assisting as aforesaid, when so arrested pursuant to the authority herein given, and declared, or shall aid, abet, or assist such person so owing service or labor as aforesaid, directly or indirectly, to escape from such claimant, his agent or attorney, or other person or persons legally authorized as aforesaid; or shall harbor or conceal such fugitive so as to prevent the discovery and arrest of such person, after notice or knowledge that such person was a fugitive from service or labor as aforesaid, shall, for either of said offences, be subject to a fine not exceeding one thousand dollars, and imprisonment not exceeding six months, by indictment, and conviction before the District Court of the United States, for the district in which such offence may have been committed, or before the proper Court of Criminal jurisdiction, if committed within any one of the organized territories of the United States, and shall moreover forfeit and pay, by way of civil damages to the party injured by such illegal conduct, the sum of One thousand dollars, for each fugitive so lost as aforesaid, to be recovered by action of debt in any of the District or Territorial Courts aforesaid, within whose jurisdiction the said offence may have been committed.

Sec. 9. And be it further enacted, That, upon affidavit made by the claimant of such fugitive, his agent or attorney, after such certificate has been issued that he has reason to apprehend that such fugitive will be rescued by force from his or her possession before he can be taken beyond the limits of the State in which the arrest is made, it shall be the duty of the officer making the arrest to retain such fugitive in his custody, and to remove him to the State whence he fled, and there to deliver him to said claimant, his agent or attorney. And to this end, the officer aforesaid is hereby authorized and required to employ so many persons as he may deem necessary to overcome such force, and to retain them in his service so long as circumstances may require.

Sec. 10. And be it further enacted, That when any person held to service or labor in any State or Territory, or the District of Columbia, shall escape therefrom, the party to whom such service or labor may be due, his, her, or their agent or attorney, may apply to any court of record therein, or judge thereof in vacation, and make satisfactory proof to such court, or judge in vacation, of the escape aforesaid, and that the person escaping owed service or labor to such party. Whereupon the court shall cause a record to be made of the matters so proved, and also a general description of the person so escaping with such convenient certainty as may be; and a transcript of such record authenticated by the attestation of the clerk and of the seal of the said court, being produced in any other State, Territory or district in which the person so escaping may be found, and being exhibited to any judge, commissioner, or other officer authorized by the law of the United States to cause persons escaping from service or labor to be delivered up, shall be held and taken to be full and conclusive evidence of the fact of the escape, and that the service or labor of the person escaping is due to the party in such record mentioned. And upon the production by the said party of other and further evidence if necessary, either oral or by affidavit, in addition to what is contained in the said record of the identity of the person escaping, he or she shall be delivered up to the claimant. And the said court, commissioner, judge, or other person authorized by this act to grant certificates to claimants of fugitives, shall, upon the production of the record and other evidences aforesaid, grant to such claimant a certificate of his right to take any such person identified and proved to be owing service or labor as aforesaid, which shall authorize such claimant to seize or arrest and transport such person to the State or Territory from which he escaped. . . .

Approved September 18, 1850

CIVIL DISOBEDIENCE

After the passage of the Fugitive Slave Law, which required citizens in free states to disclose any information they had about fugitive slaves, many people, like the fictional Huck Finn, faced a quandary. Opponents of slavery were torn between helping slaves escape and obeying what they regarded as an immoral law. Such was the outrage that not only individuals but whole communities decided to refuse to obey the Fugitive Slave Law.

"Conscience" is a key word that appears often in the arguments of those who opposed slavery and the Fugitive Slave Law. They assert that any law that goes against the conscience is a bad law and that conscience should always dictate our actions, even if it leads us to defy the law. In *Adventures of Huckleberry Finn,* however, Huck confuses what he calls his conscience with what the slaveholding society says is right. After all, he has learned these values not just from the fanatic and ignorant Pap, but from the most upstanding and religious citizens in the community. So it is really society's voice that nags him to turn Jim in. The question presents itself, then, as to whether conscience is a reliable indicator, or whether Huck has just misnamed it.

RALPH WALDO EMERSON

Generally regarded as nineteenth-century America's greatest philosopher, Ralph Waldo Emerson was one of the first to denounce the Fugitive Slave Law in a public forum. His method was to show the citizens of Massachusetts why it was immoral and then to justify breaking it. He contended that the new law advocated the serious crime of kidnapping. Moreover, it was the kidnapping of people who had fled some of the worst conditions of slavery in order to stay alive. Not only did he justify lawbreaking, he advocated it.

The objections Emerson and others raised to the new fugitive law were based on the belief that there is a higher law than the law of the state. Emerson asserted that the higher law, the law of God, is distinct from the law of man. In cases where the two contradict each other, the higher law must be obeyed and the civil law broken.

FROM RALPH WALDO EMERSON, "THE FUGITIVE SLAVE LAW," ADDRESS TO CITIZENS OF CONCORD, MAY 3, 1851, IN *THE COMPLETE WRITINGS OF RALPH WALDO EMERSON*
(New York: William H. Wise and Co., 1875)

An immoral law makes it a man's duty to break it, at every hazard. For virtue is the very self of every man. It is therefore a principle of law that an immoral contract is void, and that an immoral statute is void. For, as laws do not make right, and are simply declaratory of a right which already existed, it is not to be presumed that they can so stultify themselves as to command injustice. . . .

Here is a statute which enacts the crime of kidnapping,—a crime on one footing with arson and murder. A man's right to liberty is as inalienable as his right to life.

Pains seem to have been taken to give us in this statute a wrong pure from any mixture of right. If our resistance to this law is not right, there is no right. This is not meddling with other people's affairs: this is hindering other people from meddling with us. This is not going crusading into Virginia and Georgia after slaves, who, it is alleged, are very comfortable where they are:—that amiable argument falls to the ground: but this is befriending in our own State, on our own farms, a man who has taken the risk of being shot, or burned alive, or cast into the sea, or starved to death, or suffocated in a wooden box, to get away from his driver: and this man who has run the gauntlet of a thousand miles for his freedom, the statute says, you men of Massachusetts shall hunt, and catch, and send back again to the dog-hutch he fled from. . . .

No engagement (to a sovereign) can oblige or even authorize a man to violate the laws of Nature. All authors who have any conscience or modesty agree that a person ought not to obey such commands as are evidently contrary to the laws of God. . . .

How can a law be enforced that fines pity, and imprisons charity? As long as men have bowels, they will disobey. You know that the Act of Congress of September 18, 1850, is a law which every one of you will break on the earliest occasion. There is not a manly Whig, or a manly Democrat, of whom, if a slave were hidden in one of our houses from hounds, we should not ask with confidence to lend his wagon in aid of his escape, and he would lend it. . . .

. . . By the law of Congress March 2, 1807, it is piracy and murder, punishable with death, to enslave a man on the coast of Africa. By law of Congress September, 1850, it is a high crime and misdemeanor, punishable with fine and imprisonment, to resist the enslaving of a man on the coast of America. (1150–1153)

WILLIAM HOSMER

William Hosmer, Emerson's neighbor and friend in Concord, Massachusetts, also raised objections to the Fugitive Slave Law, based on the principle that people should always obey higher laws, even if it means breaking civil ones. To this end, Hosmer presented what he called the "limitations of civil government." It was his contention that because the laws of civil governments are imperfect, they do not always end up being in accord with moral or divine law.

FROM WILLIAM HOSMER, *THE HIGHER LAW IN ITS RELATION TO CIVIL GOVERNMENT: WITH PARTICULAR REFERENCE TO SLAVERY, AND THE FUGITIVE SLAVE LAW*
(Auburn, Mass.: Derby and Miller, 1852)

LIMITATIONS OF CIVIL GOVERNMENT

These limitations may be stated as follows:

1. Civil government cannot bind the conscience.
2. It cannot impair any other natural rights or powers of mankind.
3. It cannot release man from his responsibility to God.
4. It cannot change the nature of vice and virtue.

CIVIL GOVERNMENT CANNOT BIND THE CONSCIENCE

. . . A good man will not keep a bad law, if he is left to believe that his own conscience should govern his conduct. . . . Against this enormous outrage on the rights of man—this utter prostitution of civil authority—it behooves all who value the peace and welfare of society, to enter their solemn protest. The following considerations will place the subject in its true light:

1. It subverts the design of government. We have seen that the institution of law was intended for the benefit, and not for the injury of man; it follows, therefore, that any violence done to the human faculties, is an abuse of governmental powers. The Creator established law to operate

in conjunction with conscience, and not irrespective of it; much less did he intend that law should mar his work, by usurping control over the moral faculty.

2. But the thing is physically impossible. Conscience may be destroyed, but it cannot be bound. We may extinguish the light which God has placed in the soul, but we cannot change its nature. All attempts to bind conscience are, in reality, attempts to annihilate it. The use of the moral faculty is to judge of right and wrong, and it has no other use; hence those who interfere with its decisions, virtually say there shall be no conscience. . . .

4. Conscience is an element of our nature, and cannot be subjected to any human authority. . . . (41–43)

This moral faculty is always in accordance with the Divine law, because that law is always right, and it accords with all other laws, so far as they are right, and no farther. . . . (45)

CIVIL GOVERNMENT CANNOT IMPAIR ANY OF THE NATURAL RIGHTS OR POWERS OF MANKIND

It is not necessary to go into an enumeration of the rights or powers of man, in order to perceive their true relation to civil law. The summary statement of them in the Declaration of Independence—"life, liberty, and the pursuit of happiness"—is quite sufficient. They all stand on the same basis, and if one falls, the rest cannot stand. . . .

The slave must be allowed life, as that is not a transferable commodity, and cannot be seized upon by his master; but he must give up liberty and the pursuit of happiness, for these have a marketable value. (46–47)

STEPHEN A. DOUGLAS

In response to the immediate popular outrage against the Fugitive Slave Law and its opponents' subsequent inciting of the public to disobey the law, many other opponents, both north and south, criticized those who would advocate disobedience to any law, this new fugitive slave law included. One of the United States senators who supported the bill was Stephen A. Douglas of Illinois. When Douglas returned home to Illinois shortly after the law was passed, he found citizens in Chicago to be in a rage about it. The common council, or city council, officially denounced the law and released all Chicago citizens, including law enforcement officers,

from the obligation to carry it out. On the night after their meeting
on the law, the council was enthusiastically supported by a mass
meeting of Chicago citizenry. Douglas, a persuasive speaker, then
asked to speak in support of compliance with the Fugitive Slave
Law. His basic arguments were that the 1850 law was not essentially different from the old Missouri Compromise, that it contained no breaches of rights included in the Missouri Compromise,
that it was merely "silent" on issues regarding the rights of anyone
subject to arrest, and that disobedience was, in effect, a repudiation of the U.S. Constitution and a challenge to the Supreme Court
of the United States. After hearing Douglas speak the council reversed its position advocating disobedience of the law. The following excerpt is from Douglas' speech.

FROM STEPHEN A. DOUGLAS, "MEASURES OF ADJUSTMENT"
(Speech delivered in the City Hall, Chicago, October 23, 1850)

I am not speaking of the guilt or innocence of slavery. I am discussing
our obligations under the Constitution of the United States. That sacred
instrument says that a fugitive from labor "*shall be delivered up* on the
claim of the owner." The same clause of the same instrument provides
that fugitives from justice shall be delivered up. We are bound by our
oaths to our God to see that claim, as well as every other provision of
the Constitution, carried into effect. The moral, religious, and constitutional obligations resting upon us, here and hereafter, are the same in
the one case as in the other. As citizens, owing allegiance to the Government and duties to society, we have no right to interpose our individual
opinions and scruples as excuses for violating the supreme law of the
land as our fathers made it, and as we are sworn to support it. The
obligation is just as sacred, under the Constitution, to surrender fugitives
from labor as fugitives from justice. And the Congress of the United
States, according to the decision of the Supreme Court, are as impera-
tively commanded to provide the necessary legislation for the one as for
the other. (11)

REV. ORVILLE DEWEY: THE CLERICAL ARGUMENT

It is abundantly clear that the ordinary northerner was torn between a conviction that laws, including the Fugitive Slave Law,
should be obeyed, and reluctance to cooperate in sending anyone

back to slavery. Yet many in the North who detested slavery, as Stephen Douglas claimed to do himself, firmly believed that the laws of the land and the Constitution were inviolate and had to be respected and obeyed. Many northern ministers, taking the role of political scientist, urged their congregations to do their civic duty and support the law. They were extremely alarmed that many of the nation's moral leaders, like Emerson, were advocating civil disobedience.

An example of clerical support of the Fugitive Slave Law is found in a lecture delivered by the Rev. Orville Dewey in 1852 to the Mercantile Library Association of the City of New York. Dewey places great stress on his own displeasure with slavery and with any fugitive laws. But, in the manner of the political scientist, he argues that protest against law is a right we give up "in order to create a political community." Taking an approach similar to that of Douglas, Dewey contends that the new Fugitive Slave Law is no worse than the old one, even claiming that the new one benefits the slave.

FROM ORVILLE DEWEY, *THE LAWS OF HUMAN PROGRESS AND MODERN REFORMS*
(A lecture delivered before the Mercantile Library Association of the City of New York. New York: C. S. Francis and Co., 1852)

But I did not denounce the bill for other reasons. I felt hardly competent to do so. It had been framed by the supreme legislature of the land; and whether it was constitutional, whether it was the best law that could be made, I was not prepared to say. Besides, when the tide of public opinion was running so strong against the law, as to threaten, in my opinion, to break down the barriers of the Constitution and the Union, I did not think it right to join the malcontents in decrying the law. Moreover, I wished to put the question at once upon its ultimate merits. The main offence does not lie in *this* law, but *any* effective law. As I said in my speech—"The abolitionists ought themselves to see that they will never be satisfied. I myself feel that no bill can ever be framed that will not be distasteful to me." . . . (25)

Still it would be wrong for us to interfere between the master and slave, with any other force than that of argument. We have promised that we would not do so. It is a part of our national compact. Our Union was founded, in part, upon that agreement. No Union can stand without it.

And if we break the compact in behalf of *fugitive* slaves, *why not as well in behalf of the rest?* . . . (27)

. . . Would you, as the member of a national sovereignty, American or English, propose rudely to violate one of the written bonds of your Constitution? *Do* you, as an American citizen, mean to say to the Southern States, "We will break our covenant with *you*, come what may. We will not wait to reason; we will not wait for any legal modification; we will break the bond today." You do not, you never did, say that. There has been a Fugitive Slave Law in existence all along; you never took any such ground with regard to it. Well, then, if you do not propose to overthrow the Constitution and break up the Union, you must acquiesce in some kind of Fugitive Slave Law. And it is in vain to say that the present law is so much worse than the former, as to justify a resistance now, which you never thought of before. In fact it is not worse, but better, for the slave than the former. . . . (30–31)

. . . "I would consent"—for I said nothing of *sending* any body—"I would *consent* that my own brother, my own son, should go (i.e. into slavery)—*ten times rather* would I go myself—than that this Union should be sacrificed for me or for us;" and I am ready to stand by this as a just and honorable sentiment; and I can only wonder that any man should think it extravagant or ridiculous. Indeed, I suppose the only chance of making it appear so, was to connect with it the falsehood to which I have just referred. (32)

HARRIET JACOBS, FUGITIVE SLAVE

While theoreticians and philosophers argued over the ins and outs of disobedience to laws in the abstract, Harriet Jacobs wrote of the constant, daily effect on the lives of fugitives who had escaped to New York City, where they had lived relatively free from worry. When the provisions of the new law made it a crime to conceal the identity of a fugitive slave, all felt threatened. She describes the law as introducing a reign of terror, as many fugitives who had been longtime residents of the city had to flee again, this time to Canada, whose laws did not allow for their legal arrest and return to the South. Always there was the threat of separation from friends and family. The new law put a strain on families when free men or women discovered that their spouses were fugitives, because it followed that their children were technically slaves, even though they had been born and had always lived in freedom.

FROM HARRIET JACOBS, "THE FUGITIVE SLAVE LAW," IN
INCIDENTS IN THE LIFE OF A SLAVE GIRL
(Boston: Published for the Author, 1861)

About the time that I reentered the Bruce family, an event occurred of disastrous import to the colored people. The slave Hamlin, the first fugitive that came under the new law, was given up by the blood hounds of the north to the blood hounds of the south. It was the beginning of a reign of terror to the colored population. The great city rushed on in its whirl of excitement, taking no note of the "short and simple annals of the poor." But while fashionables were listening to the thrilling voice of Jenny Lind in Metropolitan Hall, the thrilling voices of poor hunted colored people went up, in an agony of supplication, to the Lord, from Zion's church. Many families, who had lived in the city for twenty years, fled from it now. Many a poor washerwoman, who, by hard labor, had made herself a comfortable home, was obliged to sacrifice her furniture, bid a hurried farewell to friends, and seek her fortune among strangers in Canada. Many a wife discovered a secret she had never known before— that her husband was a fugitive, and must leave her to insure his own safety. Worse still, many a husband discovered that his wife had fled from slavery years ago, and as "the child follows the condition of its mother," the children of his love were liable to be seized and carried into slavery. Every where, in those humble homes, there was consternation and anguish. But what cared the legislators of the "dominant race" for the blood they were crushing out of trampled hearts? (285–287)

I seldom ventured into the streets; and when it was necessary to do an errand for Mrs. Bruce, or any of the family, I went as much as possible through back streets and by-ways. What a disgrace to a city calling itself free, that inhabitants, guiltless of offences, and seeking to perform their duties conscientiously, should be condemned to live in such incessant fear, and have nowhere to turn for protection! This state of things, of course, gave rise to many impromptu vigilance committees. Every colored person, and every friend of their persecuted race, kept their eyes wide open. Every evening I examined the newspapers carefully, to see what Southerners had put up at the hotels. I did this for my own sake, thinking my young mistress and her husband might be among the list; I wished also to give information to others, if necessary; for if many were "running to and from" I resolved that "knowledge should be increased." (289–290)

WILLIAM SLOANE COFFIN, JR., AND THE VIETNAM WAR

Whether we are obligated to obey an immoral law has remained a controversy in American society. At no time was it more debated than during the Vietnam War, when the draft law was the one most at issue. In an address written 118 years after Americans sought to deal with the Fugitive Slave Law, William Sloane Coffin, Jr., then chaplain of Yale University, echoes the same problems faced by those who fought against slavery, the same problem faced by Huck Finn, who defied the law to save Jim. In his article, which appeared in *Christianity and Crisis: A Christian Journal of Opinion,* Coffin compares the position of draft resisters to those who opposed the Fugitive Slave Law, making reference, as Emerson and Hosmer did, to the need to obey a higher law and conscience. Like them, he defends civil disobedience, even the necessity to risk fines and imprisonment, in defense of a just cause. In 1967 Coffin was indicted for supporting and assisting young men in their refusal to be drafted and for "committing offenses against the United States." The editors of *Christianity and Crisis* quote columnist James Reston's summary of the basic conflict between the government and war resisters. The resisters, Reston wrote, "raised the basic question: Is the war not only legally but morally right or wrong? Who is 'committing offenses against the United States'—the people who oppose the war or the people who want to continue to expand it?"

FROM WILLIAM SLOANE COFFIN, JR., "CIVIL DISOBEDIENCE,
THE DRAFT AND THE WAR"
(*Christianity and Crisis,* February 5, 1968)

[*The recent indictment of William Sloane Coffin Jr. et al. brings into the courts a fundamental conflict between personal conviction and public law and brings to a head the legal and moral issues of the Vietnam War. In the words of James Reston, the indictees have "raised the basic question: Is the war not only legally but morally right or wrong? Who is 'committing offenses against the United States'—the people who oppose the war or the people who want to continue to* *expand it?" We are happy to present here the rationale for Mr. Coffin's actions as he has set them forth on two occasions during the past year.**]

Most words are dispensable. They can perish as though they had never been spoken. A few, however, must forever remain alive if human beings are to remain human. For instance: "I love my city, but I shall not stop preaching that which I believe is true; you may kill me, but I shall follow God rather than you." "We must obey God rather than men." And perhaps even "Rebellion to tyrants is obedience to God," the somewhat sloganistic motto on the seal of Thomas Jefferson.

Why are these words so indispensable? Because, in the first place, they tell us that the most profound experience of the self is still the experience of the conscience. . . .

. . . these words tell us that because there is a higher and, hopefully, future order of things, men at times will feel constrained to disobey the law out of a sense of obedience to a higher allegiance. Not to serve the State has upon occasion appeared the best way to love one's neighbor. In short, the lesson of Socrates, St. Peter, Jefferson and hundreds of history's most revered heroes is that bad subjects sometimes make good neighbors. . . .

The problem of civil disobedience is, of course, as difficult as it is ancient, and I may as well begin with my conclusion: on paper there are no answers; only in life are there solutions. I do not think any man ever has the right to break the law, but I do think that upon occasion every man has the duty to do so.

In reaching this conclusion I have been greatly helped by the New Testament treatment of what St. Paul calls "principalities and powers." If we assume that these include the legal order, then there are three things we can say about laws in general. In the first place they are good, even God-given, for without them creation would be chaos. But secondly, as with individuals so with laws, they can become rebellious. Instruments of order, instead of serving, begin to dominate. . . .

When laws begin to dominate rather than to serve men, far from staving off chaos they begin to invite it. Therefore, it is naive to say—as so many do these days—that "only the law of the land stands between man and chaos." Finally, it is only a good law, not any law, that stands between man and chaos: the 1964 Civil Rights Act, yes; the 1850 Fugitive Slave Act, no.

---

*William Sloane Coffin Jr. is well-known as the Chaplain of Yale University and a key leader of the anti-movement. During the Korean War he served in Army counterintelligence. Later he aided in the establishment of the Peace Corps and was arrested in one of the earliest freedom rides. [Original footnote.]

Thirdly, the New Testament concludes that men must respect but never worship the law; respect what is legal, but be more concerned with what is right. Man's chief task is not to stand awestruck before the legal order, but rather to bend every effort to the end that it reflect and not reject his best understanding of God's justice and mercy. . . .

. . . both the Congress and the Administration itself are seriously divided on the issue of the war. Far more vocal is the protest of thousands of university professors and thousands of clergy. Also many of our most able correspondents have seriously questioned both the aims and conduct of the war, as have 200 student body presidents, including seven from the Big Ten, and 50 Rhodes Scholars presently studying in England. These are all people who know the anguish reflected in Albert Camus' words: "I should like to be able to love my country and still love justice."

In opposition to the war there have also been a good many acts of civil disobedience: a handful of draft cards have been burned, and many more returned, and several scores of citizens have refused to pay their income tax. . . .

Remembering all this, Americans would better be able to applaud the spirit of those who refuse today to surrender their conscience to the State, even when they do not share their views. And I fervently hope we shall see the day when this country will attain such a high level of democracy that any action to which a man adheres for reasons of conscience and that harms no one will be constitutionally immune from the power of the majority.

Still, it is not enough to make the case for one man's witness to an authority higher than that of the State. What about deliberately attempting to organize massive civil disobedience in opposition to the war? . . .

And I would say again that while no one has the right to break the law, every man upon occasion has the duty to do so. This war is just such an occasion and my own conclusion is that the war is so unjust as to justify attempts at organizing massive civil disobedience. . . . "We must obey God rather than men" points first and last not to our divisions, but to that deep unity that makes these divisions possible, necessary and bearable. . . .

So both the war and the draft are issues of conscience. And an issue of conscience is one a man may not seek but hardly one he can avoid.

We admire the way these young men—who could safely have hidden behind exemptions and deferments—have elected instead to risk something big for something good. We admire them and believe theirs is the true voice of America, the vision that will prevail beyond the distortions of the moment. . . .

We hereby publicly counsel these young men to continue in their re-fusal to serve in the armed forces as long as the war in Vietnam continues, and we pledge ourselves to aid and abet them in all the ways we can. This means that if they are now arrested for failing to comply with a law that violates their consciences, we, too, must be arrested, for in the sight of that law we are now as guilty as they.

THE AFRICAN AMERICAN IN THE 1880s: "FREED—NOT FREE"

In the last major episode of *Adventures of Huckleberry Finn,* Tom and Huck make a game of freeing Jim, whom Tom knows from the start to be free already by the terms of Miss Watson's will. Critics have concluded that this section of the book is as much a comment on the condition of African Americans in the 1880s, after the Civil War and Reconstruction, as it is an exposition on slavery. The following excerpts are from George Washington Cable's *The Silent South,* a critical description of the South in the 1880s. Cable, a close friend of Twain's, was traveling with him on the lecture circuit at the time he wrote and published these essays.

To answer the question "Is the freedman free?" Cable examines a number of issues: the abridgment of African Americans' liberties, the racial segregation that reaches into every aspect of southern life, the successful attempts to exclude African Americans from participation in government and the new South's industrial progress, and, finally, the most horrible enslavement of the "freedman"— the brutal convict system.

Cable's conclusion forces him to answer no to his question. Like Jim in *Adventures of Huckleberry Finn,* which is set before the war, the African American after emancipation is legally free, but actually still in chains.

After *The Silent South* appeared in print, Cable was forced to leave the South, where he had been born and reared. He moved to Northampton, Massachusetts, where he lived for the rest of his life.

FROM GEORGE WASHINGTON CABLE, "THE FREEDMAN'S CASE
IN EQUITY AND THE CONVICT LEASE SYSTEM," IN *THE SILENT
SOUTH*
(New York: Charles Scribner's Sons, 1885)

V. FREED—NOT FREE

To be a free man is his still distant goal. Twice he has been a freedman. In the days of compulsory reconstruction he was freed in the presence of his master by that master's victorious foe. In these days of voluntary reconstruction he is virtually freed by the consent of his master, but the master retaining the exclusive right to define the bounds of his freedom. Many everywhere have taken up the idea that this state of affairs is the end to be desired and the end actually sought in reconstruction as handed over to the States. . . . There are those among us who see that America has no room for a state of society which makes its lower classes harmless by abridging their liberties, or, as one of the favored class lately said to me, has "got 'em so they don't give no trouble." There is a growing number who see that the one thing we cannot afford to tolerate at large is a class of people less than citizens; and that every interest in the land demands that the freedman be free to become in all things, as far as his own personal gifts will lift and sustain him, the same sort of American citizen he would be if, with the same intellectual and moral calibre, he were white.

Thus we reach the ultimate question of fact. Are the freedman's liberties suffering any real abridgment? The answer is easy. The letter of the laws, with a few exceptions, recognizes him as entitled to every right of an American citizen; and to some it may seem unimportant that there is scarcely one public relation of life in the South where he is not arbitrarily and unlawfully compelled to hold toward the white man the attitude of an alien, a menial, and a probable reprobate, by reason of his race and color. One of the marvels of future history will be that it was counted a small matter, by a majority of our nation, for six millions of people within it, made by its own decree a component part of it, to be subjected to a system of oppression so rank that nothing could make it seem small except the fact that they had already been ground under it for a century and a half.

Examine it. It proffers to the freedman a certain security of life and property, and then holds the respect of the community, that dearest of earthly boons, beyond his attainment. It gives him certain guarantees against thieves and robbers, and then holds him under the unearned contumely of the mass of good men and women. It acknowledges in constitutions and statutes his title to an American's freedom and aspirations, and then in daily practice heaps upon him in every public place the most odious distinctions, without giving ear to the humblest plea concerning mental and moral character. It spurns his ambitions, tramples upon his languishing self-respect, and indignantly refuses to let him buy with money, or earn by an excellence of inner life or outward behavior, the most momentary immunity from these public indignities even for his wife and daughters. . . .

. . . [I]t is in the face of all this that the adherent of the old regime stands in the way to every public privilege and place—steamer landing, railway platform, theatre, concert-hall, art display, public library, public school, courthouse, church, everything—flourishing the hot branding-iron of ignominious distinctions. He forbids the freedman to go into the water until *he* is satisfied that he knows how to swim, and for fear he should learn hangs mill-stones about his neck. This is what we are told is a small matter that will settle itself. . . .

. . . Under our present condition in the South, it is beyond possibility that the individual black should behave mischievously without offensively rearousing the old sentiments of the still dominant white man. As we have seen too, the white man virtually monopolizes the jury-box. Add another fact: the Southern States have entered upon a new era of material development. Now, if with these conditions in force the public mind has been captivated by glowing pictures of the remunerative economy of the convict-lease system, and by the seductive spectacle of mines and railways, turnpikes and levees, that everybody wants and nobody wants to pay for, growing apace by convict labor that seems to cost nothing, we may almost assert beforehand that the popular mind will—not so maliciously as unreflectingly—yield to the tremendous temptation to hustle the misbehaving black man into the State prison under extravagant sentence, and sell his labor to the highest bidder who will use him in the construction of public works. For ignorance of the awful condition of these penitentiaries is extreme and general, and the hasty half-conscious assumption naturally is, that the culprit will survive this term of sentence, and its fierce discipline "teach him to behave himself."

But we need not argue from cause to effect only. Nor need I repeat one of the many painful rumors that poured in upon me the moment I began to investigate this point. The official testimony of the prisons themselves is before the world to establish the conjectures that spring from our reasoning. After erroneous takings of the census of 1881 in South Carolina had been corrected, the population was shown to consist of about twenty blacks to every thirteen whites. One would therefore look for a preponderance of blacks on the prison lists; and inasmuch as they are a people only twenty years ago released from servile captivity, one would not be surprised to see that preponderance large. Yet, when the actual numbers confront us, our speculations are stopped with a rude shock; for what is to account for the fact that in 1881 there were committed to the State prison at Columbia, South Carolina, 406 colored persons and but 25 whites? The proportion of blacks sentenced to the whole black population was one to every 1488; that of the whites to the white population was but one to every 15,644. In Georgia the white inhabitants decidedly outnumber the blacks; yet in the State penitentiary, October 20, 1880, there were 115 whites and 1071 colored; or if we reject the summary of tables and refer to the tables themselves, . . . there were but 102 whites and 1083 colored. Yet of pardons granted in the two years then closing, 22 were to whites and only 30 to blacks. If this be a dark record, what shall we say of the records of lynch law? . . .

What need to say more? The question is answered. Is the freedman a free man? No.

SUGGESTIONS FOR FURTHER READING

By Mark Twain:

"Captain Stormfield's Visit to Heaven"

"King Leopold's Soliloquy"

Pudd'nhead Wilson

"A True Story Repeated Word for Word as I Heard It"

By Harriet Beecher Stowe:

Uncle Tom's Cabin

PROJECTS FOR WRITTEN OR ORAL EXPLORATION

1. Make a map of Jim and Huck's trip down the Mississippi River. Then make a map of the journey that Jim planned to make. Also find various maps of the Underground Railroad.

2. Note how many slave hunters make their appearance in the novel. What effect does Twain create with them?

3. What effect is achieved by Twain's having Jim reveal the instance when he struck his daughter? It is one of the only things we know about Jim's past. Why this, in particular?

4. Slave owners often promised their slaves that they would never sell them or separate their families. Yet in at least two instances in *Adventures of Huckleberry Finn* we have illustrations that such promises were not guarantees against being sold down the river. Discuss. You may find other examples in collections of slave narratives and in *Uncle Tom's Cabin.*

5. Speculate about Jim's motives for not telling Huck about the death of his father until the last.

6. Write a paper comparing the behavior of Jim (from the time he escapes from the shed on the Phelps plantation) with the behavior of the men who capture him. Draw conclusions from your comparison about Twain's opinion of slavery.

7. Write a paper on the character of Jim. With what specific episodes does Twain establish Jim as morally superior to almost anyone else in the novel?

8. Analyze all the various crises in Huck's moral quandary about whether or not to turn Jim in. Does he ever come to believe that he is being good or admirable in protecting Jim? Explain. If your answer is no, is Huck more or less admirable in acting from his heart and

his individual experience with Jim rather than from principle, as the abolitionists did?

9. Comb the novel closely for references to the idea of "property" of all kinds, including slave property, and stealing. Using what you find, discuss how rightful ownership and thievery become *relative* rather than *absolute* in a society where people themselves can be regarded as property.

10. Compare Huck's real adventures with Tom's fantasy adventures, including a comparison of Huck's escape from Pap with Tom's plan for Jim's escape. What common elements do you find, and what's the irony?

11. Underline all references to "conscience" in *Huckleberry Finn* and in the historical documents included. Exactly what do these writers and Huck mean by "conscience"?

12. Would you classify Huck as an abolitionist? Why or why not?

13. Referring to Harriet Jacobs' paragraphs on the Fugitive Slave Law, discuss what differences it made in the lives of fugitive slaves in New York.

14. Write a fictional, first-person narrative of a young runaway slave in a big city after 1850. Let your imagination have free rein, but try to be as faithful to history as possible.

15. A number of slave narratives besides those of Douglass and Jacobs have been collected and printed. Read a collection of these narratives. Can you determine whether the slave owners were successful in their efforts to destroy the slaves' family feelings by making a practice of separating families early and frequently? Explain.

16. Write a paper on the connections between the church and slavery using the complete *Narrative of the Life of Frederick Douglass,* the excerpt from David Dyer, and *Adventures of Huckleberry Finn.*

17. Compare the "slavery" that binds Huck with that which binds Jim.

18. Discuss Miss Watson as the embodiment of everything that Huck and Jim want to escape.

19. A number of writers have rewritten Twain's novel, based on their belief that the Phelps episode is out of keeping with the rest of the book and/or that it is too romanticized for Jim to be set free. Using firsthand historical materials in this chapter, outline how you might alter the ending, introducing new events and conclusions to make the ending more probable. Justify all your changes.

20. Some of the writers represented here claim that the Fugitive Slave Law contradicts the Bill of Rights (the first ten amendments to the

U.S. Constitution), while others, like Stephen Douglas, argue that to disobey the Fugitive Slave Law is to undermine the Constitution. Compare the text of the Fugitive Slave Law with the Bill of Rights to determine if, in fact, the 1850 law is consistent with the Constitution.

21. Carefully compare Huck's reasons for breaking the law with the reasons given by the abolitionists quoted and discussed in this section.

22. Write a paper on how both sides of the slavery question used scripture to endorse their point of view.

23. Explain Coffin's statement that "while no one has the right to break the law, every man upon occasion has the duty to do so."

24. Stephen Douglas argued that the Fugitive Slave Law of 1850 was essentially the same as Chapter 22 of the Missouri Compromise of 1820. Examine both texts carefully and discuss whether he is correct.

25. Abolitionists argued that the Fugitive Slave Law could very well make it possible for slave traders and bounty hunters to kidnap black people who were free, lifelong citizens of northern states and enslave them. Stage a legal debate on that point, using the text at hand.

26. Huck says that he thinks there are two Gods, that is, "Providences." Discuss this idea in light of strong clerical support of both those who would continue slavery and those who would abolish it.

27. Dramatize a debate between two anti-slavery people who take different sides on the issue of civil disobedience.

28. Analyze Brownlow's argument with care. Answer each of his points.

29. Research one of many situations in the twentieth century—such as the rise of Nazism, draft resistance, the civil rights movement, the controversy over abortion—when disobeying the law has become a moral issue. Present your findings in a paper.

30. What would you argue is the basic difference (if any) between the civil disobedience of Martin Luther King or draft-card burners in the 1960s, and the actions of the Weathermen in the 1960s and, say, the person or persons responsible for bombing the Oklahoma City federal building in 1995?

31. Discuss fully, giving as many details as you can, how the African American, after Reconstruction, could be free yet not free at the same time.

32. The pro-slavery supporters included here denounce the statement in the Declaration of Independence that "all men are created equal." In what sense did Jefferson intend that phrase, do you think? In what sense should all people be considered equal? In what ways are they obviously not equal?

33. Do a careful comparison of the final Phelps episode with the excerpt

by George Washington Cable. How might you argue that the conditions deplored by Cable are fictionally represented in the Phelps episode?

34. Explain Cable's statement, "He forbids the freedman to go into the water until *he* is satisfied that he knows how to swim, and for fear he should learn hangs mill-stones about his neck."

SUGGESTED READINGS

Adams, Sidney. *The South since the War.* Boston: Ticknor and Fields, 1866. Reprint. New York: Arno Press and the New York Times, 1969.

Barnes, Albert. *An Inquiry into the Scriptural Views of Slavery.* Detroit: Negro History Press, 1969.

Blassingame, John W. *The Slave Community.* New York: Oxford University Press, 1972.

Blassingame, John W., ed. *Slave Testimony.* Baton Rouge: Louisiana State University Press, 1977.

Bontemps, Arna Wendell. *Great Slave Narratives.* Boston: Beacon Press, 1969.

Bruce, Dickson D. *Violence and Culture in the Antebellum South.* Austin: University of Texas Press, 1979.

Butcher, Philip. *George Washington Cable.* New York: Twayne, 1962.

Cable, George Washington. *The Negro Question (and Other Civil Rights Essays).* Garden City, N.Y.: Doubleday, 1958.

Cash, W. J. *The Mind of the South.* New York: Alfred A. Knopf, 1946.

Cohen, William. *At Freedom's Edge.* Baton Rouge: Louisiana University Press, 1991.

Coleman, J. Winston, Jr. *Slavery Times in Kentucky.* Chapel Hill: University of North Carolina Press, 1940.

De Voto, Bernard. *Mark Twain's America.* Boston: Little, Brown, 1932.

Elshtain, Jean Bethke, ed. *Just War Theory.* New York: New York University Press, 1992.

Fatout, Paul. *Mark Twain on the Lecture Circuit.* Bloomington: Indiana University Press, 1960.

Fishkin, Shelley Fisher. *Was Huck Black?* New York: Oxford University Press, 1993.

Foster, Francis. *Witnessing Slavery.* Madison: University of Wisconsin Press, 1994.

Gans, Chaim. *Philosophical Anarchism and Political Disobedience.* New York: Cambridge University Press, 1992.

Genovese, Eugene D. *Roll, Jordan, Roll: The World the Slaves Made.* New York: Pantheon Books, 1974.

Johnson, Morris, William Primus, and Sharon Thomas. *From Freedom to Freedom.* New York: Random House, 1977.

Jones, Norrece T., Jr. *Born a Child of Freedom, yet a Slave.* Hanover, N.H.: Wesleyan University Press, 1990.

Katz, William Loren. *Five Slave Narratives.* New York: Arno Press, 1969.

Lloyd, Arthur Young. *The Slavery Controversy.* Chapel Hill: University of North Carolina Press, 1939.

Milne, A.J.M. *The Right to Dissent.* Amershham, England: Avebury Publishing Co., 1974.

Pettit, Arthur G. *Mark Twain and the South.* Lexington: University Press of Kentucky, 1974.

Quigley, Thomas E., ed. *American Catholics and Vietnam.* Grand Rapids: William B. Eerdmans Publishing Co., 1968.

Rawick, George P., ed. *The American Slave.* Westport, Conn.: Greenwood Press, 1979.

Robinson, Donald. *Slavery in the Structure of American Politics.* New York: W. W. Norton, 1979.

Rubin, Louis. *George Washington Cable.* New York: Pegasus, 1969.

Six Women's Slave Narratives. Oxford: Oxford University Press, 1988.

Slave Narratives. St. Clair Shores, Mich.: Scholarly Press, 1976.

Turner, Arlin. *George Washington Cable.* Austin, Tex.: Steck-Vaughn, 1969.

Weinstein, Allen, and Otto Gatell, eds. *American Negro Slavery.* New York: Oxford University Press, 1973.

Wilson, Theodore Brantner. *The Black Codes of the South.* University: University of Alabama Press, 1965.

Woodward, C. Vann. *The Burden of Southern History.* 3rd ed. Baton Rouge: Louisiana State University Press, 1993.

5

The Code of Honor

In Chapter 12 of *Adventures of Huckleberry Finn,* Huck and Jim come across a rapidly sinking ship occupied only by three dangerous double-crossing thieves who are secretly plotting each other's murders. This vessel, the *Walter Scott,* which eventually disappears beneath the waves as Huck and Jim scurry away, represents, for Twain, an entire culture—that of the plantation aristocrats of the Old South—formed in imitation of novelist Walter Scott's tales of knights in shining armor in a medieval world that existed chiefly in fiction. Scott, a Scottish writer of the early nineteenth century, was extremely popular in America, especially the South, between 1830 and the Civil War, a time during which his books were reportedly brought in by the railroad car load to be devoured by eager readers. Southern aristocrats named their houses and children and patterned their games and manners after what they saw in such novels as *Ivanhoe, Kenilworth,* and *The Fair Maid of Perth,* all of which made the Scotsman one of the most successful novelists in English history. What is pertinent in this discussion of the code of honor is not so much what Scott actually wrote as the effect his novels had on the society that adored him.

In *Adventures of Huckleberry Finn* the ship named for Scott has been boarded by criminals and is sinking. The obvious interpretation is that Twain is depicting the "Walter Scott" *society* of the

Old South, in its dying years, as being dominated by thugs, thieves, and killers—not by noble men involved in a noble cause.

What, then, were the cultural characteristics associated with the pernicious influence of Scott that Twain and others so despised? Fortunately, we do not have to guess the answer, for Twain himself discloses precisely what he meant in *Life on the Mississippi,* written shortly before he completed *Adventures of Huckleberry Finn.* Scott, he wrote in this remembrance, enchanted the South with "dreams," "decayed . . . systems of government," "silliness," and "sham grandeurs" of a "worthless long vanished society"—a society identified, among other things, with duels, elaborate forms of chivalry, fancy titles, bragging, vows, insults, challenges, and other forms of extreme rhetoric.

While the institution of slavery and its legacy form two of the main targets of Mark Twain's criticism, equally pervasive is his satiric portrayal of what he called the Walter Scott character of society by means of scenes at both the beginning and end of *Adventures of Huckleberry Finn,* thus forming a framework or bookend effect for the adventurous trip of Huck and Jim down the river. His satiric scorn is directed particularly at what was called the code of honor, a pattern of conduct that incorporated both the love of romantic fancy and severe class distinctions, all based on the aristocratic bearing of fancy titles and the attraction of romantic death—like medieval knights of old who lived by a code which required them to defend their "honor." In Scott's novels, the chief occupation of a knight seemed to be trying to determine if he or anyone he liked or was kin to had been insulted. According to the code by which the knights lived, a reputation for courage and truth was one's most important asset. If a knight caught anyone insulting him, as he inevitably did, the code of honor required him to challenge the insulter to fight him in a tournament or to meet him in a duel. Someone usually got killed or wounded as a result. In a nutshell, this was the medieval code of honor popularized by Walter Scott that was carried over to America. Dueling was an acceptable practice in America in the eighteenth century, when, for example, Aaron Burr killed Alexander Hamilton in a duel. Even after the code of honor and dueling had declined or been outlawed in the northern United States, they lingered on in the South as a deadly game of supersensitive pride and absurdity. (See Figure 5.1.)

Specific values were associated with the code of honor as it de-

Figure 5.1. A "gentleman" (note the elegant attire) submitting to a whipping, obviously as a result of some breach in the code of honor. Note the document being held by a bystander. Courtesy Roland Harper Photograph Collection, W. S. Hoole Special Collections Library, The University of Alabama.

veloped in the South before the Civil War. Its linchpin was reputation. Scholars who have studied the southern code of honor find
that it was driven almost entirely by the opinion of other people.
Those who most "genteelly" adhered to the code of honor in the
South—that is, the South's imitation knights on their plantations—
were usually supersensitive about what other people might think
or say about them. "Honorable" men in the South were obses-
sively concerned about their own reputation (or personal honor)
or the reputation of their families (family honor). One would be
more likely to hear a person say, "I would like to be *regarded* as
an honest person or a good person" than "I would like to *be* an
honest person or a good person." Self-worth, then, usually came
from what people thought about you rather than from what you
were.

Another characteristic of the southern code of honor was the
value placed on property as visible proof of a high place in society
and a distinguished family. So when they weren't defending their
own or their families' reputations, these knights were protecting
the property (which, as we have seen, consisted partly of slaves)
upon which honor rested.

The most cherished *personal* trait for one who adhered to the
code of honor was bravery, a virtue associated with manhood. Most
duels, it has been found, were fought in defense of one's reputation for courage. Indeed, failing to challenge an enemy to a duel,
or refusing to fight a duel if challenged, was a sign of cowardice
in the eyes of the world.

Revenge was also integral to the code of honor. The honor of a
man or his family was so important that any insult to either was
never forgiven. There may have been some Christian elements associated with a code for which knights once went on crusades, but
forgiveness was not one of them. The opposite of forgiveness—
revenge—was the fuel of feuds.

Feuding was also perpetuated by clannishness, also in evidence
in Walter Scott's Scottish Highlands (from which came many of
those in the South who loved his novels). The man of honor was
always more comfortable sheltered within the limited groups
where he was important. In his own groups he was somebody to
reckon with. He knew the rules and traditions necessary to play
the game. Perhaps for this reason, he was always ready to rush to
the defense of the various groups to which he belonged, whether

it be his family, his region, or his race. Perhaps this is the reason why Mark Twain, in *Life on the Mississippi,* claims that Walter Scott caused the Civil War!

So the evidence on which the reputation of the honorable man rested included overt acts of bravery in defending himself and his own kind against verbal insult. Other evidence consisted of external signs: high social position, property in land and slaves, proper attire, close adherence to rules of etiquette, proper accent, knowing the appropriate topics for conversation, general social grace, athleticism, physical height, bearing, and physical attractiveness.

As in the old days of knighthood that Walter Scott wrote about in *Ivanhoe,* forms and rules assumed immense importance. There was an honorable and a dishonorable way to conduct a duel, for example, and an honorable and a dishonorable way to ask a lady to dance.

For a variety of reasons—perhaps the stress on external evidence, perhaps the stress on bravery, perhaps the supersensitivity involved—the code of honor frequently led to violence, classically culminating in the duel and the feud.

An integral part of the code of honor, in what Twain saw as the Walter Scott society, was romanticism—courtly adventure by the rules, and fascination with titles, aristocracy, and the glories of the past. The mansions on plantations were likened to old English manor houses in the Middle Ages; the poor whites and the slaves were considered to be happy serfs who lived for a kind word from the master. Young plantation owners were the South's knights in shining armor, often to be found astride horses and carrying weapons to which lower-class people were less likely to have access. Like the knights of old, they were ready to resort to violence to defeat their enemies and, in so doing, to prove their manliness to those around them.

The code of honor, as it unfolds in *Adventures of Huckleberry Finn,* is embodied in a number of characters. What Mark Twain called the "silliness" of the code is chiefly seen in the character of Tom Sawyer, whose nonsense is a parody of romance. The code's violent destructiveness is seen in Colonel Sherburn, the Grangerfords, and the Shepherdsons. The fascination with aristocracy and titles is ridiculed in the characterizations of the king and the duke.

Tom's gang has all the trappings of the romantic code of honor. The very concept of the "gang" is equivalent to the clan, or group of knights, in effect a kind of extended family. Loyalty to the group is of first importance and is reinforced with oaths written in blood, the guarding of the group's secrets with their lives, and plans to avenge any disloyalty with violence. Like the knights of King Arthur's Round Table, they give themselves elevated titles, in this case "Captain." Their sign, like that of the knights on crusades, is the cross, which, ironically, they intend to carve into the chest of anyone who harms the gang. Like the upper-class plantation owner involved in a duel, Tom plans to kill and maim by the rules, in genteel fashion. Yet because it is romance, it is all ridiculous pretense: their guns and knives are really broomsticks; their Arabs and Spaniards are children on a Sunday School picnic; their loot consists of hymn books and religious tracts. Is Twain saying that those committed to the romantic knightly code of honor are really just silly boys playing games?

In the chapters that follow, Huck's genuine adventures, the very real dangers he faces, and the grueling moral dilemma with which he struggles all make a mockery of Tom's early romantic sham adventures.

Soon after Huck and Jim leave St. Petersburg, the games become deadly and the ridiculous side of romance is matched with the dark side as Huck and Jim board the sinking *Walter Scott.* In a grim echo of the code of honor and the rhetoric of the antebellum South, one of the thieves who has boarded the ship contemplates avenging himself by killing a gang member who interfered when "we stood on our rights." The thieves, obsessed with the *appearance* of honor rather than its *reality,* decide it would be "good morals" just to allow their old comrade to go down with the ship and drown rather than to shoot him.

Kids playing games and lower-class thugs don't have a monopoly on honor, however, for the next adherents to the tradition of honor are older men, who, like the typical southern planter, have taken the military title of Colonel. Colonel Grangerford has all the earmarks of the gentleman of honor. He is well born and has an aristocrat's pale complexion and a thin aquiline nose. He is impeccably dressed in white, has flawless manners, and takes comfort in ceremony, ritual, and hospitality extended to his friends. He and his male kin are the only people we see in the novel who are almost always on horseback and armed. The dark side of the gentleman and his family and neighbors, however, is that their code has resulted in endless revenge and killing. The mindlessness of the constant slaughter is apparent in that no one remembers the insult that started it all.

The next gentleman who is known by his military title is Colonel Sherburn, described as a "proud-looking man," "a heap the best dressed" in town. When the town drunk, Boggs, continues to insult and challenge him, this man of honor calmly issues an ultimatum, and, true to his word, shoots the retreating Boggs dead. It has hardly been a fair duel, but the gentleman has kept his word and defended his honor. Later Colonel Sherburn, who, ironically, has just shot an unarmed and retreating drunk down in the street, chastises the members of a lynch mob for not being "real men," as he himself claims to be, and for not having courage, a trait he automatically arrogates to himself. While Colonel Sherburn's speech is a bitter indictment of the mob, it is also an unconscious self-indictment. After all, he may have acted alone, but like the lynch mob he acted outside the law, and while the mob lacked the courage to string up the Colonel, it certainly didn't take any courage on his part to kill an unarmed drunk.

Twain, using a lighter touch, parodies the fascination with titles and royalty through the two river rats who invade the raft. These rascals are common, petty thieves who thrive on other people's ignorance and sorrow. Drunken and filthy, they call themselves a king and a duke. By assuming these titles, they believe they can demand respect. Huck and Jim must kneel when they speak to the king, call him "Your Majesty," and wait on him hand and foot.

When Jim notices that the king and the duke "smell so like de nation," Huck explains, "Well, they all do, Jim. *We* can't help the way a king smells; history don't tell no way" (154). Though Huck knows the king and the duke aren't real royalty, he contends that even with all their smelliness and dishonesty, "you couldn't tell them from the real kind" (155).

Adventures of Huckleberry Finn ends with Tom Sawyer, who sees the freeing of Jim as an opportunity to put into practice all the romantic ideas he has been seduced by in the novels of Alexandre Dumas, Charles Dickens, and Walter Scott. Alluding to novels by these three writers, with which Twain's audience would have been thoroughly familiar, is one of the main ways the author ridicules romance and the code of honor in the antebellum South. Some of the details in these romances are directly alluded to in

Tom Sawyer's complicated plan to free Jim. The novels to which Twain seems to allude most often are by the French writer Alexandre Dumas—*The Man in the Iron Mask* and *The Count of Monte Cristo.* The first work builds upon the legend in French history that a famous prisoner (a man who did, in fact, spend his entire adult life in prison with his face hidden behind an iron mask) was actually the twin brother of the monarch, Louis XIV, and so could never be allowed to show his face or to escape from his terrible cage to threaten Louis' place on the throne of France. Historically, and in Dumas' novel, the prisoner carved a mysterious message on a metal plate and threw it out the prison window to a passing stranger.

The Count of Monte Cristo, also by Dumas, is the story of an innocent man, Edmond Dantes, who, during the Napoleonic era, is wrongly imprisoned in the terrible Chateau D'If. He finally escapes after many years, having discovered a fabulous treasure.

Another novel that makes use of the escape motif parodied by Tom Sawyer on the Phelps farm is Sir Walter Scott's *Ivanhoe.* The hero, Wilfred of Ivanhoe, is disowned by his father because of his loyalty to the English king, Richard the Lion Hearted, who is imprisoned in France. Scott's popular novel is filled with feats of daring and knightly action.

These are only three of the many stories Tom is drawing on to rescue Jim in the "right," "honorable" way. Though Huck somewhat meekly goes along with Tom's pretenses and Jim has again been reduced to the stereotype he carries in the Tom Sawyer/ Walter Scott dominated society, Tom's romanticized foolishness results in pain for Jim and in such disillusionment for Huck that he decides to "light out for the territory" rather than remain in such a civilization.

Throughout the novel, in fact, Huck seems always to be the complete antithesis of the man of honor. For one thing, he is always an outsider. He has no family, no class, no club to defend. He also has an embarrassing tendency to see reality for what it is instead of romanticizing it. To him the Sunday School picnic is a Sunday School picnic, not a band of Arabs. Unlike the typical man of honor, who always exaggerates his achievements, Huck is humble; he always tends to think the worst of himself instead of bragging about his accomplishments. He never challenges others—for example, the king or the duke—but simply goes along with their lies and pretenses as the most expedient course. Even though he is surrounded by a violent and brutal society, he himself never resorts to violence. And rather than reveling in revenge when someone like the king or the duke has injured him, he can feel sorry for them in their bad luck. Most of all, Huck can forgive and he can apologize, even to a lowly slave.

Why exactly are "honor" and romanticism either ridiculous or destructive in Twain's view? To Twain there seems to be no way to live in the world and not at some time feel threatened and insulted, especially if society punishes you for refusing to react "bravely," and especially if you have been conditioned to believe that you are only worth what other people think of you. The novel illustrates that this Walter Scott syndrome inevitably leads to vengeance and violence.

More than this, the Walter Scott code of honor and romance provide their adherents with ways of prettying up ugly realities and escaping the truth. Romance of the Walter Scott variety (as Twain sees it) is all about external appearances rather than inner truths—what other people think, forms, rules, manners, physical appearance, no matter that what is underneath is something else entirely. So instead of facing up to the world's problems, adults spend their time playing games, chief of which is "let's pretend."

Five documents are included to stimulate a discussion of the question of honor in *Adventures of Huckleberry Finn:* a description of the southerner who lives by a code of honor by Thomas Nelson Page, an antebellum novelist; excerpts from an official nineteenth-century guide book to dueling according to the code of honor; Mark Twain's description from *Life on the Mississippi* of the values inherent in the southern code of honor and Walter Scott's influence on them; an interview with a former gang member about the code of the streets in the 1990s, which resembles in many ways the pre–Civil War code of honor; and excerpts from a study of the code of the streets as it exists in the 1990s.

THOMAS NELSON PAGE

There ain't a coward amongst them Shepherdsons—not a one. And there ain't no cowards amongst the Grangerfords, either. (112)

Col. Grangerford was a gentleman, you see. . . . He was well born. . . . every day of his life he put on a clean shirt and a full suit from head to foot made out of linen so white it hurt your eyes to look at it. (108)

The passage that follows includes a description of the southern temperament by Thomas Nelson Page, one of the Old South's chief spokesmen and an admitted admirer of Sir Walter Scott. Note the characteristics praised by Page: loyalty and courage above all, then purity, nobility, romance, conservatism, honesty, leadership, rhetorical display, impulsiveness, recklessness, and violence.

THOMAS NELSON PAGE, *THE OLD SOUTH*
(New York: Charles Scribner's Sons, 1892)

As the azure fields that stretch away through space are filled with stars which refuse their individual rays to the naked eye, yet are ever sending light through all the boundless realms of space, so under this brilliant exhibition of the South's public career lies the record of a life, of a civilization so pure, so noble, that the world to-day holds nothing equal to it.

After less than a generation it has become among friends and enemies the recognized field of romance.

Its chief attribute was conservatism. Others were courage, fidelity, purity, hospitality, magnanimity, honesty, and truth.

Whilst it proudly boasted itself democratic, it was distinctly and avowedly anti-radical—holding fast to those things which were proved, and standing with its conservatism a steadfast bulwark against all novelties and aggressions. . . . (43)

That the Southerner was courageous the whole world admits. His friends claim it; his foes know it. Probably never has such an army existed as that which followed Lee and Jackson. . . . It was not discipline, it was not *esprit de corps,* it was not traditional renown, it was not mere generalship which carried that army through. It was personal, individual courage and devotion to principle which welded it together and made it invincible, until it was almost extirpated.

The mills of battle and of grim starvation ground it into dust; yet even then there remained a valor which might well have inspired that famous legend which was one of the traditions of the conflict between the Church and its assailants in earlier ages, that after the destruction of their bodies their fierce and indomitable spirits continued the desperate struggle in the realms of air.

The tendency to hospitality was not local nor narrow; it was the characteristic of the entire people, and its concomitant was a generosity so general and so common in its application that it created the quality of magnanimity as a race characteristic. . . . (44–45)

Government was the passion of the Southerner. Trained from his earliest youth by the care and mastery of slaves, and the charge of affairs which demanded the qualities of mastership, the control of men became habitual with him, and domination became an instinct. Consequently the only fields which he regarded as desirable were those which afforded him the opportunity for its exercise.

Thus every young Southerner of good social connection who was too poor to live without work, or too ambitious to be contented with his plantation, devoted himself to the learned professions—the law being the most desirable as offering the best opportunity for forensic display, and being the surest stepping-stone to political preferment.

Being emotional and impulsive, the Southerner was as susceptible to the influences of rhetoric as was the Athenian, and public speaking was cultivated as always a necessary qualification for public position.

The South on this account became celebrated for its eloquence, which, if somewhat fervid when judged by the severe standard of later criticism, was, when measured by its immediate effects, extraordinarily successful. It contributed to preserve through decades preceding the war the supremacy of the slave-holding South, even against the rapidly growing aggressiveness of the North, with the sentiment of the modern world at its back.

It is not necessary to make reference to those orators who in the public halls of the nation, and in their native States, whenever questions of moment were agitated, evoked thunders of applause alike from rapturous friends and dazzled enemies. Their fame is now a part of the history of the country.

But in every circuit throughout the length and breadth of the South are handed down, even now, traditions of speakers who, by the impassioned eloquence of their appeals, carried juries against both law and evidence, or on the hustings, in political combat, swept away immense majorities by the irresistible impetuosity of their oratory.

That the Old South was honest, no sensible man who reads the history of that time can doubt, and no honest man will deny. Its whole course throughout its existence, whatever other criticism it may be subjected to, was one of honesty and of honor. Even under the perils of public life, which try men's souls, the personal integrity which was a fruit of civilization in which it flourished was never doubted.

In confirmation of this proposition, appeal can be made with confidence to the history of the public men of the South. They were generally poor men, frequently reckless men, and infrequently insolvent men; but their bitterest enemies never aspersed their honesty. . . .

If it has appeared to modern civilization that life has not been held sufficiently sacred at the South, this may be urged in her defence: that a comparative statement, based on the statistics, does not show that homicide is, or has ever been, more general at the South than at the North, when all classes are embraced in the statement; and if it has been tolerated among the upper classes under a form which has now happily passed away, it was in obedience to a sentiment which although grossly abused, had this much justification—that it placed honor above even life. (46–48)

A GUIDE TO DUELING

> He was standing perfectly still in the street, and had a pistol
> raised in his right hand—not aiming it, but holding it out with
> the barrel tilted up towards the sky. (143)

The official rule book governing dueling in South Carolina, written
by John Lyde Wilson, was undoubtedly one with which Thomas Nelson Page was very familiar. Wilson's essay was the authorized code
for "gentlemen," used throughout the South for as long as dueling
was practiced. Note his justifications for dueling, the reasons he
gives for challenging someone to a duel, and the elaborate ritual he
recommends for wounding or killing someone in a genteel way.

JOHN LYDE WILSON, *THE CODE OF HONOR: OR RULES FOR THE
GOVERNMENT OF PRINCIPLES AND SECONDS IN DUELLING*
(Charleston, S.C.: James Phinney, 1858)

How many cases are there, that might be enumerated, where there is no tribunal to do justice to an oppressed and deeply wronged individual? If he
be subjected to a tame submission to insult and disgrace, where no power
can shield him from its effects, then indeed it would seem, that the first law
of nature, self-preservation, points out the only remedy for his wrongs. The
history of all animated nature exhibits a determined resistance to encroachments upon natural rights,—nay, I might add, inanimate nature, for
it also exhibits a continual warfare for supremacy. . . . (4, 5)

It [dueling] will be persisted in as long as a manly independence, and
a lofty personal pride in all that dignifies and enables the human character, shall continue to exist. . . . (6, 7)

1. Whenever you believe that you are insulted, if the insult be in public
and by words or behavior, never resent it there, if you have self-command
enough to avoid noticing it. If resented there, you offer an indignity to
the company, which you should not do.

2. If the insult be by blows or any personal indignity, it may be resented
at the moment, for the insult to the company did not originate with you.
But although resented at the moment, you are bound still to have satisfaction, and must therefore make the demand.

3. When you believe yourself aggrieved, be silent on the subject, speak
to no one about the matter, and see your friend, who is to act for you,
as soon as possible.

4. Never send a challenge in the first instance, for that precludes all negotiation. Let your note be in the language of a gentleman, and let the subject matter of complaint be truly and fairly set forth, cautiously avoiding attributing to the adverse party any improper motive. . . . (11, 12)

[To the Party Being Warned that He Might Be Challenged]

1. When a note is presented to you by an equal, receive it, and read it, although you may suppose it to be from one you do not intend to meet, because its requisites may be of a character which may readily be complied with. But if the requirements of a note cannot be acceded to, return it, through the medium of your friend, to the person who handed it to you, with your reason for returning it [which will mean that you will meet him in a duel]. . . .

3. You may refuse a note, from a minor, (if you have not made an associate of him); . . . one that has been publicly disgraced without resenting it; one whose occupation is unlawful; a man in his dotage and a lunatic.

[Duty of Challengee and His Second Before Fighting]

1. After all efforts for a reconciliation are over, the party aggrieved sends a challenge to his adversary, which is delivered to his second.

2. Upon the acceptance of the challenge, the seconds make the necessary arrangements for the meeting, in which each party is entitled to a perfect equality. The old notion that the party challenged, was authorized to name the time, place, distance and weapon, has been long since exploded; nor would a man of chivalric honor use such a right, if he possessed it. The time must be as soon as practicable, the place such as had ordinarily been used where the parties are, the distance usual, and the weapon that which is most generally used, which, in this State, is the pistol. . . . (12)

. . . If either principal on the ground refuses to fight . . . it is the duty of his second to say to the other: "I have come upon the ground with a coward, and do tender you my apology for an ignorance of his character. . . . (27)

[The Degrees of Insult Justifying a Challenge to a Duel]

1. The prevailing rule is, that words used in retort, although more violent and disrespectful than those first used, will not satisfy,—words being no satisfaction for words.

2. When words are used, and a blow given in return, the insult is avenged; and if redress be sought, it must be from the person receiving the blow.

3. When blows are given in the first instance and not returned, and the person first striking, be badly beaten or otherwise, the party first struck is to make the demand, for blows do not satisfy a blow.

4. Insults at a wine table, when the company are over-excited, must be

answered for; and if the party insulting have no recollection of the insult, it is his duty to say so in writing, and negative the insult. For instance, if a man say: "you are a liar and no gentleman," he must, in addition to the plea of want of recollection, say: "I believe the party insulted to be a man of the strictest veracity and a gentleman."

5. Intoxication is not a full excuse for insult, but it will greatly palliate. If it was a full excuse, it might be well counterfeited to wound feelings, or destroy character.

6. In all cases of intoxication, the seconds use a sound discretion under the above general rules.

7. Can every insult be compromised? is a mooted and vexed question [that is, must you challenge everyone who insults you to a duel, or can you accept an apology instead?]. On this subject, no rules can be given that will be satisfactory. The old opinion, that a blow must require blood, is not of force. Blows may be compromised in many cases. . . . (32, 33)

[For the information of his readers, Wilson includes some rules from the Irish Code of Honor.]

"Rule 1.—The first offence requires the apology, although the retort may have been more offensive than the insult.—Example: A. tells B. he is impertinent, etc.; B. retorts, that he lies; yet A must make the first apology, because he gave the first offence. . . .

"Rule 9.—All imputations of cheating at play, races, etc, to be considered equivalent to a blow; they may be reconciled after one shot, on admitting their falsehood, and begging pardon publicly. (37)

"Rule 10.—Any insult to a lady under a gentleman's care or protection, to be considered as, by one degree, a greater offence than if given to the gentleman personally, and to be regulated accordingly. (40)

LIFE ON THE MISSISSIPPI

> "All I say is, kings is kings, and you got to make allowances.
> Take them all around, they're a mighty ornery lot. It's the way
> they're raised."
>   "But dis one do smell so like de nation, Huck." . . .
>   . . . "Sometimes I wish we could hear of a country that's
> out of kings." (154, 155)

Twain's discourse from *Life on the Mississippi* makes clear why he
thinks Sir Walter Scott actually caused the Civil War by cultivating
all the characteristics found in the southern man of honor, some
of which are listed by Thomas Nelson Page. The first paragraph of
the following excerpt, from a chapter called "Enchantments and
Enchanters," sets up one of Twain's basic objections to what he
called the Walter Scott culture: he notes the forward steps Western
culture took in overthrowing monarchies in the French Revolution
and in the reign of Napoleon Bonaparte when merit was set above
birth. Scott, according to Twain, reversed that progress toward democracy, "enchanting" the world by romanticizing monarchies
and their ways of life.

Twain mentions some of the same southern characteristics Page
does—the violence, the inflated rhetoric, the romance—but instead of praising them, he finds them silly and backward. To Page,
southern speech is noble; to Twain it is "windy" and "flowery."
In Twain's view, the attitudes Scott encouraged not only caused
the Civil War but thwarted the growth of southern literature.

In his closing paragraph, Twain makes reference to medieval
chivalry, which Cervantes, in *Don Quixote,* had unveiled as "silliness." Scott enchanted the South with the same silliness.

FROM MARK TWAIN, *LIFE ON THE MISSISSIPPI*
(New York: Harper and Brothers, 1911)

Against the crimes of the French Revolution and of Bonaparte may be
set two compensating benefactions: the Revolution broke the chains of
the *ancien regime* and of the Church, and made a nation of abject slaves
a nation of freemen; and Bonaparte instituted the setting of merit above
birth, and also so completely stripped the divinity of royalty that, whereas
crowned heads in Europe were gods before, they are only men since,

and can never be gods again, but only figure-heads, and answerable for their acts like common clay. Such benefactions as these compensate the temporary harm which Bonaparte and the Revolution did, and leave the world in debt to them for these great and permanent services to liberty, humanity, and progress.

Then comes Sir Walter Scott with his enchantments, and by his single might checks this wave of progress and even turns it back; sets the world in love with dreams and phantoms; with decayed and swinish forms of religion; with decayed and degraded systems of government; with the sillinesses and emptinesses, sham grandeurs, sham gauds, and sham chivalries of a brainless and worthless long-vanished society. He did measureless harm; more real and lasting harm, perhaps, than any other individual that ever wrote. Most of the world has now outlived a good part of these harms, though by no means all of them; but in our South they flourish pretty forcefully still. Not so forcefully as half a generation ago, perhaps, but still forcefully. There, the genuine and wholesome civilization of the nineteenth century is curiously confused and commingled with the Walter Scott Middle-Age sham civilization, and so you have practical common-sense, progressive ideas, and progressive works, mixed up with the duel, the inflated speech, and the jejune romanticism of an absurd past that is dead, and out of charity ought to be buried. But for the Sir Walter Scott disease, the character of the Southerner—or Southron, according to Sir Walter's starchier way of phrasing it—would be wholly modern, in place of modern and medieval mixed, and the South would be fully a generation further advanced than it is. It was Sir Walter that made every gentleman in the South a major or a colonel, or a general or a judge, before the war; and it was he, also, that made these gentlemen value these bogus decorations. For it was he that created rank and caste down there, and also reverence for rank and cast, and pride and pleasure in them. Enough is laid on slavery, without fathering upon it these creations and contributions of Sir Walter.

Sir Walter had so large a hand in making Southern character, as it existed before the war, that he is in great measure responsible for the war. It seems a little harsh toward a dead man to say that we never should have had any war but for Sir Walter; and yet something of a plausible argument might, perhaps, be made in support of that wild proposition. The Southerner of the American revolution owned slaves; so did the Southerner of the Civil War; but the former resembles the latter as an Englishman resembles a Frenchman. The change of character can be traced rather more easily to Sir Walter's influence than to that of any other thing or person.

One may observe, by one or two signs, how deeply that influence penetrated, and how strongly it holds. If one takes up a Northern or Southern literary periodical of forty or fifty years ago, he will find it filled with

wordy, windy, flowery "eloquence," romanticism, sentimentality—all im-
itated from Sir Walter, and sufficiently badly done, too—innocent travesties of his style and methods, in fact. This sort of literature being the
fashion in both sections of the country, there was opportunity for the
fairest competition; and as a consequence, the South was able to show
as many well-known literary names, proportioned to population, as the
North could.

But a change has come, and there is no opportunity now for a fair
competition between North and South. For the North has thrown out
that old inflated style, whereas the Southern writer still clings to it—
clings to it and has a restricted market for his wares, as a consequence.
There is as much literary talent in the South, now, as ever there was, of
course; but its work can gain but slight currency under present conditions; the authors write for the past, not the present; they use obsolete
forms and a dead language. But when a Southerner of genius writes
modern English, his book goes upon crutches no longer, but upon wings;
and they carry it swiftly all about America and England, and through the
great English reprint publishing houses of Germany. . . . Instead of three
or four widely known literary names, the South ought to have a dozen
or two—and will have them when Sir Walter's time is out.

A curious exemplification of the power of a single book for good or
harm is shown in the effects wrought by "Don Quixote" and those
wrought by "Ivanhoe." The first swept the world's admiration for the
medieval chivalry-silliness out of existence; and the other restored it. As
far as our South is concerned, the good work done by Cervantes is pretty
nearly a dead letter, so effectually has Scott's pernicious work under-
mined it. (327–330)

THE VALUES OF THE STREETS

LARRY WATTS' "THE CODE OF THE STREETS"

> Now, we'll start this band of robbers and call it Tom Sawyer's
> Gang. Everybody that wants to join has got to take an oath,
> and write his name in blood. . . .
>   . . . And if anybody that belonged to the band told the se-
> crets, he must have his throat cut. (17)

The code of honor Mark Twain satirizes in *Adventures of Huck-leberry Finn* arises from Walter Scott's medieval romances as adopted by antebellum southerners. Ironically, the code is also relevant to street gangs of the 1990s, as the following interview with a former gang member shows.

Twain equates the powerful romantic code of honor with law-lessness through his descriptions of both the fairly harmless ado-lescent gang of Tom Sawyer and the dangerous gangs of desperadoes that prowled the Mississippi Valley at the time. The word "gang" is explicitly applied to two groups in *Adventures of Huckleberry Finn*—Tom Sawyer's gang in the beginning of the novel and the gang that Huck and Jim find aboard the *Walter Scott*. Twain also associates the two con men, the self-proclaimed king and duke, with the English and French aristocracy, after which the southern ruling class patterned themselves. So it should come as no surprise to find parallels between the nineteenth-century gangs Twain satirizes and the gang culture of the 1990s or to find par-allels between the nineteenth-century code of honor and the late twentieth-century code of the streets.

Those parallels are clearly discernible in a comparison of the nineteenth-century values embedded in the code of honor with those revealed in the following interview, conducted by Larry Watts, a professor at Stillman College in Tuscaloosa, Alabama, with a former gang member.

The specific parallels to look for in the interview are (1) the fantasies that inspire activity; (2) their literature and codes; (3) the love of hierarchy and military trappings; (4) the importance of property or money-making, often of a lawless or violent nature; (5) the importance of respect and a reputation for courage and loyalty; (6) the swiftness with which insults are avenged; (7) the use of violence; and (8) the similarity between gang activity and boys' games.

Don't I tell you it's in the book? (18)

Curiously, both Tom Sawyer's gang and Ted's 1990s gang thrive on fantasy. Just as Tom Sawyer was inspired by the fantasy in nineteenth-century romantic novels in the formation of his gang and in his attempt to free Jim, so Ted sees that young men are attracted to gangs in order to live out what he calls "a fantasy" of twentieth-century culture. "You see it in the movies and what not. . . . It's like your chance to really experience it," he explains.

As Tom continues to be guided by the literature of "the authorities," as he calls them, so Ted makes frequent reference to the importance of the gang's "literature," established by its leaders. "Well, we have quite a literature," he says. "You've got to know your lit." He means by this the various secrets and rituals that any gang member must master to communicate with other members through code.

> [W]hen he wants to send any little common ordinary mysterious message to let the world know where he's captivated, he can write it on the bottom of a tin plate with a fork and throw it out of the window. (235)

One aspect of the literature of both gangs involves secret codes. While Tom finds it necessary, in following the proper rules of behavior, to have Jim send coded messages to the outside world by writing in blood on a shirt or scratching on a tin plate with a fork, as in a nineteenth-century romance, Ted explains that part of the literature of *his* gang is the coded language of graffiti, which members use to identify territory and to convey secret messages.

> And if anybody that belonged to the gang told the secrets, he must have his throat cut, and then his carcass burnt up and the ashes scattered all around and his name blotted off the list with blood and never mentioned again by the gang. (17)

Furthermore, the literature or codes of both Tom's and Ted's gangs are its most zealously (one might say violently) guarded secrets. The special codes and signs Tom Sawyer incorporates into his gang are, he says, to be guarded with one's life; any disclosure will be punished brutally. Tom's gang literature parallels that of many secret societies, including the infamous KKK and Knights of the Camellia, groups that began to flourish in the South at the time Mark Twain was writing his novel. In these groups, as in Ted's, signals, signs, and gestures are sacred—they identify members, territory, and strategies. The language is so secret that Ted cannot, under any circumstances, reveal it to Professor Watts, even under promise of anonymity.

> [H]e said it often made him feel easier and better for a while if people treated him according to his rights, and got down on one knee to speak to him, and always called him "Your Majesty," and waited on him first at meals, and didn't set down in his presence till he asked them. (126)

There are other similarities between the various gangs of *Adventures of Huckleberry Finn* and Ted's street gang. Like the hierarchy of kings and dukes and the "colonels" of the southern code of honor, Ted's street gang has a distinct love of the military and royal trappings. He takes pains to describe his gang in terms of a hierarchy with generals and enlisted men. The kings in the hierarchy of his 1990s gang are called "high supremes." They always know best. They are the wise men of the gang, and the lower orders respect them and do what they say.

> "Now," says Ben Rogers, "what's the line of business of this Gang?" (18)

"Business" or making money is the central purpose of the gangs in *Adventures in Huckleberry Finn* as well as Ted's gang. The business of Tom Sawyer's gang is to rob stagecoaches. The gang aboard the *Walter Scott* is engaged in the "business" of stealing money, as is the gang that has deserted the death house, for Jim and Huck find stolen loot and the masks of robbers there. Then there are less lethal forms of business. For example, Colonel Sherburn, who shoots Boggs, is the town's chief businessman, and the king and the duke (supposedly like real kings and dukes) are intent on numerous forms of "business" to con and cheat people out of their money. Ted's gang is also committed to "business" of an unsavory sort. He says, "It's all about making money," and mentions "selling dope," proportioning out "weed" for sale, and keeping "cribs" for the purpose of making money from prostitutes.

> Your newspapers call you a brave people so much that you think you are braver than any other people. . . . you're afraid to back down—afraid you'll be found out to be what you are— cowards. (146)

The most significant parallels between the southern code of honor and the 1990s code of the streets may be their common values. Just as the southern gentleman was concerned above all with what people thought of him, the chief value in Ted's gang is one's personal reputation for bravery and loyalty, which had to be proven repeatedly, in this case through acts of violence. Buck Grangerford, for example, is very proud of the courage of his own family. He is even proud of the courage of his family's mortal enemies. In keeping with the southern code of honor that Twain parodies, Colonel Sherburn taunts the prospective lynch mob by calling them cowards. Similarly, Ted names bravery as one of the most desired attributes of a gang member.

> Shore's you're born, he'll turn state's evidence; now you hear me. I'm for putting him out of his troubles. (74)

> "Well," says Buck, "a feud is this way: A man has a quarrel with another man, and kills him; then that other man's brother kills him; then the other brothers, on both sides, goes for one another; then the cousins chip in—" (111)

Like courage, loyalty is held in high value by the adherents of both the code of honor and the code of the streets. This is interpreted as loyalty to one's own kind. It is also necessary to display that loyalty by seeking vengeance through violence against others who are not in the clan or have been disloyal to the gang. To illustrate, the first order of business in Tom Sawyer's gang is to exact an oath of loyalty and set up a way to deal with those who are disloyal to the gang. The Grangerfords and Shepherdsons represent the ultimate in clannish loyalty. Similarly, in the 1990s one finds competing gangs, somewhat like the Grangerfords and the Shepherdsons. Like these two feuding families from *Adventures of*

Huckleberry Finn, Ted ranks loyalty to the gang as the most important quality of its members.

Another similarity between the antebellum southern man of honor and members of the 1990s street gang is their refusal to tolerate insults or threats. The southern gentleman was obliged to challenge to a duel with swords or pistols anyone who insulted him. So it is with Ted's gang: any insult or threat, especially from a member of another gang, might "get handled," as Ted ominously reports—someone might well find himself, he says, "in cement shoes."

> All of a sudden, bang! bang! bang! goes three or four guns—
> . . . and as they swum down the current the men run along
> the bank shooting at them and singing out, "Kill them, kill
> them!" (117)

Violence was an inevitable part of the southern code of honor, as the manual on dueling and the history of lynching make clear. Violence is implicit in the southern gentleman's need to prove his loyalty, for only actions of a violent nature could sufficiently redress insults and threats to one's own kind, as the feud demonstrates. Violence was also a way to prove one's courage and manhood, as the Colonel Sherburn/Boggs incident illustrates. In the nineteenth-century South, this violence often took the form of a duel. In the streets of the twentieth century, it takes the parallel form of fighting, and, as Ted implies, sometimes a more mysterious and horrible form.

> He said we must slick up our swords and guns, and get ready.
> He never could go after even a turnip-cart but he must have
> the swords and guns all scoured up for it; though they was
> only lath and broom-sticks. (22)

As Ted's interview comes to a close, he acknowledges that, while the gang members see themselves as making a passage into manhood, their rites are often like the games of little boys—another reminder of Tom Sawyer's gang. Little boys, Ted says, are naturally violent: they play and fight and blow things up and love their toys of war. They have their own in-crowds and bullies like the gangs of older boys. The youth gang, even with all its violence, is a natural extension of these boyish games.

Tom Sawyer's gang's pretend swords and guns made of slats and broomsticks are early, harmless versions of the serious weapons carried by the gang aboard the *Walter Scott* and used by the Grangerfords and Shepherdsons, Colonel Sherburn, and Ted's street gang.

In many essential ways, contemporary society—like the gang culture in the 1990s—sheds light on *Adventures of Huckleberry Finn.* Perhaps equally important, however, Twain's novel throws light on the complex issue of group psychology. The novel also tells us something about the adolescent struggle into manhood, and, at the same time, exposes the monstrousness of the character who never loses the adolescent need to prove his manhood. And ironically, in a novel with a character—Huck Finn—who has always lived in the public imagination as an eternal adolescent, it is not Huck who prolongs adolescence, but rather the seasoned, more powerful adults of the novel, armed with deadly toys and the respect of their communities. When Huck flees civilization, he is not so much fleeing maturity and responsibility (as some critics have argued) as he is fleeing a world dominated by perpetual boys.

FROM LARRY WATTS, "THE CODE OF THE STREETS: AN INTERVIEW WITH A FORMER GANG MEMBER" (1995)

Watts: Before we begin, I would like to assure you that you will not be identified in the published version of this interview. Please feel free to let these questions take our conversation wherever you want it to go. Enlarge and expand whenever you feel the need. To begin with, I wonder if you could please describe the extent of your experience with street gangs? At what age did you get involved, what general area of the country are we talking about, and how did you get involved?

Ted: Right in high school, the freshman year of high school. I guess that's just how it worked out.

Watts: Could you give an age?

Ted: I was probably fourteen—about fourteen years old. Just coming into high school.

Watts: And what area of the country are we talking about?

Ted: The Midwest—a big city in the Midwest.

Watts: How did you get involved?

Ted: Through some friends of mine, a couple of friends. I mean, shortly, even as a young guy, you're aware of what's going on. You knew who they were. You might not know the extent of the business, but you see them with cars and rags and things like that, and you get curious.

Watts: So you got involved from curiosity?

Ted: Yeah, basically, basically.

Watts: What is your situation now?

Ted: Well, I'm in college now, and, I mean, I finished high school and went to college, and I'm presently pursuing a degree. I got out of the gang, but—

Watts: You got out of the gang?

Ted: Basically. I left it alone.

Watts: What attracted you to a gang? You hinted at it earlier, but expand on that a little bit more.

Ted: I guess—my family—I didn't have—I wasn't raised with brothers and sisters, even though I had half brothers and sisters in other states. But I didn't interact with them. Basically, all my "brothers" were people who stayed around me, people who were tight-knit, got close. And a lot of them—I was the kind of guy that hung with older people, people not my age. And they accepted me because I didn't talk too much, and I was a little mature for my age. You see a gang hanging together. You walk to school or something like that, and you see them hanging in the halls. They give each other the secret handshake and are standing up with each other, and, you know, it was just like—wow!—this is unity; this is something. This is something interesting. This is something I have in common, you know, and you see them throwing gang signs and at parties and always together. And just groups of people. And I guess it was different. It was something I hadn't seen.

Watts: So what I can extract from you is you were fascinated because you are an only child, and you saw this sense of family? brotherhood?

Ted: Right, but I don't want to say the fact that I was an only child would be a reason for a youth to get into a gang.

Watts: And, number two, your second point was your level of maturity. You saw the gang members as older people; you were attracted to older people. You felt too mature to be with youngsters your own age?

Ted: Right.

Watts: Since we are on the question of maturity, what was the age of most of the boys involved in the gang?

Ted: Sixteen through twenty-three, basically. I mean there were younger members but you don't really consider them—you know—brothers. You don't consider them to be real G's because most of them were turned on by their older brothers or older sisters. So although they might have had the title of—whatever the gang gave them—they hadn't done anything, and they were just doing it to be doing it. They don't count. But from sixteen to twenty-three, those were the main people actually doing the dirt, starting the fights, selling the dope, and going to school.

Watts: What kind of home life did *they* have?

Ted: We had people from all walks of life. People that shared my condition—middle class, and we had upper class and people straight down from the projects. A lot of single parents, a *lot* of single parent homes.

Watts: Would you say mostly single parents, mostly poor kids? in your gang? from poor families?

Ted: Actually my high school was in a middle-class neighborhood. It was a good high school.

Watts: You have used some terminology—the term "G." What is "G"?

Ted: "G" means gangster.

Watts: And you have used the term, "business," about "taking care of business." What do you mean by "business," able to "handle business?"

Ted: The real terminology which I should use is "down for yours." It means basically doing whatever you have to do to survive.

Watts: A survivor attitude. Based in selfishness and greed?

Ted: Somewhat.

Watts: Down for yours?

Ted: Down for yours. That's doing whatever it takes to get you yours, to get your money, to get your props, to get your acceptance, to get your rank.

Watts: Your props?

Ted: Your props is like, yeah, your respect.

Watts: What kind of personality did the average, the typical member have in your gang?

Ted: They are like loose cannons. Just people that were so spontaneous—
so—so—it's just about trying to get a rep. And I mean they'd do
whatever it took to be noticed, and to get some compliment. Like
trying to be known.

Watts: Like the center of attention?

Ted: Right. In a mix, they're just in the forefront. Because you can have
a gang that's three hundred members strong, but out of three hundred members, there's only twenty who are basically running the
gang.

Watts: You have kind of answered this question, but give a more concrete
and focussed answer this time. What do you think most of the members were looking for in a gang?

Ted: Security.

Watts: Security? There are different kinds of security—emotional, financial, family?

Ted: You've named all three. Perfectly. Financial, family—I mean you can
get in a gang, and something happens to you, somebody wants to
fight you, somebody wants to stick you up, somebody wants to steal
your things, and you've got your gang to back you up. And chances
are—you're in a gang, people won't mess with you, because they
know they have all the gang to deal with. Family—because—because—when I need something, I can go to one of my members
before I can go to somebody that's not affiliated with a particular
gang.

Watts: So there appears to be a support network.

Ted: Right, right. That's good. That's good. That sums it up, as far as
reasons. I mean, everybody has his own individual reasons.
Somebody might be scared. Somebody might just be tired of being
the one that's sitting back with no props, no girls, no nothing, and
wants to get known real quick, and wants to be in the cool crowd
and be in the forefront. Like somebody else might just jump in for
the wrong reasons. But once you're in, people are bound—people
will know. It'll spread like wildfire. And there's a certain amount of
respect that you automatically get for doing that. If you make it in,
you must have had some kind of heart.

Watts: Could you define "down" for me? What you mean by "being
down"?

Ted: Yeah, "down." You know, being with it. It's like—more concrete—
being down is basically being with whatever they say is going to be.
You know, if our particular gang is fighting and you're down, that

means *you're* going to fight too. I'm *with* it. If you want to make some money, I'm down—hey—I want to get in too. I have your back.

Watts: How did the gang choose its members?

Ted: Well, it's like, everybody is always constantly being watched. I mean you see a guy who's handling his, who's real, who's not afraid, doesn't back down from somebody else or who might have some sense. You might have somebody who might do cars real well, might paint cars, who might do graffiti real well, be able to work on auto body material real well. The high supremes, some of them, see that and notice that it's a good quality, and they might want you, but it's like most of the time the gang doesn't come to you, you come to the gang. And if the gang does come to you, it's probably one of your friends that says—"Hey, Man, why don't you come and get down?" You know what I mean? But the gang doesn't seek you. *You* seek the gang.

Watts: You seek the gang. But the gang has a mechanism for recognizing.

Ted: Right.

Watts: And what do you mean by "recognizing"?

Ted: Noticing. To be recognized, you can see over here, like I said, the guy with the car. And he might not particularly—and we might not necessarily mess with him, or we might give him a little more respect than say an average Joe because he's handling his own things. He's got something. He's got a little fire to him. He's got a talent or a trade or some kind of sense, and you know he can walk like—certain people can't even come around in the world or the circle we're talking about. And if he's recognized, it's like, well, it's cool; we can talk. We can sit down and mingle.

Watts: You have used the phrase, "he can handle his own" a couple of times. What do you mean by that?

Ted: Handle his own, fighting. He has heart. He can protect himself.

Watts: He has heart?

Ted: Right. Like when a guy can handle things, that means he's man enough. He can maintain his own. If there's a fight, he's gonna fight. And chances are, usually, he wins if he's handling things. He's got that respect going for him. Being able to handle his business. Handle things.

Watts: You have answered what characteristics they were looking for. What were the characteristics of the supremes? I imagine the supremes are the higher echelon, the higher level, the bosses.

Ted: Right. Usually pretty intelligent.

Watts: What characteristics did they look for in new recruits?

Ted: Loyalty and, like I said, any trades or skills he might have. See what I want to clarify now is that my gang compared to other gangs—we worked on a different system. Most gangs just try to get as many members as they can and just work out and want to fight and be known as being the badness on the block. We were more about business AND being on the block. You know?

Watts: What kind of people might they reject?

Ted: Would they reject?

Watts: What kinds of people were not "down"?

Ted: Oh, punks, sissy kind of people like fags, homosexuals; we weren't really down with those. Just tender-hearted, we called them. People that were afraid—fear is like a big part of everything. If you're quiet and someone tells you something and gets all up in your face and you don't handle your business and you don't, you know, stand up for yourself. I don't need that—I don't need that. Or somebody that has a big mouth and just likes to run on and be in the mixing all the time. You don't want them. They'd *love* to be in, but then they can talk crap and have *us* handling their back. You know, they start things. It's like, that's not necessary. That's the sort of shallow people we don't want.

Watts: Do they associate homosexuality with fear?

Ted: With fear? It's usually the mental, the mind state of the homosexuals I've encountered. I mean they're not real to me. They're not violent people. They're not—they're not—they don't fit this description. We filtered them out, basically. I mean, there's some wherever you go most likely—hear what I'm saying? And no one knows unless you're with that man, unless he's out there saying, "I am"—you wouldn't claim to be homosexual; you wouldn't admit it—

Watts: In the gang.

Ted: No. *Heck* no.

Watts: What qualities in a person did gang members most admire?

Ted: Back then, I had intelligence and heart at the same time.

Watts: You're equating heart with—?

Ted: Not being afraid, yeah. Cause most of the time you encounter people, if they're smart, then usually they're not something else. Well, not *usually,* but chances are they're not something else. But if they're all hard and thuggish, you know, chances are that's *all* they are. And if you can combine two qualities, hey, that's a plus. If you have skills, if you're intelligent, if you can handle your business, you're cool, within the system, as far as the school, popularity, cool with ladies, if you're a ladies' man. Hey, that's all a plus, you know.

Watts: So it's a manhood thing?

Ted: Right, right, couldn't find a better word.

Watts: Partly, I think, it's a manhood thing, but isn't business supreme?

Ted: Oh yeah, that's first and foremost.

Watts: Money-making supreme?

Ted: Definitely. In my particular set.

Watts: I'm going to throw out a bunch of character nouns, and you tell me how they would rate—loyalty, tolerance, action, reflection, honesty, friendship, family, diversity, respect, and reputation.

Ted: Okay. Courage is a main thing. It's not the only thing, but you must understand that there are certain things that I'm not at liberty to put out on the streets. But, at the same time, courage is very strong.

Watts: Courage is number one?

Ted: Ummmm. Yeah, and loyalty. You must have loyalty. Out of those—

Watts: What about humility? To be humble.

Ted: Oh yeah, that's—that could save your life. But it is not something exactly you would search for, you know. Because you going to gain it whether you want it or not. You'll have it when you're confronted with a situation. And, I mean, because there'll always be someone with more rank than you and you don't just speak to anybody without respect, you know. That's how it is. You got to know when to shut the hell up—who you can talk to and who you can't talk to, when to say something and when not to say something. And it may make the difference between life and death in some situations. It's how you maintain order.

Watts: How about determination?

Ted: Oh yeah. Because if you not determined, what's the purpose?—I mean, there's a goal behind this which I have to illustrate for you, at least as a goal. And if the determination wasn't there, or distilled within its members, the gang wouldn't be around today.

Watts: Clearly loyalty speaks for itself?

Ted: I mean, if I didn't see any kind of sign of loyalty in a person or a person didn't have loyalty, he wouldn't be able to—I mean I wouldn't want him in my cell. Cause if I tell you something or I entrust my life in your hands, and you're not loyal to me or you're not loyal to some—or the gang itself, you're—you put us *all* at risk.

I mean, yeah, its like stabbing somebody in the back. You're a back-stabber and you do not *need* that in—if it happens—hey—it's handled quickly.

Watts: Handled quickly? What do they do with a disloyal person?

Ted: It depends on the crime. You know, I mean, a person can get a violation. And you don't want a violation. And basically, when you get a violation, you get your ass beat—or even worse.

Watts: Give me a concrete example of one or two violations.

Ted: Violations?

Watts: Of loyalty.

Ted: Money, that would be a violation definitely. Cause if you're making it—you're making money, and you short us for what's ours—that's a capital crime right there. Because it's all about making money, you know what I'm saying? You're making money, and you short me some money, or you come up short—Say I appoint you whatever, say I appoint you a pound of weed, and you only come back with $400, it doesn't matter the amount that you took; it's personal. If you only took a dollar, you did not handle your business. That's not loyal. That's not loyal. And you will pay a consequence.

Watts: What about ratting?

Ted: Ooh! ummm! That's about the number two [violation] right there. You sell out—OOH! I really cannot *tell* you the prices you would pay for these violations. Like I say, I'm not at liberty to tell you that. But you *really* wouldn't want to do that. Second of all, another thing, ratting to a police officer or ratting to another gang member—you messing around with our rival gang, and you supposed to be down with us, and you tell them some business, that's a violation. That's a *big* violation.

Watts: So gang members look for people exactly like themselves?

Ted: No, not exactly. Well, to an extent. You want to be with someone that fits you, that has your qualities and will benefit you.

Watts: Let's move on to action. We are still talking about the order of the most desired traits. What about action? Let's think about Beowulf. One of the characteristics of such a hero is that he acts.

Ted: Actions speak louder than words. You can say whatever you want to say, but—a man who will say, "We oughta do this,"—that's one thing. But a man who will say, "Come on let's go on and make this move," and will go on and actually *make* this play and, go on and handle this business, go sell that, is appreciated. This is a quality that all of us show.

Watts: So—"let's do it."

Ted: Get it *on.* What good do you do to *talk* about it? You lose respect if you don't act. One small slip up will impact on us. If we don't act immediately, that might be seen by another rivalry as a weakness, and we don't make that mistake.

Watts: Well, reflection doesn't rank highly in the gang structure, then.

Ted: That happens, but that's not a responsibility. The high supremes and everybody who runs things, that's *their* responsibility. That's why they are where they're at—because they have that quality. You listen to the one who has the rank. Cause he earned his. He went through a lot to be where he is. If you are on top of things, you have definitely paid your dues.

Watts: How about honesty? How does honesty rank in the gang structure?

Ted: Well, I think from the perspective of the high supremes again, be-cause, to them, loyalty, honesty—that's the quality they want to see. I like to know that if I tell this man that I want this sold or I want you to take such and such and do such and such, and maybe it didn't happen, maybe you didn't follow my order exactly the fact that maybe you came back and told me the truth would make me think a little higher of you, but the fact is that you are still in violation. But as far as somebody on a lower level—I mean—like a guy can be honest but, really, I'm not really worried about it because the things I'm doing. Whether you're telling me the truth about something or not, I'm *going* to find out about it. What's in the dark's going to come into the light, and it's not for me to be worrying about it. You understand? We're dealing in ranks again. A lot of them on the lower rank might have the mental, but most of them don't. And as you go farther up on the scale, you know, you encounter more intelligent people, if you ask me.

Watts: So you cannot steal from the gang?

Ted: Oh, no. You can *try.* Even if you pull it off, that would be the *stu-pidest* thing you'd want to do. Cause you *will* be caught.

Watts: You can't lie to the gang.

Ted: Oh No. It's like a rule. You're not supposed—but no one's perfect, is what I'm saying. I'm sure someone's lied—someone's got over one once in a while. But most of the time, so much fear in a person and so much respect for their set that they won't do that.

Watts: Even if they are not honest ordinarily, they will be honest with the gang?

Ted: Now what he does with somebody *else;* hey, he can lie. He can say whatever in hell he wants to say. But when it comes to *us*, you better come *correct*, you'd better come *real*.

Watts: As far as the gang is concerned—if they ask you, you have to turn against the family?

Ted: That's all individual again, I must tell you. Because—you know what you're supposed to do. You're supposed to respect your family. Your family comes first. Your family is what got you here. Now when it comes to handling business, the rule might be—Hey—you need to do such and such to your cousin because he messed us up; he slipped up. He did such and such, but that individual has to make that decision.

Watts: He would do his family member in?

Ted: Yes, regardless of repercussions.

Watts: So, does the gang try to make you disloyal to your family?

Ted: Oh, no. Any disloyalty to your family is because you decided to do that. They're not going to tell you to do—like say, my cousin *did* slip up and snitch, they're not going to ask me to do my cousin, out of admiration for me. They'll get somebody else to do it. I might not even *know* about it until it happened, if they did do a rebellious act against my family. They try, they're not going to—they're not trying to hurt their own members.

Watts: The question of diversity—in your particular gang were the members all black?

Ted: Blacks, yeah. They were. We had like one Hispanic dude, and he was—he thought he was black. And he was cool, and he knew how to pitch business. He was cool with everybody so he was in.

Watts: How about respect? Is that an important attribute?

Ted: There's enough respect. Age has a lot to do with it. The more you've been around, the more businesses you own, the more respect you have. And what I own helps me get my respect and for the gang to have respect. But I mean, I know a lot of things we have. Most people are ignorant of the things we have. Most people think we're just a bunch of guys on the street fighting and killing each other. And they miss the whole—and a lot of what we do might be wrong. But there's the business side, there's the money. That's what it's about.

Watts: What about the respect you have for each other?

Ted: Oh, there's a lot of respect, and anytime you don't have respect for a man—I'm going to tell him. We have a meeting, and me and that man will get in there. Me and that man will have it out. It will come to light. You got a problem with somebody, you tell him or you tell somebody so it can get handled. You go before them and let them decide it.

Watts: How do they rank reputation?

Ted: Reputation means a lot. Reputation's like—it's your resume almost. I mean, you've got a good reputation, you've earned that reputation. And talk about a new member coming in, how do we view him? The guy with the badest reputation we view him a little higher, see what I'm saying? And when I say bad, I don't mean bad as far as, you know—I mean successful, accomplished, can produce.

Watts: Well since we're on this issue of reputation, if bravery is an important element in the gang, how does one show this bravery or courage?

Ted: Fighting. Like when things—business—needs to be handled, getting his. Like the man is on the street fighting, and you got a man that's showing out and whipping everybody's behind, hey, he's showing his, he's showing his, he's showing how. Like every time you embark on something, you try your best so you can get known. So maybe someone will see you and notice and see how you produce. So maybe you can move up. If you're out there and making some money and producing the money, you're doing it cause they told you to, but you're also doing it to impress.

Watts: How did you feel that YOU proved you were a courageous person?

Ted: I guess it was the fighting. I mean this hammer of mine—whatever I said went. If it was said up high and it got to me, it was carried out. You know, it wasn't, like—even if the odds were against me, it was just showing, hey, I was trying to move up, you know.

Watts: Give me your first concrete example, your first instance of proving you were courageous.

Ted: In the cafeteria back in our high school, we sat on one side and they sat on the other side.

Watts: Who was they?

Ted: The rival gang. And one guy—he got hit in the head with a brick. He was walking home by himself, and they were put out with something he said. They just caught him by himself. I guess I was already mad from earlier in the day, and I didn't give a damn. They told me what the hell happened, and I said, fine, let's handle this right now. And this is in school. This is in the cafeteria. I walked over there with the tray and I busted him right across the head pretty hard. And a couple of seconds later, I'd say three seconds later, they didn't have to see, they didn't sit back, they said, "Damn, this nigger just got up and just went and handled his—all of them sitting over there. And I got tore down for a minute, but it wasn't but three seconds before the rest of my boys were with me, throwing the dogs, you know, just getting it on, and that just shows, you know, I didn't have to have the unit with me to go get lobbed. I was lobbed cause I was mad. *Damn. Damn* what *yawl* talking. *Damn* what *they're* talking—*I* was mad. You let him disrespect you. You let him get my boy. And my boy's face was swollen up. He's still got a little twist in it, like a stagger in his eye. And I was just—*No.* That's not gonna ride. That's not gonna ride. It's doesn't *happen* like that. And basically, after the instance, I didn't get into that much anymore, because I had already showed that—hey—ain't no fear here. Even if it was, it didn't show. It was more impulsive. I was real impulsive. I still thought—but in that instance, I think that was the one instance that I didn't care or didn't think about a repercussion. And it happened to work out good for me. It might not have been the wisest decision in the world, but it got me respect.

Watts: I guess you've already explained that respect and reputation were important, but how important?

Ted: Vital. You don't mess with the man. You don't mess with the man who's handling his and who's got the respect. You mess with the man who's a little shaky, the man just in there—the stupid person, the inexperienced person.

Watts: So the opinion of other people was a major issue?

Ted: Yeah! Definitely. Definitely. The only opinion you cared about was the opinion of gang members. Basically, because—even—I mean, the only reason the opinion of other gang members was a big deal was because we didn't want to show weakness, that would be a sign of weakness, you know. So you had to handle your things so that someone wouldn't view you as weak, that could be a possible threat to you, but as far as the everyday people were concerned, they don't know. They're ignorant of us. They don't know what it's about.

Watts: Was a person's size admired?

Ted: Oh yeah, the big guys got a lot of respect. Cause most time if you were pretty large, you were feared by other people, you know. You might get a little more respect from somebody. You might get a little bit more respect from somebody else because they say "Damn, that's a big nigger; he might do such and such. He might be able to take on such and such." Size is a thing when it comes to the fighting and the brawling. But, like, the people that were running things—they weren't the biggest people in the world—and it kind of made you wonder—why'd he get it like that? How'd he survive? You know?

Watts: What about clothing, as a way of identifying a member?

Ted: Yeah, if you were going to do some dirt, like something bad and yawl have made a certain plan and we gonna go over here and whup them or we going to go over here and shoot that, say, put on their rags, their jeans or their khakis and go on out. Might have a rag in your back pocket. Might have a ring on your finger, with a special emblem on it. I mean a guy can lean up against the wall in a certain position, and you know (if you are in) who he was and who he was associated with. But for the most part, in everyday life, or as far as going to school everyday and tripping out, we weren't big on wearing rags and being—having clothes identification. Makes a problem. Creates a problem. Why I let the world know—it's the safety in numbers. And they don't *know* the numbers—hey—you're at an advantage.

Watts: Any importance attached to personal posture, style, how you carried yourself?

Ted: How you carried yourself—Yes, I mean it's real trivial. I mean it's like—this isn't a big issue. You don't want someone walking around wearing high cut pants and looking nerdy and unfashionable, you know what I'm saying? And then again you have those that are just nice dressed, look like they can handle things, big thick, broad shoulders. You know just from the way you walked. You're perceived stronger if you have a little manliness to you. You don't want to be looking like—awful like. But it varies.

Watts: What about possessions? Were they important?

Ted: Cars and things like that were not really important unless you're talking about guns and things like that. I guess to a certain extent, but not really. It's not a big issue. Anything we want, we can get. So far as your local image and people seeing you kicking around town, you like to have a nice car. You got an Am. You like to hear people say—most of the people in this gang's got some pretty straight rides. Most of them got some good gears; most of them got some nice ladies. They're doing things. It's an image.

Watts: How did you support this life style?

Ted: A couple of us had our own cribs.

Watts: Would it be fair to equate the gang with the clan? That is, protection of people who're alike in most ways.

Ted: Yeah, definitely.

Watts: Race? Age? Territory? Clan?

Ted: It was. It was very important for those reasons. In a certain sense, nowadays we don't have some of the threats and problems we had back then. We had a lot of racism, and all that before I became down. If you were black back then, it was about the struggle, you know? It was about making your dollars, coming up, protecting your own.

Watts: Describe the kind of person that a gang person would scorn.

Ted: A bigot, a racist, a police officer, snobs.

Watts: How about "Uncle Toms"?

Ted: Same thing. I'm talking about everybody that has a problem with race or a man's color.

Watts: What about the code of the gang. Did the gang have what you might describe as rituals?

Ted: Definitely.

Watts: Initiation ceremonies? or oaths or any other ceremonies that might be a part of the gang's continuing activities? Were there, for example, any secret signals? Any special greetings?

Ted: Definitely. Want me to elaborate on that? I don't want to say too much, but, it's like, there were rituals for getting in; there were readings that were held. Every whatever day we decided and you showed up. There were balls, birthday parties; there were religious ceremonies. And when I say religious ceremonies, I don't mean anything occult or anything like that. Say a man was getting married—everybody would turn out at church or whatever—whatever suited the brother, whatever the occasion rose to. We adapted; we went and held guard, and gave our tribute, you know. There's a lot of things that I really can't reveal.

Watts: Any secret signals?

Ted: Any secret signals? There's grips; there's codes; there're handshakes, rituals, which were signs, you know, that identify who you are and what rank you are.

Watts: Any special greetings?

Ted: Yeah, definitely.

Watts: Do you feel free in saying—describing in some detail?

Ted: Nah. I mean I could tell you that there were some signs and things we throw up to signify "we're here" or we could be in a club, with a bunch of people and I could throw something up and every member of my gang in the room would know what that means and would act accordingly. We don't go with the intent to wrecking something or putting people in fear of us. Whatever happens, it happens.

Watts: You'd be violating the code to tell me any of the secret signals?

Ted: Right. That would be wrong on my part. But they are there. I'm going to tell you so that you can relate. Compare us to a military: military you have colonel, sergeants, generals, presidents, guards, you know, ranks. Then you have the mediocre—the enlisted personnel. And it goes just that deep within a gang. Every person has a job; every person has a rank. And we call them by different names.

Watts: So there was a hierarchy or ranks within the group. How did they become higher ranks?

Ted: Actions, deeds, what they did, what they displayed, who they knew, what they could produce.

Watts: What they could produce? What they brought in?

Ted: Right, right. You know—I just hate—I don't like to lose you and just put you off to the side and not tell you something; but, I mean there's a lot of things that cannot be said. So I'm not evading you. I just cannot break their code.

Watts: I understand.

Ted: Even though I'm pursuing things and doing things for myself now, I am what I am and what I was. I WAS a part of it.

Watts: Although you're out now, you have to maintain a past loyalty—to get out.

Ted: Right.

Watts: To maintain that what's past is past?

Ted: Basically. There you go. Now you're catching on to it.

Watts: Let's look for a moment at the special naming and language of the gang—words peculiar to the gang and to gangs in general?

Ted: "Rangers," "gd" for gangster disciple in a rival gang, "bd" for black disciples. It's like slang. Just rhetoric. Each set of gangs has its own name. Each rank has its own name. Our gang—when you come in— the lowest rank we have is a foot soldier. And I'm not going any farther than that because—that's the guy that's just in there with no rank—like in the military; a guy that's fresh out of boot camp. Special language? Well, we have quite a literature. You've got to know your lit. If there's something on the wall, you've got to be able to read it. You've got to see certain things that we can write on the wall, or you wouldn't understand it because you wouldn't know, but any member of the gang can look at it and say, "Oh, ok" or "This is his or this belongs to such and such." You know what I'm saying?

Watts: So graffiti was like the weekly newspaper?

Ted: Graffiti was used to tag off territory at certain times, to send a message to a rival gang. And then the literature—like you can get a page of literature written to you. I can get a paragraph of literature sent to me, and it's written with certain signs. It's almost like hieroglyphics. And if someone else were to get it, they wouldn't know what it meant or what it said. They might be able to determine a few words, maybe, like—it's like coded language.

Watts: Coded language? Could you share some of the special language? Do you feel free?

Ted: No, not as far as speaking on it. See what I'm saying? As far as coded language—nah, nah. I couldn't even *think* of anything to tell you.

Watts: You know, it is generally assumed that gangs exist in part to exact some kind of revenge through violent confrontation. Do you think gangs exist to exact revenge through violent confrontation?

Ted: They do. Not always. See that's something—the violent confrontation. All that—what would you call it? That's an aftermath; that's a result; that's an effect of something that went sour. It happens. But that's not what we're about. That's not what we're for. The circumstances make themselves, and when you have a situation, that's the result, you know? In certain situations—but that's not the purpose of the gang—what we're here for. That's not what we stand for. That's just something that has to be done sometimes to maintain order.

Watts: So you're suggesting that you are something like a business. For what sorts of things do gang members seek vengeance? You've said that it's not the main reason for your existence, but gang members DO seek vengeance?

Ted: We do—when we're threatened, or we're struck against, or we're attacked in any way, you just react. If everything were perfect which it's not, there probably wouldn't be any violence. If people would recognize when they should recognize. If we weren't human beings, maybe there wouldn't be any violence. Even without gangs, you could *still* see violence, and you could apply that to everyday people. Has nothing to do with gangs; every day men and women commit acts of violence and attack people and harm other people—politicians—

Watts: How serious is a verbal insult, as compared to a physical blow?

Ted: It all depends on the mood a person is in. Talk is nothing. You can say whatever hell you want to say—it's more like—if I was around one of the supremes, and you said something, shot it off, probably, it's like, you ain't nobody, why let you make me act stupid? Now if it's something serious, something important, you know,—depends on what the situation is—it should be handled, and it might be handled. But a lot of them, they'll just be talking trash.

Watts: Could you give examples of verbal insults? And comment on how serious they were?

Ted: If someone said that the gang had a rough-neck mentality—you know what I'm saying?—chances are someone might get themselves whipped or something like that. It all depends on who you're around. Now there's also a chance that you say, "Go to hell," and we just say, "YOU go to hell," and go on about our business. I mean it wouldn't hurt, but then again, it might be something a little more serious, like, say—what would be a good example?—you could say, "Yawl ain't nothing but a bunch of wannabee Muslims." And "Yawl don't do anything but kill and do this or do that" and "You messed over such and such a person or whatever," and "Yawl ain't nothing for that, you know. And I'm going to get you for that." It's threatening the gang, you know. That would be a major offense. Well, I mean, not a major offense, but that would require some action. I mean we're dealing with high school, you know what I'm saying?

Watts: So threats are more important than verbal insults.

Ted: Yeah. Verbal threats can get you only when you question someone of high calibre or someone with some real respect, someone that's important. You can't have that. I mean it's just like the mob. You wouldn't go to Al Capone and sit in his chair and spit in his face and say, "Damn you." You'll be in cement shoes. But—you go around some of these boys and say some stuff and *still* be in cement shoes. Or they might just get shunned off.

Watts: One would assume that being in a gang was a way to prove one's manhood. Would you agree?

Ted: I can see that. Yeah. I can see that. I agree with that. Because someone's in a gang—to get in the gang, you went through some stuff, some ass-whipping. And a coward—

Watts: What do you mean?

Ted: Getting in—getting what's called "blessed." It's called jumping in.

Watts: So, when you are jumped in, you have to take a good whipping?

Ted: We call that getting blessed or walking the gauntlet or whatever you want to call it. And, you know anything about Indian history—

Watts: You mean Native American?

Ted: Right. *They* ran the gauntlet, went through a line of people to get beaten, you know.

Watts: That gauntlet structure is used in a lot of fraternities.

Ted: Indeed, it is.

Watts: To an outsider, it might appear, ironically, that the rites of manhood were more like the games of little boys, even as ugly and violent as they might be. How would you respond to such an observation?

Ted: I could see how you could say that. I could see how you could say that. I mean—but without being in the gang, you really can't know.

Watts: Are these rites ugly and violent?

Ted: Yes, definitely.

Watts: So are they like the games of little boys?

Ted: Yes, when you're talking about the games of little boys—how we play and fight and break things up and shoot things up and toys. Yes, I think so.

Watts: And wanting to be accepted with the in-crowds, by the bigger boys, and the bullies and appeasing the bullies?

Ted: Yeah, like a fantasy, man. You really get a chance. You see it and you play it. You see it in the movies and what not. And I'm not talking just about gangs. I'm talking about the whole violence, the whole violence in the whole spectrum in the games of little boys. It's like your chance to really experience it, to let things out—to let all your desires—I don't know how to say this—channel—all that's inside.

Watts: You have been saying everything very well. You are, I would suggest, very articulate, very well spoken and intelligent. The last question I want to ask you as we close out this interview is, have you put the gang experience behind you?

Ted: Yeah, I put it behind me. I put it behind me as far as—physically. But it is always up here.

Watts: It occupies your mind?

Ted: Not constantly. But it's there. And it's good in a way. And it's bad. Because I have a lot of bad memories. And then again I've learned a lot. It gave me a sense of order; it gave me an appreciation of structure in my life; it gave me self-determination. It gave me the determination to be somebody that can help other misguided youths "to be somebody."

ELIJAH ANDERSON'S "THE CODE OF THE STREETS"

By and by a proud-looking man about fifty-five—and he was a heap the best-dressed man in that town, too—steps out of the store. . . .

"I'm tired of this, but I'll endure it till one o'clock. Till one
o'clock, mind—no longer. If you open your mouth against me
only once after that time you can't travel so far but I will find
you. . . ." (142, 143)

The final document continues the examination of the code of
honor as it exists in the late twentieth century. In excerpts from
Elijah Anderson's "The Code of the Streets" one finds an amazing
irony: The code of the streets that governs the lives of young African-American gang members in inner cities in the 1990s is in
essential ways identical to the code of honor adhered to by the
white gentleman of the nineteenth-century, slaveholding South.
Note the similar characteristics outlined by Anderson. First, to
those who live by the street code, as with those who lived by the
nineteenth-century code of honor, "honor" means the opinion
that other people have of them. Second, those who live by the
code are supersensitive; their honor must "constantly be
guarded," he writes, and "such people become very sensitive to
advances and slights." Third, appearance is extremely important—
not just the clothes they wear but their bearing, the way they walk,
and their speech. Fourth is the place of "challenges" in the street
code, just as it was to men who dueled in the nineteenth century.
Fifth is the element of vengeance in both codes. And, finally, protecting one's honor is intimately connected with proving that one
is a man or manly.

FROM ELIJAH ANDERSON, "THE CODE OF THE STREETS"
(Atlantic Monthly, May 1994)

At the heart of the code is the issue of respect—loosely defined as
being treated "right," or granted the deference one deserves. . . . In the
street culture, especially among young people, respect is viewed as almost an external entity that is hard-won but easily lost, and so must
constantly be guarded. . . . The person whose very appearance—including his clothing, demeanor, and way of moving—deters transgressions
feels that he possesses, and may be considered by others to possess, a
measure of respect. . . . If he is bothered, not only may he be in physical
danger but he has been disgraced or "dissed" (disrespected). . . . (82)
. . . The code revolves around the presentation of self. Its basic require-
ment is the display of a certain predisposition to violence. Accordingly,
one's bearing must send the unmistakable if sometimes subtle message

to "the next person" in public that one is capable of violence and mayhem when the situation requires it, that one can take care of oneself. The nature of this communication is largely determined by the demands of the circumstances but can include facial expressions, gait, and verbal expressions—all of which are geared mainly to deterring aggression. Physical appearance, including clothes, jewelry, and grooming, also plays an important part in how a person is viewed; to be respected, it is important to have the right look.

. . . he risks being "tried" (challenged) or "moved on" by any number of others. To maintain his honor he must show he is not someone to be "messed with" or "dissed." . . . (88)

. . . For many inner-city youths, manhood and respect are flip sides of the same coin. (89)

SUGGESTIONS FOR FURTHER READING

By Mark Twain:

> *A Connecticut Yankee in King Arthur's Court*
>
> *The Prince and the Pauper*

By Charles Dickens:

> *A Tale of Two Cities*

By Alexandre Dumas:

> *The Count of Monte Cristo*

By Walter Scott:

> *Ivanhoe*

PROJECTS FOR WRITTEN OR ORAL EXPLORATION

1. Conduct a debate on the question of whether Colonel Grangerford is to be admired. Use the choice of wording and events in the text itself to support your thesis.

2. Conduct a similar debate on the Colonel Sherburn incident: did Colonel Sherburn do what he had to do? If not, what should he have done?

3. According to Mark Twain, those who adhered to the code of honor adored hierarchies, royalty, and titles. In contrast to the Walter Scott attitude, one of the revolutionaries in France once stated, in effect, that "it is a crime to *be* a king." What exactly do you think he meant? Debate the validity of this statement as well.

4. What techniques does Twain use to ridicule royalty?

5. Why would it be uncharacteristic, if not impossible, for Huck Finn, if he were a teenager today, to belong to a gang?

6. Write an essay comparing the code of honor in the nineteenth-century South with the code of the streets today.

7. Identify someone you would define as an "honorable" person and write an essay explaining why you think so.

8. We have seen what traits the nineteenth-century man of honor valued most. Construct a list, according to their importance in that time, of those characteristics. What is *the* most valued trait? Are there traits which are glaringly absent from the list? Then construct your own list of values, indicating how and why what you value most might differ from what the nineteenth-century man of honor valued.

9. Courage was probably the most valued trait in a nineteenth-century man, as it well may be in those who adhere to the street code of today. In either case, does this extend to the courage to ignore the opinion of one's peers? To be one's own person, no matter what others around you think? Discuss or debate fully.

10. Write an essay on courage in *Adventures of Huckleberry Finn.*

11. Contrast the romanticism of Tom Sawyer and the realism of Huck Finn.

12. Is it somehow easier for Colonel Sherburn and Colonel Grangerford to be "brave" in standing up to others than it is for Huck or Jim? What makes the difference?

13. In your own society to what extent do honor and respect rest on the "things" a person has rather than on the person's intrinsic nature?

14. To what extent do honor and respect in your own society rest on the appearance rather than the reality of a person?

15. Define "romance," in the broad sense, carefully. What does it contribute to a person's life? How can it be harmful?

16. Write your own essay on the code of honor among your acquaintances.

SUGGESTED READINGS

Cash, W. J. *The Mind of the South.* New York: Alfred A. Knopf, 1946.

Couch, W. T., ed. *Culture in the South.* Chapel Hill: University of North Carolina Press, 1934.

Eaton, Clement. *Freedom of Thought in the Old South.* Durham, N.C.: Duke University Press, 1940.

——. *The Mind of the Old South.* Baton Rouge: Louisiana State University Press, 1964.

Page, Thomas Nelson. *The Old South: Essays Social and Political.* New York: Charles Scribner's Sons, 1892.

Taylor, William R. *Cavalier and Yankee.* Garden City, N.Y.: Doubleday and Co., Anchor Books, 1963.

Wyatt-Brown, Bertram. *Southern Honor: Ethics and Behavior in the Old South.* New York: Oxford University Press, 1992.

Cultural Satire: Shakespeare, Home Decor, Sentimental Verse

Despite what is often the darkness of Mark Twain's message, he is also America's great comic writer. Twain contended that "the Sweet Singer of Michigan," Julia A. Moore, whom he parodied in the portrait of Emmeline Grangerford, was funny when she intended to be serious and pathetic when she intended to be funny. The relationship of comedy and tragedy in Twain's own work is decidedly different because he *intends* to be both tragic and comic at the same time. Behind the humorous sketches involving Tom Sawyer, the king, and the duke is a darkly serious vision of human life. Twain's comedy took the form of parody and satire, of which he became the undisputed master in America.

Satire is defined as literature in which vice and folly or certain human weaknesses are held up to ridicule, often with the purpose of instigating reform. Much of the comedy on that long-lived TV program, *Saturday Night Live,* is satire. The other important form, parody, is defined as a humorous or satirical imitation of a serious work of literature, musical composition, person, or event. Musical variety shows often include parodies of films like *Gone with the Wind,* with costumes and southern accents so exaggerated as to be comical. Scarlett, the southern belle, might appear in a hoop skirt so big no one else could enter the room with her, and Rhett Butler's moustache might droop down to his shoulders.

Satire and parody have several things in common: both are humorous, use scorn or ridicule, and exaggerate certain salient characteristics, usually weaknesses, of human activity. But whereas a satire is an original composition, a parody is an imitation of another work.

Twain uses both forms in *Adventures of Huckleberry Finn.* And in the classic manner, he does this with both humorous and serious intent. The novel is filled with satirical sketches, sometimes subtle and sometimes broad, from the opening pictures of Miss Watson and the Widow Douglas to Huck's final decision to "light out for the territory" to escape civilization. Twain's nineteenth-century audience would have recognized his allusions to frontier revivals, the stock market, romantic legends, and popular literature. Tom Sawyer's gang and his high jinks at the end of the novel are parodies of much of the popular romantic fiction of the day (see references to Dumas, Dickens, and *Ivanhoe* in Chapter 5) as well as satires of the mean outlaws, like John Murel, who tried to take over the Mississippi Valley in Mark Twain's boyhood. Pap's tirade against a government that allows a free black man to vote is one of the novel's bitterest parodies—of a nineteenth-century bigot. Huck and Jim's conversation about Jim's "investment" in a cow makes fun of the rampant speculation in the stock market after the Civil War, and Huck's garbled accounts of King Solomon and Jim's responses show what happens when one takes a literal, commonsense approach to a fanciful, symbolic story of a king threatening to cut a baby in half. Jim and Huck's conversations about royalty are satires of one of the most popular legends of the nineteenth century: speculation about what happened to the infamous lost prince (the Dauphin) of France after the French Revolution and the execution of Louis XVI and Marie Antoinette.

When the king and the duke enter the novel, Twain resorts to the most absurd satire, appropriate for such uncouth figures. The king and the duke satirize European royalty, for they have all the characteristics of dishonesty and meanness Twain attributed to real kings and dukes. When the king manages to take up a large offering from the revival crowd by pretending to be a reformed pirate who intends to be a missionary, Twain is satirizing the confidence man of his day, who often preyed on the generosity and good will of simple people.

Thus Twain can indulge an almost endless train of literary and popular allusions that all his educated readers at the time would have recognized.

As with most satirists, so with Mark Twain: the object behind the fun was to expose pretentious, phony, and stupid people, and to bring down the mighty, whether it be con men or rich men, exalted authors of great reputation or the royalty they adored.

In *Adventures of Huckleberry Finn* Twain extends his satire of nineteenth-century culture to include the production of Shakespearean plays, house decor, and sentimental verse. His parody of Shakespeare is part of the king and the duke's exploitation of the simple people of the Mississippi Valley frontier. Two of his other targets, sentimental verse and home decoration, are found in the Grangerford household.

SHAKESPEAREAN BURLESQUE

Assisted by the whole strength of the company! New costumes,
new scenery, new appointments! (139)

In deciding to stage the balcony scene from *Romeo and Juliet* and
the sword-fight from *Richard III,* using Hamlet's "To Be or Not to
Be" soliloquy as an encore, the duke (a sometime itinerant actor)
is playing to his rural audience's appetite for any kind of enter-
tainment and, supposedly, their particular love of Shakespeare. In
this, Mark Twain reflects an accurate picture of frontier life, for
Shakespeare's plays were those most frequently produced in a
drama-hungry nineteenth-century America. *Hamlet, Macbeth, Julius Caesar, Richard III, Romeo and Juliet,* and *Othello* were
standard fare in theatrical companies in cities like New York, Boston, and San Francisco and in traveling theatrical companies, large
and small, throughout the United States. These traveling companies performed in hotel lobbies, saloons, barns, and even, in one
case, a pigsty. It was said that even the roughest miners in the
wilds of the far West could quote the famous speeches from Shakespeare's plays. These productions were well advertised with elaborate flyers and advertisements in the local papers, usually
outrageously exaggerating the renown of the traveling actors and
the sets to which the audience would be treated.

In *Adventures of Huckleberry Finn,* the duke, in typical fashion,
has printed up a playbill calling himself and the king world-
renowned tragedians, using the names of famous British actors,
Garrick and Kean, one of whom (Garrick) had been dead for over
eighty years. Without the slightest ghost of a set, he also advertises
"new costumes" and "new appointments" (139).

What Mark Twain intends with this sequence (but what the duke
does *not* intend) is also in the tradition of nineteenth-century en-
tertainment—the burlesque of Shakespeare. The duke intends to
play Romeo and casts the older, stouter, bald, gray-bearded king
as Juliet. When the king wonders how he can play a young girl
with his bald head and beard, the duke assures him that the audience "won't ever think of that" (133). (Actually, as in Shakespeare's own time, boys sometimes did play the parts of girls in
some of these little companies, but a bald-headed, bearded Juliet

was definitely going too far.) Moreover, the king is not a supremely talented actor; as the duke tells him, "Juliet's a dear sweet mere child of a girl, you know, and she don't bray like a jackass" (137). Finally, Twain gives us the complete text of the duke's version of Hamlet's soliloquy. This is a senseless hodgepodge of many disconnected famous lines in *Hamlet* mixed up with famous lines from *Macbeth*.

Twain's parody of Hamlet's speech may also have been his way of observing that the lines from Shakespeare so beloved by Americans were really just fancy words that didn't really make much sense to the people (like the duke) who had committed them to memory. Such an observation would certainly be in keeping with Twain's theme throughout the novel of contrasting elegant, romanticized, and superficial appearances with the cruel or meaningless reality that lies beneath them.

Four documents follow. The first is a typical burlesque advertisement of the time (much like the one the duke runs off). This is followed by three parodies of Hamlet's soliloquy. Instead of considering "To Be or Not to Be," one burlesque Hamlet considers "To Bake or Not to Bake," another whether "To Dye or Not to Dye," and a third, entitled "A Dental Soliloquy," whether "to have it out or not." Many others were written on the subjects of "To wed or not to wed," "To dance or not to dance," "To diet or not to diet," and so on.

FROM GEORGE C. D. ODELL, *ANNALS OF THE NEW YORK STAGE*
(New York: Columbia University Press, 1931, V, 44)

Mr. Mitchell
Has much pleasure in announcing to the Public that he has, at an enormous expense, effected an engagement with himself for a few days, during which he will appear
in a series of
Shakespearean Characters,
In the true Tragic-Comico-Illegitimate style
During this engagement he trusts he shall be able to induce himself to appear as
Hamlet!
   With Comic Songs!
      Richard No. III!
         And
            Macbeth!

Mr. Bengough the Artist, has been engaged for nearly twenty minutes a day, during the past week, and the Costumer has not slept much except at night, during the same period . . .

N.B. A roll of red flannel has been imported expressly for this occasion.

FROM *PARODIES OF THE WORKS OF ENGLISH AND AMERICAN AUTHORS*
(London: Reeves and Turner, 1885)

A Dental Soliloquy

> To Have it out or not? that is the question—
> Whether 'tis better for the jaws to suffer
> The pangs and torments of an aching tooth,
> Or to take steel against a host of troubles;
> And, by extracting end them? To pull—to tug!
> No more; and by a tug to say we end
> The tooth-ache, and a thousand natural ills
> The jaw is heir to; 'tis a consummation
> Devoutly to be wished? To pull—to tug!
> To tug—perchance to break! Ay, there's the rub. (153)

An Apropos Soliloquy By a Girl of the Period

> To Dye, or not to dye, that is the question:—
> "Whether 'tis nobler in the mind to suffer"
> Th' outrageous colour of Dame Nature born,
> The very "head and front of my offending"
> Against the fiat of chameleon Fashion,
> Or summon Art to aid me? Shall I end
> This heart-ache by the "hazard of a dye"
> That Fashion dooms my hair to?—Dye:—a wash:—
> No more:—Poison, perhaps? ay, that's the rub
> To bring paralysis: the *'harmless wash'*
> With lead and sulphur . . . (153)

Paterfamilias as Hamlet

> *Ham.*—To BAKE, or not to bake, that is the question:—
> Whether 'tis better for ourselves to make
> Digestive, light, sweet wholesome home-made bread;
> Or to take in tradesmen's loaves against our sense,

And, nothing heeding, eat them?—To eat—eat what?—
The trough's abominations without end;
The cockroach! a thousand unnatural things
The bakehouse teems with,—'tis adulteration
Devoutly to be shun'd. Impure? Pure?
For in this loaf of bread what dirt may come
From unclean baker at his midnight toil,
Must give us pause: There's the respect
That takes all relish from the staff of life:
For who that reads his *Lancet* or his *Times*
Would eat this stuff the baker sends, contentedly,
Knowing full well from analysts' reports
And sanitary officers' returns,
The noisome mysteries of the baker's art,
When he himself bread, cakes, and scones may make
With Borwick's Baking Powder? (148)

HOME DECOR

> On the table in the middle of the room was kind of a lovely
> crockery basket that had apples and oranges and peaches and
> grapes piled up in it, which was much redder and yellower
> and prettier than real ones is, but they warn't real because you
> could see where pieces had got chipped off and showed the
> white chalk, or whatever it was, underneath. (104)

When Huck finds himself with the Grangerfords, for the first time
in his life he sees the inside of a fashionable, "stylish" household.
Twain uses this decor as an occasion for both comedy and a bitter
comment on society.

The Grangerford home is decorated in a nineteenth-century style
that a twentieth-century eye would find cluttered and artificial. Notice how many details of the decor are imitations of nature and are
not tied intrinsically to function: the bricks are often painted; the
clock is not just a clock, but has a scene painted on it. Never mind
that the clock strikes 150 times; it is a work of art in the Grangerfords' eyes. Excess instead of simple function seems to be the valued commodity. Parrots, a china dog and cat that squeak through
the bottom, and huge turkey wing fans crowd all these other decorations on the mantle.

On the table is a basket made not of natural fibers but of "crock-
ery." It is a fake basket filled with fake fruit, which is brilliantly
colored but, like the mantle animals, chipped.

The books and pictures in the room are standard fare, the im-
plication being that the Grangerfords have them not so much because they chose them as favorites, but because they know that
this was what the fashionable household should display.

Huck's naive point of view creates the humor in the description
since he views the room with fresh eyes, seeing things as they are
rather than as the family sees it.

Many home decorating magazines of the time instructed housewives in do-it-yourself projects designed to get as far away from a
"natural" look as possible. Fruit made of wax, painted in what
Huck describes as gaudy colors, artificial flowers, and leaves made
of fabrics and woven around the legs of tables were favorite
decorations of many homes of the period. Almost everything was

covered with something. Pianos, tables, chairs, mantels, floors, windows—all were covered with thick fabrics with heavy fringes. Little individual ruffles were often made for each leg of furniture. It seems an appropriate strategy for a civilization that tried to cover its savagery with polite manners. In one of the most bizarre practices of the period, real wood would be painted over with a shade of brown and then "grained" with darker paint to look like wood!

The way in which this so-called stylish decor fits into the whole story of the Grangerfords' life emphasizes the tragedy of their story. For the household decor is veneer, something false on the surface. Underneath the elaborately painted dog and cat and parrots and fake fruit one can see the common materials they are made of. Underneath the fancy painting of a town on the clock is a faulty machine that makes 150 strikes at a time.

Veneer and pretense symbolize the way they live their lives. On the outside is a thin veneer of fashionable and stylish society with its self-conscious display of polite manners, Christian books, churchgoing, and elegant parties. At the core, however, is not civilized society at all, but savagery, as they slaughter their neighbors in the manner of the most primitive of tribes.

Twain seems to be making fun not only of the unnatural and cluttered decor, but of the magazines that provided housewives with ideas for decorating. The following excerpt is from one of those favorite magazines, *The Decorator and Furnisher*.

J. R. PUGH, "THE BEST ROOM"
(The Decorator and Furnisher, October 1888)

The fireplace should be left open, so that it will always be possible to have the fire burning and crackling on the hearth. . . . In front of the fireplace, can be thrown a black bear skin.

Diagonally across from the fireplace, the upright piano can stand, pulled out from the wall and covered with a scarf of dark terra-cotta plush. If the fair mistress of the house is skilled in embroidery, this scarf would be much improved by a design of conventionalized pomegranates and leaves, worked in shades of pink and greens and outlined in gold thread. . . . A bric-a-brac table on which pretty ornaments, not necessarily expensive, can be arranged, a square table more massive in effect, the top covered with a rich fringed velour square, on which can be placed a low lamp and a few handsome books [may also be displayed] . . . If in the room, there is a narrow space between the windows or the door frames, a very pretty effect can be produced by putting a pedestal table on it.

On this, place the owner's handsomest ornament and if it be of marble or bronze, back of it throw a plush curtain depending from a slender rod of brass. . . . Around the entire base of the recessed window, we will imagine a low wooden seat covered with a cushion, either of figured velour or terra cotta plush; on it thrown will be two square pillows. The effect of this recess would be heightened by a flooring of Mosaic setting with a fox skin thrown on it. (Vol. 13, 18, 19)

SENTIMENTAL VERSE

"And Art Thou Gone Yes Thou Art Gone Alas." (105)

They got him out and emptied him;
   Alas it was too late: (106)

When Huck enters the Grangerford household, he comes across the artistic renderings of the family's daughter Emmeline, who had died at fifteen. Emmeline wrote and drew pictures about one subject only—death. These included dark drawings about death and dying as well as obituary verses, usually about gruesome accidents. Huck sees a picture of a girl leaning on a tombstone, one of a girl grieving over a dead bird, one of a sorrowful girl who evidently has received a letter informing her of the death of someone she loved, and one of a girl about to jump off a bridge. (See Figure 6.1.)

Emmeline's scrapbook, composed of clippings from the *Presbyterian Observer,* contained obituaries and stories about "accidents and cases of patient suffering." These provided her with subjects for many of her poems, including one about Stephen Dowling Bots, who drowned in a well. She also wrote poems when anyone she knew died—except, one assumes, any of the hated Shepherdsons, with whom her family was constantly feuding. Thus, from everything Huck can find out about her, Emmeline Grangerford was obsessed with death.

Several things throw light on Emmeline's preoccupation with death. First, since the inspiration for so many of her poems came from a religious newspaper, presumably she didn't even know most of the people whose misfortunes she wrote about. Furthermore, her brother, Buck, reports that she "didn't even have to stop to think" to write a poem. What really mattered to her was the rhyme, the *sound* of the word, and if one word didn't work, she immediately came up with another one. Finally, Huck admits that sometimes all the pictures began to "aggravate" him, something about which he feels profoundly guilty.

Emmeline represents a very real characteristic of nineteenth-century society, for the newspapers were filled not only with obituaries, but with obituary poems written by "obituary poets" who

Figure 6.1. A typical mourning scene, illustrating the nineteenth-century obsession with death and its focus on the mourner instead of the deceased. A weeping willow, signifying grief, is in the background. From the collections of Henry Ford Museum & Greenfield Village. Reprinted with permission.

were hired for that purpose. With little or no knowledge of the deceased, these poets would memorialize those who had died.

Ironically, Huck, too, was obsessed with death, as was nineteenth-century society as a whole. The difference between Huck's and Emmeline's obsessions and what makes her and her society easy targets for ridicule is that she overly sentimentalizes death. Her emotion seems phony and self-indulgent. That is, she appears to take delight in grief and death rather than to suffer the profound loss of someone she has known and cared about. It is, in a sense, a cheap high. One might even say, as Huck actually implies, that it makes Emmeline feel good to think about just anybody dying. She wallows in her emotions. As Huck says, "with her disposition, she was having a better time in the graveyard" (105).

Moreover, Emmeline's fascination with death, as well as her family's mawkish memorializing of her, rings especially false in the whole context of the Shepherdson-Grangerford incident, which is marked by the senseless slaughter of members of both families, from boys to old men, in the bloody feud. Note, for example, Emmeline's lovely, spidery young woman about to end her life, with great sad drama and romance, by jumping from a bridge. Compare that with the reality of Buck's corpse, riddled with bullets and pulled out of the river by a devastated Huck. The contrast here makes her sentimentality about death and dying not only false, but callously cruel, insensitive, and absurd.

JULIA A. MOORE

> Buck said she could rattle off poetry like nothing. She didn't
> ever have to stop to think. (106)

Professional obituary poets and other writers fascinated by death constituted what was known in the nineteenth century as the Graveyard School. Among these was Julia A. Moore, born a humble Michigan farm girl. In 1876 her first collection of verses appeared as *The Sentimental Song Book*. Shortly before Mark Twain wrote *Adventures of Huckleberry Finn*, he bought a copy of Moore's book, and declared her to be "the Empress of the Hogwash Guild." In *Following the Equator* (1897), with tongue in cheek, he writes the following of her:

I have been reading the poems of Mrs. Julia A. Moore, again, and I find in them the same grace and melody that attracted me when they were first published, twenty years ago, and have held me in happy bonds ever since. "The Sentimental Song Book" has long been out of print, and has been forgotten by the world in general, but not by me. I carry it with me always—it and Goldsmith's deathless story. . . . Indeed, it has the same deep charm for me that the Vicar of Wakefield has, and I find in it the same subtle touch—the touch that makes an intentionally humorous episode pathetic and an intentionally pathetic one funny. (339, 340)

Mrs. Moore is obviously one of the members of the Graveyard School on whom Mark Twain based Emmeline Grangerford.

Included below are two of Mrs. Moore's poems, which may seem more like parodies than Emmeline's. Her preface announces her preference for the subject matter of death, and the two poems themselves are, typically, about the death of children, very much in the manner of Emmeline Grangerford's "Stephen Dowling Bots." Note how Moore's total disregard of cadence, her single-minded attention to rhyme, and her curious juxtaposition of flat, mundane words like "Chicago" with high-sounding sentiment results in what Mark Twain found to be hysterically funny.

FROM JULIA A. MOORE, *THE SENTIMENTAL SONG BOOK*
(New York: Platt and Peck Co., 1879; rpt. 1912)

PREFACE

This little book is composed of truthful pieces. All those which speak of being killed, died or drowned, are truthful songs; others are "more truth than poetry." They are all composed by the author.

I was born in Plainfield, and lived there until I was ten years of age. Then my parents moved to Algoma, where they have lived until the present day, and I live near them, one mile west of Edgerton.

Little Andrew
Air—*Gypsy's Warning*

Andrew was a little infant
    And his life was two years old;
He was his parents' eldest boy,
    And he was drowned, I was told.
His parents never more can see him

In this world of grief and pain,
And oh! they will not forget him
  While on earth they do remain.

On one bright and pleasant morning
  His uncle thought it would be nice
To take his dear little nephew
  Down to play upon a raft,
Where he was to work upon it,
  And this little child would company be—
The raft the water rushed around it,
  Yet he the danger did not see.

This little child knew no danger—
  Its little soul was free from sin—
He was looking in the water,
  When, alas, this child fell in.
Beneath the raft the water took him
  For the current was so strong,
And before they could rescue him
  He was drowned and was gone.

Oh! how sad were his kind parents
  When they saw their drowned child,
As they brought him from the water.
  It almost made their hearts grow wild.
Oh! how mournful was the parting
  From their little infant son.
Friends, I pray you, all take warning,
  Be careful of your little ones.

From *William House and Family*

Come all kind friends both far and near
Come listen to me and you shall hear—
It's of a family and their fate,
All about them I will relate.

They once did live at Edgerton,
They once did live at Muskegon.
From there they went to Chicago
Which proved their final overthrow.

It was William House's family,
As fine a family as you see—
His family was eleven in all,
I do not think it was very small.

Two children died some years ago,
Before they went to Chicago,
Five children there he had with him,
When death his home there entered in.

The small-pox then was raging there,
And Oh! it would not their house spare,
For all but one was sick of them.
A dreadful house it must have been.

The eldest girl was married then,
The eldest boy was in Michigan,
The second boy he was at home,
And took care of them all alone.

His father and his mother dear,
And dear sister, too, I hear,
Were very sick and in his care,
And no kind friends to help him there:

Two little brothers, and a baby too,
Made six in all—what could he do,
He had to take care of them all,
The baby, too, was very small.

OTHER PARODIES OF OBITUARY POETS

> Every time a man died, or a woman died, or a child died, she
> would be on hand with her "tribute" before he was cold.
> (107)

Mark Twain was not the only writer to parody obituary poets.
In fact, the main response to Mrs. Moore's popular volumes was
a flood of parodies. One of the humorists who published parodies
of obituary poets was Max Adeler. In *Out of the Hurly-Burly; or,
Life in an Odd Corner,* Adeler created a poet named Mr. Slimmer
who is hired by a newspaper to write obituary poems. The disas-

trous results of the fictional Mr. Slimmer's efforts are caused, in part, by the newspaper editor's instructions to him to "lighten the gloom," "to divert their minds from contemplation of the horrors of the tomb" (Philadelphia: P. Garrett and Co., 1879, 115).

FROM MAX ADELER, *OUT OF THE HURLY-BURLY*
(Philadelphia: P. Garrett and Co., 1879)

Alexander McGlue

He wore a checked shirt and a Number Nine shoe,
    And he had a pink wart on his nose.
No doubt he is happier dwelling in space
    Over there on the evergreen shore.
His friends are informed that his funeral takes place
    Precisely at quarter-past four.

Little Willie

Willie had a purple monkey climbing on a yellow stick,
And when he sucked the paint all off it made him deathly sick;
And in his latest hours he clasped that monkey in his hand,
And bade good-bye to earth and went into a better land.

Oh! no more he'll shoot his sister with his little wooden gun;
And no more he'll twist the pussy's tail and make her yowl for
    fun.
The pussy's tail now stands out straight; the gun is laid aside;
The monkey doesn't jump around since little Willie died.

Little Hanner

We have lost our little Hanner in a very painful manner,
And we often asked, How can her harsh sufferings be borne?
When her death was first reported, her aunt got up and snorted
With the grief that she supported, for it made her feel forlorn.
She was such a little seraph that her father, who is sheriff,
Really doesn't seem to care if he ne'er smiles in life again.
She has gone, we hope, to heaven, at the early age of seven
(Funeral starts off at eleven), where she'll nevermore have pain.

PROJECTS FOR WRITTEN OR ORAL EXPLORATION

1. Some of the same criticism Mark Twain levels against aspects of his culture in *Adventures of Huckleberry Finn* has been leveled against art in our own culture—for example, soap operas or romances. In a parody, criticize something from your own culture—for example, a film, a television program, particular books or ways of dressing or decorating.

2. Write a parody of Hamlet's soliloquy.

3. Produce the duke's parody of *Romeo and Juliet* as you think Twain might have meant it to be played.

4. Write and produce a brief parody of a Shakespearean play.

5. Write a parody of a soap opera.

6. Produce a parody of the performance of any popular musician.

7. Have a round-table discussion of what makes the parody funny.

8. Produce a parody of a TV commercial.

9. Produce a parody of a fashion show.

SUGGESTED READINGS

Blair, Walter. *Mark Twain and Huck Finn.* Berkeley: University of California Press, 1960.

Blair, Walter, and Hamlin Hill. *America's Humor.* New York: Oxford University Press, 1978.

Bode, Carl. *American Life in the 1840s.* New York: New York University Press, 1967.

Covici, Pascal, Jr. *Mark Twain's Humor.* Dallas: Southern Methodist University Press, 1962.

Dunn, Elizabeth Cloudman. *Shakespeare in America.* New York: Macmillan, 1939.

French, Lillie Hamilton. *Homes and Their Decoration.* New York: Dodd, Mead and Co., 1903.

Grow, Lawrence. *American Victorian.* New York: Harper and Row, 1984.

Halttunen, Karen. *Confidence Men and Painted Women.* New Haven: Yale University Press, 1982.

Jackson, Charles O., ed. *Passing: The Vision of Death in America.* Westport, Conn.: Greenwood Press, 1977.

Johnson, Claudia D. "Burlesques of Shakespeare: The Democratic American's 'Light Artillery.' " *Theatre Survey* 21 (May 1980): 49–62.

Leopold, Allison Kyle. *Victorian Splendor.* New York: Stewart, Tabori and Chang, 1986.

Lowenherz, Robert J. "Mark Twain Laughs at Death." *Mark Twain Journal* 10 (Spring 1958): 2–5.

McKay, Janet Holmgren. " 'An Art So High': Style in *Adventures of Huckleberry Finn.*" In *New Essays on "Huckleberry Finn,"* edited by Louis J. Budd, 61–81. Cambridge: Cambridge University Press, 1985.

Pike, Martha V., and Janice Gray Armstrong. *A Time to Mourn: Expressions of Grief in Nineteenth Century America.* Stony Brook, N.Y.: Museums at Stony Brook, 1980.

Schlereth, Thomas J. *Victorian America: Transformations in Everyday Life, 1876–1915.* New York: HarperCollins, 1991.

Sloane, David E.E. *"Adventures of Huckleberry Finn": American Comic Vision.* Boston: Twayne, 1988.

———. *Mark Twain as a Literary Comedian.* Baton Rouge: Louisiana State University Press, 1979.

Wade, John Donald. "Southern Humor." In *The Frontier Humorists.* Hamden, Conn.: Archon Books, 1975.

Well, Stanley. *Nineteenth-Century Shakespearean Burlesques.* 5 vols. London: Diploma Press, 1977.

Winkler, Gail Caskey. *Victorian Interior Decoration: American Interiors, 1830–1900.* New York: Holt, 1986.

Index

About the Author

CLAUDIA DURST JOHNSON is Professor of English at the University of Alabama, where she chaired the Department of English for 12 years. She is series editor of the Greenwood Press "Literature in Context" series, which includes her works *Understanding To Kill a Mockingbird* (1994) and *Understanding The Scarlet Letter* (1995). She is also the author of *To Kill a Mockingbird: Threatening Boundaries* (1994), *The Productive Tension of Hawthorne's Art* (1981), and *American Actress: Perspectives on the Nineteenth Century* (1984), and coauthor (with Vernon Johnson) of *Memoirs of the Nineteenth-Century Theatre* (Greenwood, 1982), and (with Henry Jacobs) *An Annotated Bibliography of Shakespearean Burlesques, Parodies, and Travesties* (1976), as well as numerous articles on American literature and theatre.